SHAKESPEARE AND THE IRISH WRITER

Shakespeare and the Irish Writer

edited by

JANET CLARE

and

STEPHEN O'NEILL

UNIVERSITY COLLEGE DUBLIN PRESS

PREAS CHOLÁISTE OLLSCOILE
BHAILE ÁTHA CLIATH

First published 2010
by University College Dublin Press
Newman House
86 St Stephen's Green
Dublin 2
Ireland

ISBN 978-1-906359-39-3

Cataloguing in Publication data available from the British Library

Typeset in UK in Plantin and Fournier by Elaine Burberry
Text design by Lyn Davies
Index by Jane Rogers
Printed on acid-free paper in England by
Antony Rowe, Chippenham

Contents

Acknowledgements

We wish to express our gratitude to Barbara Mennell for being such a supportive and energetic editor at UCD Press and to Noelle Moran for exemplary efficiency. The anonymous readers for the Press offered thoughtful comment and advice. Philip Edwards's essay 'Shakespeare and the Politics of the Irish Revival' originally appeared in *The Internationalism of Irish Literature*, edited by Joseph McMinn (Lanham, MD, 1992). We are grateful to the author for permission to reprint this essay. For a generous subvention towards publication we are most grateful to the National University of Ireland. We would especially like to thank our contributors for responding so well to our comments and queries and helping to make this project such a stimulating and enjoyable experience. We have incurred many other debts of gratitude in the completion of this volume, the idea for which emerged, in part, out of a conference we organised that was held at NUI Maynooth in February 2006. Thanks are due to the School of English, Media and Theatre Studies, NUI Maynooth and the School of English, Drama and Film, University College Dublin for their organisational and financial support; to Pauline Slattery, Amanda Bent, Shaun Regan, Aoife Leahy, Selene Scarsi, John Gallagher; and to the Research office, NUI Maynooth, in particular Professor Ray O'Neill, Vice-President for Research. Additionally, thanks to Liam O'Dowd for his work on the manuscript of the volume as part of the innovative Summer Undergraduate Research Programme at NUI Maynooth.

JANET CLARE, *Hull*
STEPHEN O'NEILL, *Maynooth*
January 2010

Contributors to this Volume

JANET CLARE is Professor of Renaissance Literature at the University of Hull and formerly taught at University College Dublin. Amongst her publications are '*Art Made-Tongue Tied by Authority*': *Elizabethan and Jacobean Dramatic Censorship* (Manchester, 1990; 2nd edn, 1999), *Drama of the English Republic, 1649–1660* (Manchester, 2002) and *Revenge Tragedies of the Renaissance* (Northcote, 2006). She has published numerous articles on Shakespeare and Renaissance drama including 'Shakespeare Productions in Ireland, 2002–2004', *Shakespeare Survey*, 2006.

BRIAN COSGROVE taught for 25 years at University College Dublin and was Professor of English at the National University of Ireland Maynooth from 1992 to 2006. His publications include *Wordsworth and the Poetry of Self-Sufficiency* (Salzburg, 1982); numerous articles on Wordsworth, Joyce, and Heaney; *Literature and the Supernatural* (Dublin, 1995), a collection of essays in honour of the Maynooth bicentenary; and a memoir, *The Yew-Tree at the Head of the Strand* (Liverpool, 2001). His study of Joyce, *James Joyce's Negations*, was published by UCD Press in October 2007.

MATTHEW CREASY is a lecturer in the Department of English, University of Glasgow. He is currently writing a monograph about James Joyce and mis-quotation.

CARY DI PIETRO currently lectures in English and drama at the University of Toronto at Mississauga. He is the author of *Shakespeare and Modernism* (Cambridge, 2006) and of related articles on Shakespeare and the early twentieth century in *New Theatre Quarterly*, *Shakespeare Survey* and *Shakespeare*. He is editor of Volume 9 in the forthcoming series *Great Shakespeareans* (Continuum), and author of a biographical essay on A. C. Bradley in the volume. He is also the contributor of numerous entries on modernist Shakespeare criticism to the forthcoming *Shakespeare Encyclopedia* (Santa Barbara, 2009).

NOREEN DOODY is a lecturer in the Department of English, St Patrick's College, Drumcondra, Dublin City University. Her research and publications are in Irish Studies and nineteenth-century literature, especially the work of Oscar Wilde and W. B. Yeats.

PHILIP EDWARDS is Emeritus Professor of English at the University of Liverpool and formerly taught at Trinity College Dublin. His publications include *Threshold of a Nation: A Study in English and Irish Drama* (Cambridge, 1979); *Shakespeare: A Writer's Progress* (Oxford, 1986), *Shakespeare's Styles: Essays in Honour of Kenneth Muir*, edited with Inga-Stina Ewbank and G. K. Hunter (Cambridge, 2004). He has edited *King Lear* (Basingstoke, 1975); *Hamlet* (Cambridge, 1985); *Pericles* (Harmondsworth, 1976); *The Spanish Tragedy* (Manchester, 1977), and, with Colin Gibson, *The Plays and Poems of Philip Massinger* (Oxford, 1976).

HEATHER INGMAN is a member of the School of English, Trinity College Dublin. She has published widely on women's writing, including women's inter-war fiction and Irish women's writing. Her publications include *Women's Fiction Between the Wars: Mothers, Daughters and Writing* (Edinburgh, 1998) and *Mothers and Daughters in the Twentieth Century: A Literary Anthology* (Edinburgh, 1999). Her most recent book is *Twentieth Century Fiction by Irish Women: Nation and Gender* (Aldershot, 2007).

DECLAN KIBERD is Professor of Anglo-Irish Literature and Drama in the School of English, Drama and Film, University College Dublin. His publications include *Synge and the Irish Language* (London, 1979; 2nd edn 1992); *Men and Feminism in Modern Literature* (London, 1985; 2nd edn 1987); *Inventing Ireland: The Literature of the Modern Nation* (London, 1995); *Irish Classics* (London, 2000); *The Irish Writer and the World* (Cambridge, 2005); numerous essays on Irish literature in English and Irish; and most recently *Ulysses and Us* (London, 2009).

HELEN HEUSNER LOJEK is Professor of English and Associate Dean of the College of Arts and Sciences at Boise State University, Idaho. She is the author of *Contexts for Frank McGuinness's Drama* (Washington DC, 2004) and has written extensively on Brian Friel, Charabanc Theatre Company, and the drama of Northern Ireland. She is currently working on a book about space in Irish drama.

RICHARD MEEK has taught at the University of Reading, King's College London, and the University of York. He has recently published essays in *SEL* and *English*, and *Narrating the Visual in Shakespeare* (Aldershot, 2009). He has co-edited a collection of essays exploring the notion of a 'literary' Shakespeare, entitled *Shakespeare's Book: Essays in Reading, Writing, and Reception* (Manchester, 2008). An article on the relationship between *King Lear* and *Heart of Darkness* is forthcoming in *Borrowers and Lenders*.

ANDREW MURPHY is Professor of English at the University of St Andrews. He is the author, most recently, of *Shakespeare for the People: Working-Class Readers 1800–1900* (Cambridge, 2008) and *Shakespeare in Print: A History and Chronology of Shakespeare Publishing* (Cambridge, 2003). His first book was *But the Irish Sea Betwixt Us: Ireland, Colonialism, and Renaissance Literature* (Kentucky, 1999). His edited collections include *A Concise Companion to Shakespeare and the Text* (Oxford, 2007) and *Shakespeare and Scotland*, co-edited with Willy Maley (Manchester, 2005).

TADHG Ó DÚSHLÁINE is Senior Lecturer in the Department of Modern Irish, National University of Ireland Maynooth. His research is on Gaelic literature, especially from the seventeenth century. His publications include *An Eoraip agus Litríocht na Gaeilge 1600–1650: Gnéithe den Bharócachas Eorpach i Litríocht na Gaeilge* (Dublin, 1987) and essays on Irish-language writers Séan Óg Ó Caomhánaigh and Jer Ó Cíobháin.

STEPHEN O'NEILL is Lecturer in English Literature in the School of English, Media and Theatre Studies, National University of Ireland Maynooth. His publications include *Staging Ireland: Representations in Shakespeare and Renaissance Drama* (Dublin, 2007) and essays on Elizabethan drama. His current research is on Shakespeare and new media.

Note on Procedures

All quotations of Shakespeare are from the Oxford Shakespeare *Complete Works* ed. by Gary Taylor and Stanley Wells (Oxford, 1988), unless otherwise stated.

Interpreting Shakespeare in Ireland

Janet Clare and Stephen O'Neill

'After all, Ireland is not England, and if she does homage to Shakespeare it must be more or less in her own way!' wrote Douglas Hyde, leader of the Gaelic League, to Victor Gollancz, Professor of English at King's College, London and Honorary Secretary of the Shakespeare Tercentenary Committee.[1] Writing in the year before the Easter Rising and in the decade before the War of Independence, it is to be expected that Hyde's response to the genius of Shakespeare should be guarded and qualified. It is nonetheless characteristic both of an Irish generosity to Shakespeare – that homage should be done – and of a determination to disengage from post-Romantic bardolatry. If Hyde's nationalist sensitivities at once suggest an Irish language and literary tradition independent of Shakespeare, at the same time there is a sense of a shared tradition of reading, commenting on and indeed acting Shakespeare that has produced an intimacy with the works, one which surfaces again and again in Irish writing, both in English and in Gaelic. Of course, interpreting Shakespeare from a specific national context in the way Hyde does here has always been integral to the study of the plays and their changing meanings and has become increasingly widespread: in disparate national contexts, from Australia and Canada to China and Romania, the Shakespeare canon con- tinues to enjoy a considerable literary and cultural afterlife. Recent studies of Shakespeare's reception in these and other contexts have revealed the various local histories at play in that afterlife.[2] As Fintan O'Toole has commented, 'Shakespeare's plays are one of the few sets of narratives that are available across national and religious lines.'[3] But the reception of Shakespeare in Ireland is especially interesting as it involves a history of performing, studying and responding to the plays in English and in Irish translation, in colonial and post-colonial settings. Focusing specifically on the work of Irish writers, mod- ernist and contemporary, and their response to Shakespeare, this collection seeks to build on earlier work devoted to the larger question of Shakespeare and Ireland.[4] Much of the earlier work in this area has been concerned with the Irish subtexts and contexts of Shakespeare's plays.[5] In contrast, the present volume shifts the focus to the reciprocal relationship between Shakespeare and the Irish writer. Shakespearean texts have stimulated Irish writing, while Irish writers in their appropriations of and responses to Shakespeare have given a great deal to Shakespeare studies. The enlargement of meaning that Irish writing has afforded Shakespeare's plays constitutes a legitimate form of Shakespeare criticism.

Hyde's comment draws attention to the extent to which Shakespeare has occupied a liminal position in Ireland, at certain points in history being associated with British imperialism or its cultural legacy. It was not until 1933, for example, that Dublin's Shakespeare Society changed its name from the British Empire Shakespeare Society; according to one member 'the words British Empire in the name of the society has the effect of keeping out many people'.[6] Proximate and contentious as Shakespeare is and has been in relation to Irish writing, he has elicited double and, occasionally, paradoxical perspectives. For example, in this volume, Tadhg Ó Dúshláine notes how Seán Ó Ríordáin's poem 'Fill Aris', which is on the Leaving Certificate Gaelic syllabus, contends that the Irish race must break free of the dominance of English literature as epitomised in Shakespeare, Keats and Shelley. Yet, in his diary, amongst many references to Shakespeare, Ó Ríordáin brackets him with Homer, Virgil, Plato and Dante as 'world giants'.[7] Similarly, Andrew Murphy's discussion in this volume of the poem that Hyde composed for the Shakespeare tercentenary text reveals a fractured response: in the poem, an Irishman journeys to Stratford where he condemns English control in Ireland but exempts Shakespeare from implication. One could further argue that the bi-cultural inheritance of Irish writers has been creatively enriching, at once outside and invested in a tradition while in the direct line of another. In the early twentieth-century this enabled a critical vantage point, demonstrated in the writings of Shaw, impossible for a British writer at the time to attain.

The relationship between Shakespeare and Ireland has been, unsurprisingly, theorised in terms of Ireland's colonial past. Irish responses to the plays from the late nineteenth century onward have been interpreted as decolonising moments, whereby the master author and texts of empire are seized and adapted to articulate a subaltern experience and perspective. Declan Kiberd's *Inventing Ireland*, in a chapter on Irish engagements with Shakespeare by Yeats and Joyce, persuasively theorises the Shakespeare–Ireland relationship in these terms and has established the interpretative terrain that the current volume seeks to evaluate.[8] More recently, Robin Bates, drawing on Kiberd's post-colonial analysis, has attempted to connect responses by Irish writers to Shakespeare's representation of the Irish or their 'cultural impressment' in the plays. Understood in such terms, the use of the Irish in 'Shakespeare's presentations of Britain and the superiority of Englishness [. . .] creates a continuing conflict for the Irish writer attempting to operate within a dominant language and literature inherited as part of belonging to the empire'.[9] But this formulation improbably suggests a uniformity of response by the Irish to Shakespeare and filters the specificities and nuances of individual responses and reactions through a one-fits-all post-colonial reading. While it is important to note the ways in which Irish engagements with Shakespeare were shaped by the historical relationship between Britain and Ireland, it is also necessary that we avoid producing Manichean or over-determined understandings and interpretations of those engagements. Accordingly, in attending to different kinds and forms of response to Shakespeare by writers in Ireland at various points in history, this collection is intended to provide some new parameters for interpreting Shakespeare and his cultural associations in and from Ireland.

SHAKESPEARE'S RECEPTION IN IRELAND

Irish actors, directors, scholars and creative writers have always contributed to what is now increasingly regarded as the Shakespeare industry and have done so in both English and also in Irish translation. And, generations of Irish people have grown up familiar with Shakespeare's plays, which continue to be a core component of post-primary education. Shakespeare continues to be a recurring feature of the Irish theatrical scene, with innovative productions by indigenous companies such as the Abbey, Classic Stage Ireland, Rough Magic, as well as visiting companies.[10] Fiona Shaw is among the best known Irish actors to appear in Shakespearean productions in Ireland and Britain; indeed Shaw's performance as Richard II in the Royal National Theatre's 1995 production is part of a long tradition of Irish actresses playing male roles that dates back to Fanny Furnival, the first female Hamlet, in Dublin's Smock Alley Theatre in 1741, and one that includes Millicent Bandman-Palmer playing Shakespeare's troubled young prince in Dublin's Gaiety Theatre in June 1904.[11] It is Bandman-Palmer's performance that gives rise to the comic observation in Joyce's *Ulysses*: 'I hear that an actress played Hamlet for the fourhundredandeight time in Dublin. Vining held that the prince was a woman. Has no one made him out to be an Irishman?'[12] If the Irish can subvert Hamlet's gender why not his nationality, Joyce playfully asks.

The business of theatre has always subverted national boundaries. Actors playing Shakespeare have moved freely between Ireland and Britain since the early seventeenth century, if not before.[13] One of the earliest Shakespeare performances in Ireland was a production of *Othello* by John Ogilby in Dublin's Smock Alley Theatre in 1662, thus laying the ground for a long and continuing history of Shakespeare on the Irish stage.[14] But the traffic of players flowed both ways: actors from Smock Alley, whose repertoire included *Hamlet*,

Julius Caesar, King Lear, Macbeth and *The Tempest,* performed both in Edinburgh as well as in their native city.[15] In the eighteenth century, Dublin-born Thomas Sheridan was regarded on London's stages as second only to the pre-eminent Shakespearean actor David Garrick, renowned for his Hamlet, which he played for the first time on a Dublin stage.[16] In the nineteenth century, major Shakespearean productions by Sir Henry Irving and F. R. Benson regularly played in Dublin's Theatre Royal and Gaiety Theatre. In the early twentieth century, Shakespeare formed an integral part of the repertoire of the Gate Theatre, where the expressionist style of its founders Hilton Edwards and Micheál MacLiammóir drew recognition at home and abroad.[17] And the Abbey Theatre, while fostering a national Irish drama, also staged Shakespeare, with its first Shakespearean production – *King Lear* in 1928 – initiating an enduring commitment to Shakespeare's plays. Clearly, these plays constitute a theatrical history shared by Ireland and Britain.

The theatrical tradition of Shakespeare in Ireland predates the scholarly one. There had been individual editions of the plays published in Dublin since the early eighteenth century as well as editions of the complete works – such as Alexander Pope's 1725 edition – but in the history of the editing of Shakespeare, the contribution of the eighteenth-century Irish editor Edmond Malone is particularly central.[18] Malone, who came from a legal family and for a time pursued a legal career, had discovered Shakespeare at an early age, acting in his plays at Dr Ford's school on Molesworth Street in Dublin.[19] When he moved to London in 1774, Malone became part of the circle of Dr Johnson, and made only occasional return visits to Ireland.[20] He collaborated with George Steevens in his edition of Shakespeare and for the second edition produced the first chronological study which he entitled 'Attempt to Ascertain the Order in which the Plays attributed to Shakespeare were Written'. For the third collaborative edition, Malone produced two additional volumes for which he wrote 'History of the Stage' and produced an edition of the non-dramatic poems. In 1790, Malone's own edition of Shakespeare was published, which was now a rival to that of Steevens. 'The fruit of all this labour', Malone wrote, is 'a genuine text'.[21]

In a series of lectures on Shakespeare in the eighteenth century, David Nichol Smith saw Malone as the culmination of the later school of eighteenth-century editors and asserted that 'he remains the greatest of all our Shakespearian scholars'.[22] If this is so, more recent bibliographical work has identified how, as much as he consolidated earlier scholarship, Malone equally determined later. In a sense Malone revolutionised the way Shakespeare was read. While his editorial procedures have been seen as conservative, Malone's 1790 edition, with its emphasis on documented materials in compiling and annotating the plays, provided future generations of editors with what has been described as 'the apparatus' of the Shakespearean text.[23] Further, his editorial recovery of the *Sonnets* was instrumental in transforming Shakespeare from the public dramatic poet of the Restoration and the eighteenth century into a private lyric poet who could be embraced and appropriated by the Romantics.[24]

Nichol Smith's comments set Malone firmly in the tradition of English scholarship. Yet to some of his detractors Malone's nationality formed part of the ammunition in their attacks on his scholarship. Joseph Ritson in *Cursory Criticisms on the edition of Shakespeare published by Edmond Malone* refers to Malone as 'our Irish editor' and 'our Hibernian'.[25] He implies that the textual errors of the 1790 edition are linked to the author's ethnicity. As an Irishman, Malone could not expect to understand the mentality of an English author, Ritson claimed: the 'ears of Shakespeare were made very differently from Mr Malone'. And, commenting on the perceived shortcomings of Malone's editing of *Coriolanus*, Ritson concluded 'But such is the absurd consequence of an Irish editor attempting the illustration of an English author'.[26] Through these slurs, Ritson vented his professional jealousy of Malone, whose 1790 edition had frustrated Ritson's own ambitions to produce a Shakespearean edition.[27] Ritson's comments are curious in view of Malone's pro-Union sympathies and his integration into the literary circles of eighteenth-century London; it seems that when scholarship wished to claim Malone as one of the editorial tradition, his Irish identity was submerged, only to be revived in the criticisms of hostile editors and reviewers. For his part, Malone modestly registered satisfaction that his work had been well received in Ireland: 'I was not a little pleased to learn from every quarter that my work had not been disapproved of by the public.'[28]

The importance of Malone in bibliographical history is matched by Edward Dowden's significance as the first biographer of Shakespeare. Dowden, who in 1867 and at the age of twenty-four became Professor of English Literature at Trinity College Dublin, was the author of *Shakspere: A Critical Study of his Mind and Art* (1874). In an address delivered in the Chapel of Trinity College Dublin on Trinity Monday, 1943, Dowden's successor H. O. White coupled Dowden with Malone in terms of his permanent place in the history of Shakespearean scholarship. Dowden saw himself as a Liberal Unionist (as opposed to an English Tory) but his Protestant, Unionist position meant that he was seen as a 'reluctant Irishman' by some.[29] His indifference to the work of the Irish Literary Revival could only reinforce this view. Although he was a friend of Samuel Ferguson, who was so instrumental in the Celtic revival and in the foundation of a national literature in the English language, Dowden could 'never more than half enter' Ferguson's epic *Congal* which preceded *Shakspere: A Critical Study of his Mind and Art* by two years.[30] Ireland was developing its national literature as the first Professor of English Literature at the University of Dublin was producing a biography of England's national poet, which was to gain him worldwide recognition. In the 'nationality' versus 'cosmopolitan' debate in which cosmopolitanism was seen as obliterating all nationality from critical and creative work, Dowden's position was clear.[31]

For Dowden, writing about Shakespeare, as about Wordsworth, Shelley, Goethe, Montaigne and Whitman, was a non-nationalist undertaking, though in some respects Dowden's universalising of literature may have involved a deliberate avoidance of contemporary political differences and debates. Yet, intriguingly, Dowden's approach bears comparison to that of several Gaelic revivalists, who saw English literature, and Shakespeare especially, as being beyond questions of national difference; 'the Gaelic Leaguer loves his Shakespeare' claimed Eamon O'Neill at a meeting of the League attended by Yeats and Lady Gregory.[32] As Philip Edwards has commented, de-Anglicising did not necessarily equal de-Shakespearising.[33] For instance, Frank O'Connor in his book *Shakespeare's Progress* was generally uninterested in Shakespeare's national identity. Furthermore, several Irish republicans including Ernest O'Malley, Seán O'Faoláin and Peadar O'Donnell expressed admiration and respect for Shakespeare. And, Thomas MacDonagh, who taught with Padraig Pearse at St Enda's school in Rathfarnham and later fought alongside him in the 1916 Easter Rising, wrote approvingly of Shakespeare.[34] Dowden was far from an isolated figure and indeed his admiration for Shakespeare may have been more equivocal than that of contemporary nationalists.

In *Shakespeare: A Critical Study of his Mind and Art*, through a chronological treatment of the plays, Dowden attempted a spiritual and psychological biography of the dramatist. Dowden was not altogether happy about his work on Shakespeare. He recognised that for the sake of Britain Shakespeare must be praised, but he struggled with the difficulty of finding what he sought: the personality of a dramatic poet. This was inevitable when, as Philip Edwards points out, the texts that Dowden was discussing were not, as with Wordsworth and Shelley, confessional or meditative. As is clear, and he was not alone at the time, Dowden had little interest in Shakespeare as a writer for theatre or – despite all the scholarship of Malone – as the author of plays dependent on other plays, rather than solely expressive of mind and personality. Dowden sensed this himself when he wrote to Aubrey de Vere after the publication:

> This 'Study of Shakespeare' I only partly like myself . . . one who loves Wordsworth and Browning and Newman can never be content to wholly abandon desires and fears and affinities which are extra mundane, even for the sake of the rich and ample life of a mundane passion and action which Shakespeare reveals.[35]

It is evident that in working on Shakespeare, Dowden may in a strange way have engaged with a subject against the grain. Elsewhere in the letters he talks of Shakespeare being 'a discipline', 'alien to my most vital self'; he was concerned that he had put some of himself into Shakespeare as part of a defence in an only partly congenial undertaking. Philip Edwards in the essay in this volume questions the now traditional view of Dowden as celebrating a masculine, materialist Shakespeare who worshipped success.

It is the 'cosmopolitan' approach which distinguishes Dowden's approach from other near contemporary studies of Shakespeare's plays in Ireland, as evidenced by such publications as Darrell Figgis's *Shakespeare: A Study* (1911) and Plunket Barton's *Links between Ireland and Shakespeare* (1919). Barton's book reads as an antiquarian excavation of references to Ireland as well as putative Irish and Celtic sources for Shakespeare's plays, expanding earlier work by David Comyn and William Magennis.[36] As with these earlier examples, Barton's objective is to establish the presence of Ireland in Shakespeare's creative map and, in the process, forge cross-cultural connections. Figgis's part in the audacious smuggling of guns into Ireland in May 1914 meant that he was one of many nationalists rounded up in the period of martial law following the Easter Rising; he was imprisoned in Ireland and, then, Britain. But his nationality impinges hardly at all in his critical appreciation of Shakespeare. Rather than betraying hostility to Shakespeare as the national poet of the enemy, Figgis is hostile to the anti-Shakespearean polemic of Bernard Shaw and contests his fellow Irishman, as amongst Shakespeare's 'newer critics' who wear the 'cap of revolution and enmity'.[37] In the closing lines of his introduction, Figgis comments that perhaps 'there was never a time so opportune for such a task as the present'.[38] By the present opportunity for a new book on Shakespeare, Figgis is presumably alluding to critique of Shakespeare and the defence of Shakespeare from the 'new drama' of European modernism.

AT STRATFORD-ON-AVON: DOWDEN AND YEATS

In an Irish context what Dowden's work on Shakespeare is most remembered for is the response of Yeats in his essay 'At Stratford-on-Avon'. Written in April 1901, when Yeats saw Benson's production of Shakespeare's histories, the essay reads as a critique of Victorian Shakespeare criticism, a riposte to Dowden, who is regarded as exemplifying its worst excesses, and wider observations on the interpretation of art. Even as it unfolds its broader concerns, the essay is personal in tone and replays old frustrations with Dowden on the part of the poet and of his father, J. B. Yeats. For the latter, Dowden's approach to literature was 'too heavy, too moral, too intellectual' and it was a view of the Trinity professor that Yeats inherited.[39] This is especially evident in Yeats's discussion of Shakespeare's portrayal of Richard II, whom he sets out to defend from Shakespeare critics and their 'vulgar worship of success'.[40]

To Yeats, Dowden's imperialist celebration of Bolingbroke as a man of action and condemnation of Richard as a self-regarding dreamer is a fundamentally misguided reading of Shakespeare's drama and aesthetic. Yeats's Shakespeare is no utilitarian but an artist who embraces the imaginative, the contemplative, the sensitive, qualities that Yeats suggests Richard exhibits. As Yeats writes, Shakespeare 'had no nice sense of utilities, no ready balance to measure deeds'.[41] The implications of Yeats's reading have been variously considered as the co-opting of Shakespeare in the interests of Irish cultural nationalism through a disassociation from 'Britian, union, empire and shared culture';[42] or, relatedly, the restoration to the plays of 'an openness that they had lost under an imperial interpretative psychology'.[43] That some English journalists reacted negatively to the essay, regarding it as an audacious reinterpretation, gives ground to these hypotheses.[44] Yet it would be too crude to regard 'At Stratford-on-Avon' as producing an Irish Shakespeare; rather, as Brian Cosgrove shows in this volume, the Shakespeare that emerges is very much bound up with Yeatsian aesthetics and antinomies that include utilitarianism and its attendant moralism, on one hand, and freedom and wildness, on the other. Interestingly, while Dowden in his letters had written against utilitarianism, to Yeats he was exemplary of a perspective on literature and Shakespeare that was antithetical to his own. Nonetheless, as Cosgrove contends, Yeats's essay cannot be reduced to a reflex of political divisions in Ireland at the time. Moreover, it demonstrates the mutability of Shakespeare in Irish writing for, as Philip Edwards has noted, only two years before the publication of 'At Stratford-on-Avon', Yeats had seen only the mundane aspect of Shakespeare, 'his preoccupation with things'.[45]

WRITING IN SHAKESPEARE'S SHADOW: INFLUENCE AND ICONOCLASM

The centrality of Shakespeare in Irish culture as exemplified in the work, critical and creative, of Irish writers on both sides of the political divide raises the spectre of influence. Harold Bloom's controversial and singular theory of poetic influence expounded in *The Anxiety of Influence* in which an ephebe's poetry is born from an agonistic struggle with a strong precursor might not be inapt to describe the relationship of the Irish writer to Shakespeare. Joyce, Wilde and Shaw liked to associate their life or art or both with Shakespeare. In Bloom's interpretation of artistic creation, power and agency reside in the influential figure – the strong male poets of his canon – and an agonistic struggle follows with the poet in the shadow of influence. In the struggle the follower attempts to absorb and surpass the poetry of a strong precursor.[46] Interestingly, Bloom's theory of influence has classical antecedents, which, we can presuppose would have appealed to Wilde and Joyce. Longinus had employed similar eristic metaphors as Bloom in his description of Plato wrestling with Homer.[47] Such a struggle was an open one for pre-eminence; struggle, strife and competition led to the poet's attempts to match his model. Literary competence grows through the aspirant's rivalry with authors of his own day as well as of antiquity.

Several contributors in this volume have appealed – explicitly or implicitly – to Bloom's theory of influence as apposite to the relationship of the Irish writer to Shakespeare. For James Joyce, Shakespeare was the precursor who he wished not merely to emulate, but also to surpass or, in Declan Kiberd's words in his essay in this volume, Shakespeare was Joyce's antagonist whose greatest work – *Hamlet* – might be trumped. Kiberd's discussion of *Hamlet* as an intertext for *Ulysses* demonstrates how the latter keeps faith with the 'deeper thesis' of the former. To this end, Kiberd demonstrates how Joyce's novel interacts with the play's concern for the 'lost integrity of the father-son relationship' and develops one of its centrifugal questions: 'how to complete an authentic action which expresses, rather than simplifying or falsifying, the inner self?'[48] More generally, it is in *Ulysses*, and especially in the 'Scylla and Charybdis' chapter, that Shakespeare's canonicity is dissected and the corpus of English literature is critically examined.[49] As Stephen Dedalus presents his theory of *Hamlet* before various auditors in the National Library, a layered dialogue with the playwright, his plays and their motifs develops.[50] Frequently, the tone is humorous: John Eglinton mentions 'Saxon Shakespeare' and later comments 'The bard's fellowcountrymen [. . .] are rather tired of our brilliancies of theorising'; Buck Mulligan asks 'Shakespeare? I seem to know the name [. . .] The chap who writes like Synge'; Stephen asks 'Why is the underplot of *King Lear* in which Edmund figures lifted out of Sidney's *Arcadia* and spatchcocked on to a Celtic Legend older than history?' and goes on to divine a 'note of banishment, banishment from the heart, from the home' in Shakespeare's dramatic oeuvre.[51] In these readings from Ireland, various Shakespeares emerge. Eglinton references national readings and their different nuances. Mulligan is iconoclastic. Stephen more studiously identifies the intertexts of *King Lear* and – more provocatively – suggests Celtic influence. Stephen's Hamlet-theory is, of course, generally provocative and perhaps the positioning of Shakespeare as a literary forefather ripe for re-evaluation involves a challenging of colonial authority and its cultural forms, especially viewed in relation to the novel's setting in pre-Independent Ireland.[52] Yet, as Kiberd suggests, for Dedalus, and perhaps Joyce himself too, Shakespeare remains the supreme artist, one who casts different shadows depending on where and when he is read. And, *Ulysses* seems fully cognisant that the uses to which Shakespeare can be put are multivalent and are not beholden to narrowly conceived ideologies of nation and identity.

The question of 'influence' figures rather differently and to some extent more conventionally in the relationship of Wilde with Shakespeare in which there is little sense of 'anxiety' on the part of the younger poet. As both essays here amply demonstrate, Shakespeare was an authoritative presence and arbiter of Wilde's aesthetics. In her essay, Noreen Doody claims that Shakespeare was pivotal to Wilde's sense of his own identity: national, artistic and sexual. At his trial in 1895, accused of gross indecency, Wilde appealed to the Shakespeare of the *Sonnets*. An incriminating love letter sent to Wilde was thus turned into a sonnet, evoking the homoeroticism of Shakespeare's sonnets, aestheticising life as art. Through appeal to Keats's formulation of Shakespeare's negative capability, Shakespeare's aesthetic was a powerful antecedent for Wilde's view that art is a matter of 'imaginative reality' rather than 'unimaginative realism'.[53] Wilde was of course fascinated by the notion of literary influence, seemingly concurring with the view that words always belong to somebody else, thus, making writing always an act of collaboration. In his essay 'Lips that Shakespeare taught to speak', Richard Meek argues that Shakespeare's contribution to Wilde's conception of life as art can shape the interpretation of *The Picture of Dorian Gray*. In the portrayal of the Shakespearean actress Sybil Vane and Dorian's fascination with her, the novel dramatises the ethical and moral problems that emerge when one allows influence, literary or otherwise, to take over one's life. Dorian's love of Sybil Vane is bound up with his love of Shakespeare so that Shakespeare's words, their influence, improperly create feelings. More generally, Meek's analysis of *Dorian Gray* demonstrates the sheer power of Shakespeare's literary afterlife as it pervades Wilde's text and the minds of his protagonists.

What is intriguing about the relationship of Irish writers with Shakespeare is the overlapping and divergences of response. The nationalist, Jesuit-educated Joyce would seem to have little in common with the anglophone, Methodist-educated Shaw. Yet both were Irish expatriates looking to Europe for artistic inspiration rather than to the Irish Literary Revival or to the tradition of British literature. In Joyce's *Exiles*, the journalist Robert Hand seems close to Joyce when he observes 'If Ireland is to become a new Ireland she must first become European'.[54] Nonetheless, Shakespeare was a monumental figure that could not be readily dismissed as part of an outworn tradition. If Joyce sought to surpass Shakespeare, Shaw saw him as one of the 'towers of the Bastille' that must be destroyed to promote a European modernist drama. In his Preface to *Caesar and Cleopatra*, Shaw entitled provocatively a section 'Better than Shakespear'. Yet, as Cary DiPietro notes in his essay in this volume, while it may be tempting to read the essay as an expression of Shaw's anxiety of influence, of a writer anxious to defeat his literary precursor by bettering him, this was not Shaw's point. Shaw, in his response to Shakespeare's *Antony and Cleopatra* was engaged, as he was later to be in *Saint Joan*, in an act of historical revisionism. While Shaw admired Shakespeare's 'word music', he deplored the lack of noble ideas, the characters and his lack of historical understanding. In his iconoclasm, that shocked some contemporaries, Shaw claimed that there was an intellectual and philosophical paucity while also exclaiming that he pitied the man who could not enjoy Shakespeare. Shaw's relationship with Shakespeare was thus a mixture of rivalry and censure and, as DiPietro notes below, his Irishness allowed him that external perspective, a critical vantage point from which he could critique Shakespeare in ways that his English contemporaries could not. Indeed, it was Shaw who coined the term 'bardolatry' to encapsulate the uncritical worship of Shakespeare, associated, in critics like Walter Raleigh, with imperialism at the expense of what, according to Shaw, was innovative and, philosophically richer in the new European drama of Ibsen and Chekhov.

CONTESTING WORDS: LANGUAGE, PARODY AND TRANSLATION

The response of the Irish writer to the language of Shakespeare has been ambiguous. Not all Irish writers have shared Shaw's admiration of Shakespeare's word music. Caliban's retort to Prospero in *The Tempest* that his 'master' has taught him language and his profit is that he knows 'how to curse' (1.2.364) has been quoted as a post-colonial paradigm for the subversion of the language of the coloniser by the colonised. While he had no explicit sympathy for the cause of the Gaelic League, Joyce complained to his Swiss reviewer of the constraints of writing in English or at least of the limitations of writing for the English reading public: 'Writing in English is the most ingenious torture ever devised for sins committed in previous lives. The English reading public explains the reason why.'[55] Certainly, as Matthew Creasy recalls at the beginning of his essay, the case has been made for Joyce as a wrecker of inherited language structures, a kind of Celtic revenge upon imperial oppressors. Here, the use of Shakespeare as the English national poet would seem central. The 'Scylla and Charybdis' episode in particular reveals a playful preoccupation with Shakespeare's 'words, words, words'. In *Ulysses*, misapplied quotations from Shakespeare's plays can serve as a private joke but also function more pointedly.[56] Yet, for all their paradoic suggestiveness, the Shakespeareanisms in *Ulysses* are not necessarily a subversion of but a 'lyrical identification' with Shakespeare's language.[57] Parody can thus play an oblique homage.[58]

As Creasy demonstrates, appropriating Shakespeare's text and parodying Shakespeare's language is not restricted to Joyce but was part of a wider practice in political journalism in pre- and also post-Independent Ireland. Sketches in *The Leader*, which Creasy terms as a journal of national self-criticism, use Shakespeare as a vehicle of political satire in the same way as Shakespeare burlesques did on the London stage. There is, as Creasy argues here, a certain ambiguity in the sense that the revivalists who contributed to

The Leader might be making the Shakespeare allusion the object of fun or ridicule while equally accepting that he was important enough to be worth mocking. The object of the parody in these sketches may not even be Shakespeare, but the failings of the Irish who have succumbed to the excesses of English popular culture and by extension the contemporary language. Andrew Murphy develops this point in his essay and quotes Douglas Hyde: 'If by ceasing to speak Irish our peasantry could learn to appreciate Shakespeare and Milton, to study Wordsworth or Tennyson, then I would certainly say adieu to it.'[59] But since that 'language' has been lost to the people, Hyde contends, and replaced by one that is much less 'forcible' than Gaelic there is every reason for the de-Anglicisation of Ireland. As Murphy argues in his essay, Hyde's poem for the Shakespeare tercentenary volume crystallises the unresolved tension between his respect for Shakespeare and English 'high culture' and his frustration with English rule in Ireland. The differences between the English original and the Gaelic translation that appear in the imperial themed volume and that Murphy traces here reveal this fracture point. For Hyde's poem at once reads as a homage to Shakespeare and also a co-opting of him to critique the English colonial project in Ireland.

The position of the Gaelic League and other cultural nationalists like Hyde involved a desire to break free from English literary influences, yet Shakespeare appears to have occupied a privileged position. As Tadhg Ó Dúshláine demonstrates in his essay on Irish language translations of Shakespeare, cultural nationalism did not prevent engagement with the most culturally valorised of English literary figures. In an essay that introduces Irish language responses to Shakespeare – an overlooked subject to date – Ó Dúshláine notes how Gaelic writers actively debated the value of translating Shakespeare 'as Gaeilge'.[60] For some writers, such as J. L. O'Sullivan, who translated *Macbeth* into Irish in 1925, the act of translation was a way of enhancing the Irish language through a European context, for 'the great continental nations', he explained, 'have long ago realised the full educative value of making available for their peoples, through translation, the classic literatures of foreign countries.'[61] For others, there was little value in reading Shakespeare in Irish since translation could not convey the pathos of the Shakespearean text. But for others again, Shakespeare's language could curiously overlap with Irish, as in Sean Og Ó Caomhanach's gloss of 'crants' from *Hamlet*: ''Tis common with us in Irish. I thought it odd at the time but now I see that it has the same meaning in Shakespeare as it had with us.' For the same writer, writing from an internment camp in the Curragh in 1922, the words of Shakespeare resonated, conveying a sense of an ending: 'Like Hamlet, am I not going to my death?'[62] It is important to note that Irish language translations and responses to Shakespeare from cultural nationalists have not been narrowly determined by issues of national literatures; Ó Dúshláine comments on the more recent example of poet Nuala Ní Dhomhnaill who, in several Irish language poems, cites Shakespearean characters and motifs, often quite playfully, so as to disarm the gender assumptions that have traditionally underpinned them. Once again it is evident that for the Irish writer, Shakespeare can elicit a range of responses.

ALLUSIONS AND SUBTEXTS

It is probable that as an interpretative intertext Shakespeare's works are amongst the most frequently appropriated and quoted.[63] The reader's recognition of such Shakespearean intertexts or citations enhances the pleasure of reading; [64] but in an Irish context, quotation or eclectic use of Shakespeare brings with it the aura of a colonial text. Declan Kiberd has noted of Wilde and Joyce that they articulated their response to Shakespeare in their fiction and this is also true of a number of writers represented in this volume.[65] Several essays explore the resonances of Shakespeare's plays in later writing and identify this dialogic relationship as an interpretative tool. Heather Ingman has commented of Elizabeth Bowen that she was a precursor of a series of women writers who have reclaimed Shakespeare for female-centred experience and, more specifically, that Bowen uses Shakespeare to relay a critical portrayal of the Anglo-Irish in *The Last September*. The reader is alerted to a Shakespearean subtext by Marda's allusion to Shakespeare, and if this is taken to be *Twelfth Night*, as Ingman argues, the novel's preoccupation with the fragility of society and fluidities of gender and desire become more pronounced. Unlike source studies or attention only to questions of influence, awareness of intertextuality expands the meaning not only of the host text but also of the pre-text. If Shakespeare's play underpins Bowen's novel, as Ingman argues, the novel, in its turn, draws out what is only briefly referred to in Shakespeare's play, the precarious insularity of Illyria. Bowen's recourse to Shakespeare to comment suggestively on Irish politics is repeated in her short story 'Sunday Afternoon' where *The Tempest* is Bowen's subtext. Illustrative of the range of uses to which Irish writers have put Shakespeare, Bowen's perspective is far from post-colonial: in her take on the play, there is no subversion of Prospero's rule.

The aura of *The Tempest* informs Joyce's *Exiles* (1918). Like Prospero, Richard Rowan has been an exile from his home country, although Joyce's play, unlike Shakepeare's, focuses on return and Rowan's re-establishment in Ireland. Memorably, near the end of the play, Rowan returns from his walk on Merrion strand, claiming, and misquoting Caliban, 'the isle is full of voices'. Like Caliban, Rowan is on his native soil and seems to hear what others do not. But there would seem to be more submerged Shakespearean intertexts as *Exiles* evokes Shakespeare's explorations of sexual jealousy and tormented obsession with infidelity represented in *The Winter's Tale*. Wrecked with uncertainty about Bertha's fidelity, Rowan's disquietude evokes that of Othello, but more particularly Leontes. Like Leontes and Polixenes in *The Winter's Tale*, Richard Rowan and Robert Hand have been friends since boyhood and it is Bertha, like Hermione, who alludes to this intimacy. It is an intimacy that extends to the love of the same woman, imagined in Shakespeare, real in Joyce, and with the same unsettling consequences. Neither Rowan nor the audience know the truth and that both Bertha and Robert allude to the truth as a 'dream' brings us back to Shakespeare's dream play world where illusion and reality, shadow and substance, are blurred. *Exiles* with its eclectic mingling of heterogeneous Shakespeare allusions is also charged with the evocative power of the texts from which they are taken.

The plays of Samuel Beckett similarly echo and allude to Shakespeare. Writing in French and in English, his plays have been absorbed into continental theatre as much as Irish or British theatre. Arguably, of all the Irish writers discussed in this volume Beckett's work has least to do with Ireland or least reflects questions of national identity. Yet Beckett was educated in Dublin and was a close associate of Joyce, and as with Joyce the language of Shakespeare resonates in his plays and prose and is put to new and startling use. In his essay in this volume, David Wheatley does not engage specifically with Beckett as an Irish writer, although he demonstrates that Beckett's early reading of Shakespeare gave him considerable familiarity with the plays. Instead, Wheatley explores the resonance of the Shakespeare text in a text of modern Irish drama. Taking his cue from Jan Kott's pioneering essay on the two plays, Wheatley furthers the idea of *Lear* as a prototype for the tragicomedy of *Endgame* in the particular brand of clowning and the way clowning imposes in great tragic scenes.[66] However grim and unbearable, Beckett's characters go on, as do Shakespeare's. Beckett's staging, as Wheatley says, favours 'a ruthless minimalism', not so far distanced from the Elizabethan stage and for all his minimalism Beckett can recuperate the rhetorical acting of his precursor. Hamm like Lear is a dethroned patriarch and both are actors, clinging to their self-image as symbolic kings. Hamm's dramatic material threatens to dry up; Lear must abandon histrionics if he is to arrive at the self-realisation that he is 'a poor bare forked animal'. As Lear and Hamm witness their kingdoms fall away, it is the 'faithful' servants, the Fool and Clov, who can speak the truth of their empty posturing. As dramatic entities they are, Wheatley notes, pushed close to a state of nothingness, but, he infers, in their tragicomic worlds they 'fail to fail outright'. Here, as in other essays on Joyce, Wilde and Bowen, we can see the reciprocal relationship between Shakespeare and the Irish writer as the Shakespeare text is enlarged through the lens of the later work.

SHAKESPEARE AND IRISH DRAMA

A more explicit engagement with Shakespeare is evident in the dramatic oeuvre of Frank McGuinness and especially in his play *Mutabilitie* in which there is a complex and specific intertextuality. The character William, an enigmatic actor and poet, happens upon Edmund Spenser's colonial settlement in Elizbethan Ireland. The perplexing question of Shakespeare's identity – colonial and post-colonial – frames *Mutabilitie* as William tells File 'I do exist but not as you imagined'.[67] As Helen Heusner Lojek demonstrates in her essay, McGuinness not only imaginatively and iconoclastically recreates the known facts of Shakespeare's life – in this play we have a gay, Catholic, and irreverent Shakespeare – but, more interestingly, uses this figure to indicate more friable concepts of Irish history and identity in terms of the Elizabethan setting and, by extension, the play's own contemporary moment. What emerges in *Mutabilitie*, as Lojek reveals, is not simply a bricolage of Shakespearean images but a considered exploration of the role of the artist in times of conflict. In a sense, then, McGuinness's pseudo-biographical drama, with Shakespeare in Spenser's Ireland, becomes an assertion of the responsibility and also the efficacy of the artist in the present.

The Shakespearean influence on McGuinness that Helen Heusner Lojek traces from *Mutabilitie* back to his earlier plays is dramaturgic. McGuinness's idiom, blended styles, often fantastic assortments of character are, indeed, Shakespearean and, again, a reminder of how Shakespeare is a critical reference point for Irish playwrights. Shaw's reaction to Shakespeare has already been noted, but for other Irish playwrights Shakespeare's identity and his plays are tellingly cited. In Sean O'Casey's *Red Roses for Me*, written in 1943, the young protagonist Ayammon Breydon reads and rehearses his Shakespeare before his mother. An optimistic socialist, Ayammon claims Shakespeare for his fellow workers:

> It's only that they're afraid of Shakespeare out of all that's been said of him. They think he's beyond them, while all the time he's part of the kingdom of heaven in the nature of everyman. Before I'm done, I'll have him drinking in th'pubs with them![68]

On stage, Ayamonn is quite literally associated with Shakespeare as he sits reading from the plays. If, as his biographer has said, Ayamonn is a version of the young O'Casey, then the scene represents a professional identification that transcends the constraints of nationality and posits Shakespeare as playwright for the people.[69] In Teresa Deevy's neglected play *A Disciple*, performed at the Abbey in 1931, the protagonist Ellie Irwin also reads Shakespeare in a trope borrowed from Shaw's *Heartbreak House*. But, in Deevy's play, Shakespeare fails: Ellie Irwin is frustrated in her reading of *Coriolanus* because the play's model of heroism is a masculine one.[70] So, whereas Shakespeare constitutes a powerful signifying agent in O'Casey's *Red Roses*, the citation in Deevy's play suggests the inefficacy of Shakespeare as a mode of expression. Ellie's frustration with Shakespeare signifies a deeper frustration with inherited patriarchal ideologies that are rife in the early twentieth century Ireland of *A Disciple*.

As has been suggested, Shakespearean drama operates at a subtextual level in Joyce's *Exiles,* and the same could be said for Marina Carr's *Portia Coughlan.* Carr has named Shakespeare amongst her precursors: 'the poets of the theatre: Chekov, Ibsen, Tennessee Williams, Wilde, Beckett and of course the king himself – Mr Shakespeare.'[71] At first it might seem that there is little in *Portia Coughlan* other than recall of name and place from *The Merchant of Venice.* Portia Coughlan, like Shakespeare's Portia, is associated with Belmont but in this instance, tragically, as Belmont is the name of the river where her twin brother drowned and where Portia Coughlan will take her life. The play's title alerts us to a Shakespearean subtext and encourages us to consider further. Carr's intertextual reference extends to *Twelfth Night*, specifically to the twins Viola and Sebastian who each believe the other drowned. As part of the resolution of a romantic comedy they are joyfully and wonderously united and, moreover, Sebastian's timely intervention provides a marriage partner for the woman in love with his sister in the guise of a boy. Carr subverts this genre of fantasy comedy, rejecting improbability and replacing it with inevitability. Portia Coughlan is haunted by the presence of Gabriel, her dead twin, but he is not restored to her as Sebastian is to Viola. Only death can reunite the twins. Shakespearean motifs, alongside classical referents, work to defamiliarise the contemporary setting[72] while Carr's harsh, unlyrical language subverts Shakespeare's lyricism in the service of a bleak, tragic drama.[73]

SHAKESPEARE, IRELAND AND NATIONAL IDENTITIES

Just as in the Irish theatre no one play or cluster of plays has dominated production for the Irish writers surveyed here, there is no single Shakespeare play that is exemplary.[74] There is no equivalent to the significance that, say, *Macbeth* has had for Scottish writers or perhaps *The Tempest* for generations of post-colonial writers.[75] But if one play were to suggest itself it would be *Henry V*, for the good reason that it includes the Irish character, Captain MacMorris, who asks 'What ish my nation?' (III.2.66). This scene has been repeatedly alluded to in the specific context of the Irish campaign of the late 1590s led by the second Earl of Essex and, more generally, in the context of early modern conceptions of nationhood.[76] His questions have been evoked not only in critical but in literary texts. As an early instance of Irish stage stereotypes,

MacMorris's shadow cuts across representations in modern Irish drama and his questions seem to anticipate later explorations of identity in Irish writing. In *Ulysses*, Leopold Bloom answers Shakespeare's stage Irishman. In an exchange in Barney Kiernan's pub, where The Citizen expresses the opinion that there are too many strangers in Ireland, Bloom is asked if he can define a nation, leading to his assertion that 'a nation is the same people living in the same place'. And to The Citizen's 'What is your nation if I may ask', Bloom emphatically replies: 'Ireland' [. . .] I was born here. Ireland.'[77] Seamus Heaney in his poem 'Traditions' interweaves Shakespeare and Joyce:

> MacMorris, gallivanting
> round the Globe, whinged
> to courtier and groundling
> who had heard tell of us
>
> as going very bare
> of learning, as wild hares,
> as anatomies of death:
> 'What ish my nation?'
>
> And sensibly, though so much
> later, the wandering Bloom
> replied, 'Ireland', said Bloom,
> 'I was born here. Ireland.'[78]

Heaney's quotation of Bloom answering MacMorris, or Joyce answering Shakespeare, encapsulates a moment of confident national identity. As a colonised subject, MacMorris, on the stage of the Globe Theatre and in an international arena, has to counter prejudices of crude Irish stereotyping. This is repudiated by Bloom. We might also see in Heaney's appropriation of two great national writers a sense of cultural and national equality. Joyce is not in the shadow of Shakespeare. A similar answering of MacMorris's question is evident in McGuinness's *Mutabilitie*: the twentieth-century Irish playwright ironically and anachronistically reverses the sixteenth-century playwright's questioning of national identity so that it in the play, it is the English poet Spenser who asks the troubled question: 'What is my nation?'[79] By paralleling and reversing Shakespeare's text, McGuinness is suggesting that identity is a question to be asked of the self rather than the other.

The contributors to this volume have had a broad remit to engage with the question of the relationship of the Irish writer to Shakespeare and to his plays. Essays by Philip Edwards, Andrew Murphy, Matthew Creasy and Tadhg Ó Dúshláine have explored the identity and role of Shakespeare at specific moments of Irish history, particularly in the decade leading toward Independence. It has already been noted how Hyde used the occasion of the Shakespeare tercentenary to critique English rule in Ireland, but as Andrew Murphy discusses in his essay, in the year that also witnessed the 1916 Easter Rising, Shakespeare's words were equally being used to condemn the Irish rebellion. What emerges is the diversity of response to Shakespeare amongst nationalists and across traditional political dichotomies of the time. Questions of nation and ideology have not been the sole determinants of Shakespeare's reception in Ireland. Indeed, the category 'Shakespeare and the Irish Writer' reveals a level of cultural continuity within and across the contours of the history of Ireland and Britain. Moreover, as essays by Brian Cosgrove, Noreen Doody, Cary DiPietro, and David Wheatley illustrate, in significant ways, Irish writers in the early to mid twentieth century – Wilde, Yeats, Joyce, Shaw and Beckett – conceived of Shakespeare as a world writer in the broadest sense of the term, that is as a figure informed by but not restricted to local politics or geographies. In this way, they anticipated the responses of post-colonial writers like Derek Walcott, George Lamming and Salman Rushdie for whom Shakespeare was a catalyst for expression.[80]

Essays by Declan Kiberd, Heather Ingram, Richard Meek and Helen Heusner Lojek have taken a more intertextual approach, demonstrating the figuration of Shakespeare's plays in Irish writing and how this serves as both a critique of Shakespeare and as textual layering and enrichment. The response of Irish writers to Shakespeare and the treatment of his plays – whether emulative or parodic, iconoclastic or subtly allusive, or a combination of these – is a complex and fascinating one. While several of the writers explored, such as Joyce, Yeats and Shaw, are mindful of Shakespeare's historicity and the uses to which he has been put in history, especially English history, there is an artistic recognition of the freeplay of the Shakespearean text. And, transposed to an Irish context, Shakespeare has continued to be a source of creative engagement and contestation for contemporary Irish writers.

No collection of essays could claim to offer a comprehensive discussion of the presence or influence of Shakespeare in Irish writing. To an extent the writers represented here are self-selecting in that they engaged with Shakespeare as an iconic figure, of British imperialism or of world literature or of both. In England, Shakespeare has been absorbed into configurations of national identity.[81] This could hardly be said of Ireland, yet Shakespeare has been prised away from his colonial associations and absorbed into Irish writing. By tracing the response of individual writers in specific contexts, the essays remind us of changing responses to Shakespeare, not merely in Ireland but in wider contexts, and how such interpretations are historically and culturally contingent. The essays therefore combine to provide a new insight into Shakespeare's reception in Ireland and they illustrate how Shakespeare's plays have initiated a dialogue in Irish writing, and continue to do so. The Shakespeare of Irish writers – to recall Hyde – is one that is very much of their own making and infinitely mutable.

Notes

1 See Andrew Murphy's chapter in this volume.

2 The recent publications on global Shakespeares are numerous but see for example, *Postcolonial Shakespeares* ed. by Ania Loomba and Martin Orkin (London: Routledge, 1998); Murray J. Levith, *Shakespeare in China* (London: Continuum, 2004); Li Ruru, *Shashibiya: Staging Shakespeare in China* (Hong Kong: Hong Kong University Press, 2003); *Four Hundred Years of Shakespeare in Europe* ed. by Ton Hoenselaars and Angel-Luis Pujante (Newark: University of Delaware Press, 2003); Tetsuo Kishi and Graham Bradshaw, *Shakespeare in Japan* (London: Continuum, 2005). Several research projects addressing Shakespeare in national contexts are under way, including 'The Reception of Shakespeare in Spain in the Framework of European Culture' at the University of Murcia; and 'The Reception of Shakespeare in Romania' funded by Romania's National Council of Research in Higher Education. The 'Shakespeare in Asia' project is available at http://sia.stanford.edu/japan/homepage.htm.

3 *Irish Times*, 12 Feb. 2008.

4 See Mark Thornton Burnett, 'Introduction' in *Shakespeare and Ireland: History, Politics, Culture* ed. by Mark Thornton Burnett and Ramona Wray (Basingstoke: Macmillan, 1997), pp 1–5.

5 Christopher Highley, *Shakespeare, Spenser and the Crisis in Ireland* (Cambridge: Cambridge University Press, 1997); Andrew Murphy, 'Shakespeare's Irish History', *Literature and History*, 5: 1 (1996), 38–59; Willy Maley, 'The Irish text and subtext of Shakespeare's English Histories', in *A Companion to Shakespeare's Works*, ed. by Richard Dutton and Jean E. Howard, 4 vols (Oxford: Oxford University Press, 2003), II: *The Histories*, 94–124; Stephen O'Neill, *Staging Ireland: Representations in Shakespeare and Renaissance Drama* (Dublin: Four Courts Press, 2007).

6 Myles Dungan, *No Great Shakes? 1902–1982: 75 Years of the Dublin Shakespeare Society* (Dublin, 1982), p. 6.

7 University College Dublin, Ó Ríordáin Archive.

8 Declan Kiberd, *Inventing Ireland: The Literature of the Modern Nation* (London: Jonathan Cape, 1995), pp 268–85.

9 Robin E. Bates, *Shakespeare and the Cultural Colonization of Ireland* (London: Routledge, 2007), p. 131.

10 On recent and acclaimed productions of Shakespeare in Ireland by directors including Jason Byrne, Selina Cartmell, Pat Kiernan, and Conall Morrison, see Rachel Andrews, 'Something Wicked this Way Comes', *Irish Theatre Magazine*, 8: 34 (2008), 51–8.

11 On Fiona Shaw and earlier Irish Shakespearean actresses, see Tony Howard, *Women as Hamlet: Performance and Interpretation in Theatre, Film, and Fiction* (Cambridge: Cambridge University Press, 2007), pp 222–5.

12 James Joyce, *Ulysses*, ed. by Declan Kiberd (Harmondsworth: Penguin, 1992), p. 254.

13 See W. S. Clark, *The Early Irish Stage* (Oxford: Clarendon Press, 1955); Peter Kavanagh, *The Irish Theatre* (Tralee, Kerry: The Kerryman, 1946); Alan Fletcher, *Drama, Performance, and Polity in Pre-Cromwellian Ireland* (Cork: Cork University Press, 2000).

14 Clark, *Early Irish Stage*, p. 56. The first recorded place for a performance of Shakespeare in Ireland is in Coleraine in 1628, but the intended performance of *Much Ado About Nothing* was postponed at the last moment. See Fletcher, *Drama, Performance and Polity*, p. 238.

15 Clark, *Early Irish Stage*, pp 72–7; Christopher Morash, *A History of Irish Drama* (Cambridge: Cambridge University Press, 2002), p. 18.

16 Morash, *A History of Irish Drama*, p. 51.

17 See Christopher Fitzsimon, *The Boys: A Biography of Micheál MacLiammóir and Hilton Edwards* (London: Nick Hern, 1994).

18 Margreta de Grazia, *Shakespeare Verbatim: The Reproduction of Authenticity and the 1790 Apparatus* (Oxford: Clarendon Press, 1991), p. 2.

19 Samuel Schoenbaum, *Shakespeare's Lives* (Oxford: Clarendon Press, 1970), p. 163.

20 Peter Martin, *Edmond Malone, Shakespearean Scholar: A Literary Biography* (Cambridge: Cambridge University Press, 1995), p. xv.

21 *Plays and Poems of William Shakespeare*, ed. by Edmond Malone, 16 vols (Dublin: John Exshaw, 1794), I, viii.

22 David Nichol Smith, *Shakespeare in the Eighteenth Century* (Oxford: Clarendon Press, 1928), p. 56.

23 On Malone's conservatism, see de Grazia, *Shakespeare Verbatim*, p. 77.

24 Gary Taylor, *Reinventing Shakespeare: A Cultural History from the Restoration to the Present* (London: Hogarth Press, 1990), p. 156.

25 Joseph Ritson, *Cursory Criticism on the Edition of Shakespeare published by Edmond Malone, Eighteenth Century Shakespeare* (London: Frank Cass, 1970), p. 103.

26 Ibid., p. 75; p. 78.

27 Taylor, *Reinventing Shakespeare*, p. 156.

28 Edmond Malone, 'A letter to the Rev. Richard Farmer, relative to the edition of Shakespeare published in 1790, and some late criticisms of that work', *Eighteenth Century Shakespeare*, p. 2.

29 See Philip Edwards's chapter below, p. 30.

30 See Ernest A. Boyd, *Appreciations and Depreciations: Irish Literary Studies* (London: T. F. Unwin, 1917; Dublin: Talbot Press, 1917).

31 See AE, 'Nationality and Cosmopolitanism in Literature', in *Literary Ideals in Ireland* (London: T. F. Fisher Unwin; Dublin: Daily Express, 1899), pp 83–7.

32 Cited in Philip O'Leary, *The Prose Literature of the Gaelic Revival, 1881–1921: Ideology and Innovation* (Pennsylvania: Pennsylvania University Press, 1994), p. 53.

33 See Edwards's chapter below, p. 25.

34 See Richard English, 'Shakespeare and the Definition of the Irish Nation' in *Shakespeare and Ireland*, pp 136–51. See also MacDonagh's *Literature in Ireland: Studies Irish and Anglo–Irish* (Dublin: Talbot Press, 1916; repr. Tyone, Nenagh: Relay Books, 1996), where of Shakespeare in translation, he says: 'all that is great in his dramatic power, in his creation, in his philosophy, will be great in other languages, only indeed less great for want of that Shakespearean diction', p. 86.

35 *Letters of Edward Dowden and his Correspondents*, ed. by Elizabeth D. Dowden and Hilda M. Dowden (London: J. M. Dent and Sons, 1914), pp 69–70.

36 Plunket D. Barton, *Links between Ireland and Shakespeare* (Dublin: Maunsel, 1919); David Comyn, *Irish Illustrations to Shakespeare* (Dublin: Freeman's Journal, 1894); William Magennis, 'Shakespeare's debt to Irishmen', *Irish Times*, 18 Apr. 1916.

37 Darrell Figgis, *Shakespeare: A Study* (London: J. M. Dent and Sons, 1911), p. 21.

38 Ibid., p. 26.

39 Richard Ellmann, *The Man and the Masks* (London: Penguin, 1979), p. 14. See also R. F. Foster, *W. B. Yeats: A Life*, 2 vols (Oxford: Oxford University Press, 1997), I: *The Apprentice Image, 1865–1914*, pp 29–30; and Peter Ure, 'W. B. Yeats and the Shakespearian Moment', in *Yeats and Anglo-Irish Literature: Critical Essays by Peter Ure*, ed. by C. J. Rawson (Liverpool: Liverpool University Press, 1974), pp 204–27.

40 W. B. Yeats, 'At Stratford-on-Avon', in *Essays and Introductions* (London: Macmillan, 1961), p. 103.

41 Ibid., p. 106.

42 Philip Edwards, *Threshold of the Nation: A Study in English and Irish Drama* (Cambridge: Cambridge University Press, 1979), p. 207.

43 Kiberd, *Inventing Ireland*, p. 269. For a similar assessment, see Richard Foulkes, *Performing Shakespeare in the Age of Empire* (Cambridge: Cambridge University Press, 2002), p. 170.

44 Wayne Chapman, *Yeats and English Renaissance Literature* (London: Macmillan, 1991), p. 47.

45 W. B. Yeats, *Literary Ideals in Ireland* (Dublin, 1899), p. 73.

46 Harold Bloom, *The Anxiety of Influence: A Theory of Poetry* (New York: Oxford University Press, 1973).

47 Longinus, *On the Sublime*, ed. by D. A. Russell (Oxford: Clarendon Press, 1964).

48 See Declan Kiberd's chapter below, p. 99.

49 For a discussion of the chapter in terms of the literary canon and the emerging discipline of English, see John Nash, 'Reading Joyce in English' in *Joyce on the Threshold* ed. by Anne Fogarty and Timothy Martin (Gainesville: University Press of Florida, 2005), pp 110–26.

50 See William Schutte, *Joyce and Shakespeare: A Study in the Meaning of* 'Ulysses' (Yale: Yale University Press, 1957; repr. Hamdon: Archon, 1971).

51 *Ulysses*, p. 236; p. 253; p. 271; p. 272.

52 On the gendered nature of the chapter's emphasis on literary forefathers, see Cary DiPietro, *Shakespeare and Modernism* (Cambridge: Cambridge University Press, 2006), pp 70–82.

53 Oscar Wilde, 'The decay of lying' in *Collins Complete Works of Oscar Wilde* (Glasgow: HarperCollins, 2003), p. 1,082.

54 James Joyce, *Exiles* (London: The Egoist Press, 1918), p. 45.

55 *Selected Letters of James Joyce*, ed. by Richard Ellmann (London: Faber & Faber, 1975), p. 230.

56 For example, in *Joyce's Revenge: History, Politics and Aethetics in 'Ulysses'* (Oxford: Oxford University Press, 2002), p. 77, Andrew Gibson notes how Stephen's quoting of Hamlet animates his expression of frustration with the Gaelic revivalists.

57 Gibson, *Joyce's Revenge*, p. 79.

58 This could be said of allusions to *King Lear, Julius Caesar* and *The Tempest* in Joyce's *Exiles*.

59 'A plea for the Irish language', in *Language, Lore and Lyrics: Essays and Lectures*, ed. by Breandán Ó Conaire (Dublin: Irish Academic Press, 1986), p. 77.

60 See also Michael Cronin's essay, 'Rug-headed kerns speaking tongues: Shakespeare, Translation and the Irish Language', in *Shakespeare and Ireland*, pp 193–212. Cronin is primarily concerned with Irish language references in Shakespeare's plays and only briefly discusses how Gaelic writers responded to Shakespeare.

61 See Ó Dúshláine's chapter below, p. 71.

62 'Shakespeare a tháinig go hÉirinn', in *Bliainiris* 2003, ed. by Ruairí Ó hUiginn and Liam Mac Cóil (Dublin: Carbad, 2003), pp 188–97.

63 See, for example, Douglas Bruster, *Quoting Shakespeare: Form and Culture in Early Modern Drama* (Nebraska: University of Nebraska Press, 2000).

64 Julie Sanders, *Adaptation and Appropriation* (London: Routledge, 2006), pp 24–5. On different forms of Shakespeare as intertext, see Robert S. Miola, 'Seven types of intertextuality', in *Shakespeare, Italy and Intertextuality*, ed. by Michele Marrapodi (Manchester: Manchester University Press, 2004), pp 13–25.

65 Kiberd, *Inventing Ireland*, p. 281.

66 Jan Kott, '*King Lear* or *Endgame*' in *Shakespeare Our Contemporary* (London: Methuen, 1965), pp 127–68.

67 Frank McGuinness, *Mutabilitie* (London: Faber & Faber, 1997), p. 93.

68 Sean O'Casey, *Collected Plays*, 5 vols (London: Macmillan, 1967), III, Act I, lines 56–64.

69 Christopher Murray, *Twentieth Century Irish Drama: Mirror up to Nation* (Manchester: Manchester University Press, 1997), pp 89–90.

70 See Cathy Leeny, 'Ireland's exiled Women Playwrights: Teresa Deevy and Marina Carr', in *Cambridge Companion to Twentieth Century Irish Drama*, ed. by Shaun Richards (Cambridge: Cambridge University Press, 2004), pp 150–63.

71 Marina Carr, 'Dealing with the Dead', *Irish University Review*, 28: 1 (1998), 190–6 (p. 195).

72 See Paula Murphy, 'Staging histories in Marina Carr's midlands plays', *Irish University Review*, 36: 2 (2006), 389–402; and Melissa Sihra, 'Reflections across water: New stages of performing Carr', in *The Theatre of Marina Carr*, ed. by Cathy Leeney and Anna McMulan (Dublin: Carysfort Press, 2003), pp 92–113.

73 Carr's interest in Shakespeare continues: *The Cordelia Dream* was specially commissioned by the Royal Shakespeare Company (RSC) as part of its contemporary Shakespeare series in 2009. Other forms of Shakespearean influence have been detected in Irish drama, from Friel's *Translations* as a version of the histories to the use of *Romeo and Juliet*'s 'love-across-the-divide' plot device in plays treating of Northern Ireland. See Anthony Roche, 'A bit off the map: Brian Friel's *Translations* and Shakespeare's *Henry IV*', in *Literary Interrelations: Ireland, England and the World*, ed. by Wolfgang Zach and Heinz Kosok (Tübingen: Gunter Narr, 1987), pp 139–48; and Joe Cleary, 'Domestic troubles: Tragedy and the Northern Ireland conflict', in *Outrageous Fortune: Capital and Culture in Modern Ireland* (Dublin: Field Day, 2007), pp 232–60.

74 For a sample of productions of Shakespeare in Ireland, see Janet Clare, 'Shakespeare performances in Ireland, 2002–2004', *Shakespeare Survey*, 58 (2005), 260–7.

75 See *Shakespeare and Scotland*, ed. by Willy Maley and Andrew Murphy (Manchester: Manchester University Press, 2004).

76 See Andrew Hadfield, '"Hitherto she ne're could fancy him": Shakespeare's "British" plays and the exclusion of Ireland', in *Shakespeare and Ireland*; Willy Maley, 'The Irish text and subtext of Shakespeare's English histories', in *A Companion to Shakespeare's Works*, pp 94–124; Andrew Murphy, 'Shakespeare's Irish history', pp 38–59; O'Neill, *Staging Ireland*, pp 146–63. On the censorship of *Henry V*, see Janet Clare, '*Art Made Tongue-Tied by Authority': Elizabethan and Jacobean Dramatic Censorship* 2nd edn (Manchester: Manchester University Press, 1999), pp 92–5.

77 *Ulysses*, p. 430.

78 Seamus Heaney, 'Traditions' in *Wintering Out* (London: Faber & Faber, 1972), p. 32.

79 *Mutabilitie*, p. 51.

80 George Lamming, *The Pleasures of Exile* (1960), *Water with Berries* (1971); Salman Rushdie, *The Moor's Last Sigh* (1995); Derek Walcott, *A Branch of the Blue Nile* (1983). On post-colonial and post-post-colonial adaptations of Shakespeare, see *World-wide Shakespeares: Local Appropriations in Film and Performance*, ed. by Sonia Massai (London: Routledge, 2005).

81 See Michael Dobson, *The Making of the National Poet: Shakespeare, Adaptation and Authorship, 1660–1769* (Oxford: Oxford University Press, 1992).

CHAPTER I

Shakespeare and the Politics of the Irish Revival

Philip Edwards

So arrogantly pure, a child might think
It can be murdered with a spot of ink.

Yeats had swans in mind, but we might also think of marble statues, tokens of outmoded admiration, regularly murdered with a spot of ink. 'Milton's dislodgement', wrote Leavis in 1936, 'was effected with remarkably little fuss.'[1] The crowbar is under Yeats's statue. Who is safe? Certainly not Shakespeare.

That the greatness of Shakespeare's plays is an unalterable geological fact of life on this planet, like Mount Everest or the Grand Canyon or the Giant's Causeway, no one could possibly maintain. More like the bare ruined choirs of the English abbeys where late the sweet birds sang. 'It is we who make a play a "masterpiece", not Shakespeare', said Terence Hawkes at the World Shakespeare Congress in Berlin in 1986.[2] What we create we can uncreate. The arguments of Alan Sinfield in *Political Shakespeare*, and Terence Hawkes in *That Shakespeherian Rag*, and Terry Eagleton in *Literary Theory: An Introduction*, are that Shakespeare owes his position in the forefront of English literary culture to the utility of his plays in reinforcing values and attitudes convenient to ruling-class ideology and supportive of the power structures of capitalist society. 'Given a deep enough transformation of our history,' Eagleton writes, 'Shakespeare would be no more valuable than much present-day graffiti.'[3]

Surely a similar sense of the precariousness of Shakespeare's high standing, as contingent and not absolute, must have been in the minds of Irish nationalists at the end of the nineteenth century? The idea that art, and literature in particular, belonged to a nation, was an index of that nation's history and the spirit of its people, declaring its past and shaping its future, was a basic nineteenth-century idea. Irish nationalism had the urgent task of discovering and disseminating the independent literary past of Ireland, of creating an energetic and independent new literature. Thus to demonstrate a distinctive

Irish culture was to establish a right to political independence, and to provide protection against the engulfing tide of an alien Anglo-Saxon culture.

Given that the imposed Anglo-Saxon culture as expressed in its literature was alien and incongruous, what price Shakespeare, the flagship of English literature? What was to be said 'de Shakespeare nostrati', about the Shakespeare who, as Ben Jonson put it, so early and so firmly, belongs to *us*?[4] The nineteenth-century Irish nationalists should have been in the same position as the present-day new historicists or cultural materialists, bound to question the status of a writer whose position implies the acceptance of values about art and society which are alien and repugnant. They must, surely, have insisted that Shakespeare belonged to England, and that his primacy implied the primacy of English values? To accept Shakespeare, surely, was to accept the dominance of imperial England and the extinction of autonomy?

And if we take it as axiomatic that an imperial power will homogenise the culture of colonial peoples by suppressing their language, their religion, their literature, and substituting its own, we may see the majestic presence of Shakespeare in Ireland in the eighteenth and nineteenth centuries as strong evidence of that homogenisation. Ireland was steeped in Shakespeare. His plays were on the stage in every town, and Dublin printings of his works were in the parlour of everyone who could afford to have a parlour. De-Anglicising, to use Hyde's word, would seem necessarily to involve de-Shakespearising.

Yet it is evident that for a large number of educated Irish people in the nineteenth and twentieth centuries, eager for the freedom and independence of Ireland even to the point of armed rebellion, the acceptance of Shakespeare's plays as an indispensable part of their cultural life presented no problem whatsoever. The fierce John Mitchel, a prisoner in the hulks of 1850, wrote in his journal 'Thank God for Shakespeare, at any rate!'[5] The prose writings of James Clarence Mangan bristle with Shakespeare quotations, and, to judge by their inaccuracy, he must always have quoted from memory. In 1911, Darrell Figgis, who was to organise the purchase of the guns run ashore at Howth in 1914, wrote his book *Shakespeare: A Study*, which, except for one footnote, betrays not the slightest interest in a possible conflict of national culture or attitudes.[6] Frank O'Connor fought alongside Erskine Childers in the Civil War, and was intensely interested in the native Irish literary tradition which he did so much to illustrate in his writings and translations; yet his book, *Shakespeare's Progress*, gives no recognition whatsoever of Shakespeare's works as representative of a specifically English tradition.

But there *was* a great deal of resistance to Shakespeare among Irish writers at the turn of the century. The most formidable resistance of all, from Bernard Shaw, certainly has a nationalist aspect, but the breaking down of 'bardolatry' (his own word) is more fittingly seen as part of the general Shavian blitzkrieg on received opinions. The role of Shakespeare in the intellectual life of the exiles Shaw and Joyce – and Wilde – is well known, and is not my concern in this essay.

So what about AE (George William Russell)? John Eglinton had this to say: 'Of English literature in general he wrote to me in an early letter, "I see the great tree of English literature arising out of roast beef and watered with much rum and beer". He disliked Shakespeare, whose tragedies, he said, "were all about murders".' And in another place, 'He often shocked me by avowing his detestation of the Sonnets.'[7] In spite of the affable place which Joyce created for him in the Shakespeare scene in *Ulysses*, AE so disliked Shakespeare that it was not until 1911 that he was 'persuaded [. . .] to read the dramatist attentively for the first time'.[8] It made no difference. AE's essay, 'Shakespeare and the Blind Alley', in *The Irish Statesman* (9 February 1924), clearly expresses the original and continuing failure of Shakespeare to nourish the sensibility of at least one Irishman.

In this essay Shakespeare is the misleader of the human spirit, the powerful founding father of secularisation and observation, which can teach us only what we already know.

> There are certain figures in history which are pivotal, and around them myriads have wheeled to new destinies. Shakespeare was undoubtedly pivotal, more so perhaps than any except the great spiritual figures. But did he lead literature into a blind alley? [. . .]. Shakespeare was the first supreme artist in literature who seems to be absorbed in character for its own sake. Nothing before or since has equalled the art by which recognisable personalities are revealed in a few words. But nothing is revealed in the Shakespearean drama except character [. . .]. To the greater Greek dramatists life swam in an aether of deity [. . .]. We feel as we read that we are in the divine procession, and know ourselves more truly by this envelopment [. . .]. When we are absorbed in character for its own sake we are absorbed in our own illusion [. . .]. Since Shakespeare became the shepherd of the artistic soul, dramatist and novelist have become more and more absorbed by this illusion.[9]

The Jonsonian notion of Shakespeare as the genius essentially limited to observation of the world around us was extraordinarily widespread in Ireland. Yeats, in 1899, saw Shakespeare as the beginning of a decadence notable for its 'preoccupation with things'. 'Shakespeare shattered the symmetry of verse and of drama that he might fill them with things and their accidental relations to one another.'[10] That Shakespeare's vision was fundamentally 'mundane' was axiomatic for those who did not like him, such as AE and George Moore, and those who liked him in spite of it, such as Yeats and Dowden.

Before George Moore began to consider a possible identification of himself as an Irish writer, his scorn for Shakespeare was a consequence of his admiration for French literature. 'Shakespeare I had never opened,' he boasted in 1888; 'no instinctive want had urged me to read him.'[11] And when he did open him? 'Shakespeare leaves me cold.' 'I utterly fail to see in what Shakespeare is greater than Balzac.'[12]

It is interesting that in *Confessions of a Young Man* (1888), from which these statements are taken, Moore referred to Shakespeare as '*our* national bard'. The Elizabethan dramatists, he said later, were 'the real literature of *my* race'.[13] By 1901 his race had crossed the sea to the land of his birth. 'We in Ireland would keep in mind our language, teach our children our history, the story of our heroes, and the long traditions of our race, which stretch back to God.'[14]

This preludes a remarkable sentence in *Salve*, the second volume of *Hail and Farewell* (1912): 'Shakespeare is read in England, for England produced Shakespeare' (p. 267). He is now speaking as an Irishman, a lapsed Catholic admiring a liberated and liberating Protestant culture. His switches in allegiance are clearly teaching him a lot about cultural difference and cultural conditioning. But he never had much to say in favour of Shakespeare. His Baconian play, *The Making of an Immortal*, which he wrote in 1927, was based on an idea he had had in 1902. His rather shameful lecture, in French, on Shakespeare and Balzac, was delivered in 1910; and in 1924 he said he thought W. S. Landor was greater than Shakespeare.

I turn with some relief to the brilliant essays of D. P. Moran collected in *The Philosophy of Irish Ireland* (1905).[15] Moran was totally sceptical of the nineteenth-century nationalist movement, which was run largely by people of English descent. 'A family dispute,' he said contemptuously (p. 14). The foundation of Ireland was the Gael, and Ireland was nothing but the Gael. The creation of an Irish literature in English struck him as a preposterous hoax: 'one of the most glaring frauds that the credulous Irish people ever swallowed.' He was particularly scathing about the 'Celtic note', as it had been discovered and advertised by people who knew no Gaelic, Matthew Arnold and W. B. Yeats. 'We called ourselves Celts' – and were proud to find ourselves the possessors of a mystical penumbra, 'a natural magic.' 'We now knew the difference between English literature and Irish literature, and satisfied ourselves that Shakespeare was a Celt' (p. 104).

This Arnoldian taxonomy seemed to Moran a despicable muddle. It was basically a matter of identifying Ireland in English terms. But the Irish were 'absolutely different' from the English. It was impossible, he said, to 'fight England, as she now is, on her own terms – fight over her literature, her cynicism, her moral conceptions, her social ideas, her wealth'. Irish Ireland had to be rediscovered, not an English version of Ireland. And as for English literature, though Moran has little to say about Shakespeare, he writes: 'It takes an Englishman to get the most out of English literature [. . .]. A literature steeped in the history, traditions, and genius of one nation is at best only an imperfect tutor to the people of another nation.'

27

Moran's views are echoed in Thomas MacDonagh's book, *Literature in Ireland*, which he published only a few months before he was executed for his share in the 1916 Rising.[16] The tradition of Anglo-Irish literature of the eighteenth century was a 'dissent from an English orthodoxy' rather than a 'consent' in a specifically Irish orthodoxy (p. vii). He insisted that the texture of Shakespeare's writing could not be fully appreciated by those who had had a different history and a different language (pp 47–8), and regretted that many Irish people had been 'lured by the felicity of gracious words' into sympathy with the 'ravening lust and barbarity' of the English story as related by Shakespeare in his history-plays, and so found it hard to accept the more humane spirit of Gaelic literature (p. 110).

Moran has already pointed to the real Irish solution to the Shakespeare problem; hi-jack him. The discovery that the pillar of the Anglo-Saxon literary tradition was in fact a Celt was of course an Anglo-Saxon discovery; it was suggested in Matthew Arnold's confident and absurd essay of 1866, 'On the Study of Celtic Literature', which had so profound an effect on the destiny of the Irish nation. Without the Celtic element, said Arnold, 'Germanic England would not have produced a Shakespeare.'[17] Shakespeare's work evinced the 'natural magic' of the Celt, 'the indefinable delicacy, charm, and perfection of the Celt's touch' (p. 376).

The chief attribute of the Celtic temperature as Arnold described it, however, he never actually attached to Shakespeare. This attribute of course is that the Celt is not dominated by 'the despotism of fact'. This 'rebellion against fact' disqualifies him from success in political organisation and political stability. It is necessary to quote yet again that crucial sentence: '"They went forth to the war," Ossian says most truly, "but they always fell"' (p. 346). So we have 'the Celtic genius, sentiment as its main basis, with love of beauty, charm and spirituality for its excellence, ineffectualness and self-will for its defect' (p. 347). Arnold could not help adding that 'no doubt the sensibility of the Celtic nature, its nervous exaltation, have something feminine in them, and the Celt is thus peculiarly disposed to feel the spell of the feminine idiosyncrasy; he has an affinity to it; he is not far from its secret' (p. 347).[18]

It was left to Yeats to go the whole distance and incorporate Shakespeare as a Celt by emphasising his sympathy for the political failure. The whole of his brilliant essay of 1901 on Shakespeare's history plays, 'At Stratford-on-Avon', is founded on the Arnoldian binary opposition of the spiritual and sensitive failure, the Celt, to the pragmatic, materialistic, successful Anglo-Saxon. The Shakespeare criticism he had read was 'a vulgar worshipper of success', condemning Richard II as sentimental and weak, and praising the robust Henry V as 'Shakespeare's only hero'. And, Yeats explains:

I think that these emotions began among the German critics, who perhaps saw something French and Latin in Richard II, and I know that Professor Dowden, whose book I once read carefully, first made these emotions eloquent and plausible. He lived in Ireland, where everything has failed, and he meditated frequently on the perfection of character, which had, he thought, made England successful, for, as we say, 'cows beyond the water have long horns' [. . .] He [. . .] thought that Henry V [. . .] was not only the typical Anglo-Saxon, but the model Shakespeare held up before England; and he even thought it worth while pointing out that Shakespeare himself was making a large fortune while he was writing about Henry's victories. [Shakespeare] saw indeed, as I think, in Richard II the defeat that awaits all, whether they be artist or saint, who find themselves where men ask of them a rough energy and have nothing to give but some contemplative virtue, whether lyrical fantasy, or sweetness of temper, or dreamy dignity, or love of God, or love of his creatures. [. . .] Having made the vessel of porcelain, Richard II, he had to make the vessel of clay, Henry V. He makes him the reverse of all that Richard was. He has the gross vices, the coarse nerves, of one who is to rule among violent people.[19]

Here is Yeats in 1901 praising Shakespeare for his unworldliness and his anti-materialism when in 1899 we have seen him claiming that Shakespeare's concentration on 'things' beckoned in a second fall of man. This is only one of the contradictions in the strange tangle of spirituality and mundanity, femininity and masculinity, success and failure, nationalism and unionism in the Irish picture of Shakespeare in the later nineteenth century which I am now going to try to unravel.

Yeats's asperity in the passages I have just quoted towards his father's friend, Edward Dowden, first Professor of English Literature at Trinity College Dublin, was not without justification. In 1895 Dowden reprinted, as the intro-duction to his *New Studies in Literature*, an article he had published in *The Fortnightly Review* in 1888, as 'Hopes and Fears for Literature'. This article was itself a re-fashioning of a speech Dowden had given in 1883 to the Trinity College Historical Society. The reissue of this piece Yeats not unreasonably saw as an attack on him and his efforts in the nineties to found an Irish literature. There was a row in the columns of *The Daily Express* (January/February 1895).

Dowden's article notes that while a growing cosmopolitanism is estab-lishing 'a certain community [. . .] between the several literatures of Europe', 'the principle of nationality seems at the same time to have acquired increased force.' He instances Germany and Italy. Then he moves to 'nationality' in literature as it affects Ireland. Where there are differences in language there will be differences between literatures. But he takes it for granted that Britain and Ireland are a single people speaking 'one common language'. The Irish language is dead, he writes, except 'in forlorn wilds and on rugged headlands of the west'. Yet in spite of the extinction of a separate language, we hear 'plaintive demands for an Irish literature with a special character of its own'.

> Shall we in these islands of ours, who 'speak the tongue that Shakespeare spake', nurse the dream of four separate streams of literature, or shall we have our pride and our joy in one noble river broadened and deepened by various affluent waters?

Dowden attacked the Home Rule movement, which 'professedly would reduce Ireland to a dependency of Great Britain'. (This unwise sentence appears in the 1888 version, and was altered in 1895.) He acknowledged that 'our strength springs from the soil in which we grow', and continued,

> Yet it is well to remember that the spirit of a man may inhabit an ampler space than that in which his body lives and moves. 'Spartam nactus es: hanc orna.' Yes, but which Sparta is our possession – the land that has fed our bodies or the land that has nourished and enriched our souls?

Dowden expresses perfectly, from the western side of the Irish Sea, the time-honoured enthusiasm for a many-stranded unity of imperial culture which Arnold in his essay had expressed from the eastern shores. Arnold had begun his essay on Celtic literature with a fervent hope for the speedy 'fusion of all the inhabitants of these islands into one homogenous, English-speaking whole'. He deplored the encouragement of the Welsh language. 'Let the Welshman speak English, and, if he is an author, let him write English.' Dowden's use of the Roman proverb, 'Spartam nactus es: hanc orna' (originally a line from a lost play of Euripides) is fascinating. Literally it means, 'Sparta is your portion: embellish her.' But as Cicero uses it, it means that it is bad luck that in the sweepstake of life you have drawn Sparta, but you should put up with it and do your best for her.[20]

The appearance is that Dowden, a reluctant Irishman, could not accept the position which Arnold had found for Shakespeare in the literary culture of 'the British Isles'. Namely, that the dramatist, though an Englishman, had absorbed the Celtic element in this federated culture and was its most wonderful exponent. No, it would seem that for Dowden, Shakespeare was wholly and unalterably Anglo-Saxon. In Yeats's opinion he was working against the evidence of the plays themselves in order to present Shakespeare as a worldly, pragmatic success-worshipper because he admired and was envious of those qualities which prevailed in England and had led to the establishment of the Empire. But Yeats was wrong.

Dowden's best-known work, *Shakspere: A Critical Study of his Mind and Art*, was published in 1874 and remained in print for 100 years – a strange success-story for a bad book.[21] The author's political and religious prejudices are clear throughout. European imperialism, like the rise of science, was a necessary aspect of the development of mankind, 'extending . . . the dominion of civilised man' (p. 12). And so was Protestantism; Catholicism being a feature of the less advanced period of human development. Protestantism, in which the modern spirit had shown itself, had led mankind to 'a deeper and truer sanctity than can be conferred by the wand of ecclesiastical magic' (p. 13). Although only zealots would argue whether Shakespeare was a Catholic or a Protestant,

> It is certain that the spirit of Protestantism [. . .] animates and breathes through his writings [. . .] It may be asserted without hesitation that the Protestant type of character, and the Protestant polity in state and nation, is that which received impulse and vigour from the mind of the greatest of English poets (p. 38).

The list of Protestant qualities includes 'energy, devotion to the fact, self-government' – the latter meaning of course a mastery of the self.

Presenting Shakespeare as a tolerant and sympathetic observer of human beings of all kinds in all stations of life, but not afflicted by what he calls 'humanitarian idealism' (p. 325), not doctrinaire in religion, neither partisan nor radical in politics, taking things as they were and tending to think that things were best as they were, Dowden insists that he is a writer who above all else had, like the Elizabethan age as a whole, 'a rich feeling for positive, concrete fact' (p. 25). It is amazing how the word 'fact' dominates Dowden's book on Shakespeare. 'In a word,' Dowden himself says, 'we are brought back once again to Shakspere's resolute fidelity to the fact' (p. 46). 'The one supreme crime in Shakspere's eyes' was 'want of fidelity to the fact'. So what do 'fact' and 'the fact' mean? They mean things as they are, things as they really are, things authenticated by real experience, reality itself, as opposed to what is dreamed of, imagined, conceived to be, or wished to be.

Dowden's insistence on this concerning a man who wrote such works as *The Comedy of Errors*, *A Midsummer Night's Dream*, *As You Like It*, *The Winter's Tale*, and *Cymbeline*, may strike us as insane. But for Dowden, insanity is defined as the sort of 'protest against fact' which you find in Shakespeare's contemporaries, Marlowe and Greene – and they died young. Not for Shakespeare was this 'flimsy kind of idealism – this restless knocking of a man's head against the solid laws of the universe' (p. 47).

Why do we find this quite bewildering insistence on Shakespeare's scorn for anything but the hard observable realities of existence? Shakespeare worried Dowden a great deal. In the first place he was a dramatist. Dowden's whole concern as a critic was communion with a personality, tortured and tormented or serene and wise, who had a special gift as observer and judge of mortal life and its shadowy fringes. The ideal text, therefore, was

Wordsworthian or Shelleyan, a text which is a spiritual diary. From this lava we can work back to the molten stuff: the mind, the sensibility, the wisdom of the writer. 'Our prime object should be to get into living relation with a man; and by his means, with the good forces of nature and humanity which play in and through him.'[22] And so it must be with Shakespeare, as he says at the beginning of his book: 'To come into close and living relation with the individuality of a poet must be the chief end of our study' (p. 2). But when the texts are most decidedly not confessional or meditative, how can they be used to exhibit the author?

While he was writing his book, in August 1874, Dowden's exasperation showed itself in a letter to Aubrey de Vere.

> How is the personality of a dramatic poet to be discovered? . . . I want to put my hand on Shakespeare's shoulder for a moment even, and find it difficult. He eludes one at first, and much more afterwards. And yet there ought to be methods by which one could force a dramatic poet to discover himself, and announce his name, and tell you his secret.[23]

Dowden's real fear was that when he had managed to put his hand on Shakespeare's shoulder he would discover that the man had no soul. In his search for Shakespeare, Dowden, understandably, decided to start from the facts. And what the facts about Shakespeare revealed, according to the greatest biographer of the nineteenth century J. O. Halliwell-Phillips, was that Shakespeare was a worldly, mercenary, prudent exemplar of the bourgeois virtues of self-advancement and property-ownership; one who had undertaken authorship as the readiest way of making money.

Somehow the fact of Shakespeare's purchase of New Place in Stratford-upon-Avon in 1597 had to be made the pivot of the spiritual life of Shakespeare. What Dowden built round this was ingenious in the extreme. Shakespeare, we learn, was a man who 'was himself resolved, as far as in him lay, not to fail in this material life of ours' (p. 73). But, besetting him in this determination not to stay poor, were two 'temptations' which might lead him astray from worldly success. These temptations Shakespeare objectified in the twin plays, *Romeo and Juliet* and *Hamlet*; the temptations of love and thought. As Dowden notes, Hamlet resembles Romeo in his inability to maintain the will in a fruitful relation with facts, and with the real world (p. 101). Shakespeare's recognition of Hamlet's weakness is his own strength. The arrival of Fortinbras at the end of the play is 'the restoration of a practical and positive feeling', for Fortinbras excels 'the Danish Prince' in 'plain grasp of ordinary fact'. (And, he might have added, so does Claudius.)

But writing these two plays was not the only thing Shakespeare had to do in order to purge himself of his temptation to get lost in loving or thinking.

'He bought up houses and lands in Stratford, and so made a protest, superficial, yet real, against the Romeo and the Hamlet within him' (p. 48). (Has a more extraordinary reason for buying a house ever been given?) And then there are the history plays. These become Shakespeare's determined affirmation of the rightfulness of the conduct of his own life on the principle that 'to fail is the supreme sin' (p. 73). I scarcely need to stress Dowden's harsh exhibition of the failures in the history plays: 'Henry IV is a timid saint; it were better that he had been a man' (p. 73). And as for Henry V: 'He must certainly be regarded as Shakespeare's ideal of manhood in the sphere of practical achievement' (p. 210).

So, by the late 1590s, Dowden's Shakespeare had established himself in the world, and had written the plays which proclaim the moral imperative of establishing oneself in the world and the sinfulness of yielding to the distracting voices of love or thought. He was now therefore free to regard the failures of the world with more sympathy, and to acknowledge that there are higher values than 'the art of getting on in life' (p. 123). 'He was primarily not a man of action' (p. 281) and he was now able to pay more attention to those qualities in himself which were inimical to action and achievement. The history plays, we now learn, 'had not dealt with the deeper mysteries of being' (p. 220). The world of *Henry V*, we now learn, is 'a smaller, safer, world of thought, feeling, and action' (p. 228). So, in *Julius Caesar*, 'Octavius is successful. Yet we should rather fail with Brutus' (p. 281). 'The purest wreath of victory rests on the forehead of the defeated conspirator' (p. 306). Our admiration for Cordelia has nothing to do with her success. The idealist Timon was 'infinitely interesting' to Shakespeare, whereas 'the practical and limited character of Alcibiades was esteemed highly by him, but did not really interest him' (p. 392). Dowden explains: 'An Alcibiades or a Fortinbras represents that side of his character into which he threw himself for protection against the weakness of excess of passion, or excess of thought' (p. 393).

The theory underlying Dowden's Shakespeare is that the self creates an anti-self as a prophylactic against the weakness of the self. At this point in his strange argument, Dowden quotes the great Sonnet 94, 'They that have power to hurt and will do none.' In it, he says, Shakespeare 'expresses his admiration of the calm, self-possessed, successful man' but 'remains remote and unmoved in the presence of such a practical, successful, unideal character'. Inevitably, Dowden sees the portrait of Prospero as summing everything up. Prospero initially despised worldly success, and for that reason lost his dukedom. But he won it back, knowing however that material success was only a part of the insubstantial pageant we call reality. He had 'entered into complete possession of himself'; very powerful, but indifferent to power.[24]

Did Dowden approve of his own ingenuity in explaining the hardness of Shakespeare as a carapace deliberately assumed as a survival technique?

When he had finished the book, and was waiting to see a printed copy, just after Christmas, 1874, Dowden wrote as follows to Aubrey de Vere:

> This 'Study of Shakespeare' I only partly like myself, and I expect you will only partly like it. One who loves Wordsworth and Browning can never be content to wholly abandon desires and fears and affinities which are extra-mundane, even for the sake of the rich and ample life of mundane passion and action which Shakespeare reveals.[25]

Now this really is a poser. The person whom I succeeded in Dowden's chair in 1960, H. O. White, had been a student of Dowden, and apparently he used to carry the professor's books back to his room after the lectures. White told me that after a lecture on Ben Jonson he went up to Dowden in the usual way, and told him how much he had enjoyed the lecture. Dowden, he said, turned on him and said with some fierceness, 'Couldn't you see it was all against the grain?'

Was the book on Shakespeare, which expresses the strongest admiration for the mundane vision of the practical man Shakespeare, and yet assures us that Shakespeare was basically soulful, compassionate, altruistic, also 'against the grain'? Was the worship of success, which Yeats found so repugnant a feature of the book, a dissimulation of Dowden's real feelings? And was the endeavour to provide his author with the requisite spiritual equipment an embarrassing and finally unsuccessful duty?

Dowden wrote frankly about his problems with the Shakespeare book to Elizabeth West, the girl whom he had taught at Alexandra College and whom, years later, in 1895, he married, after the death of his first wife. Back in 1871, long before the book, or the lectures from which the book was made, had been thought of, Dowden was writing to her about the attractiveness of failure in Shakespeare; that failure is only apparent; being in truth 'the highest success'. 'Who would not willingly be Cordelia?'[26] It is a striking question. But, as he began to work on the book, the fact (as he believed it to be) of Shakespeare's worldliness became a great problem. In January 1874, Dowden wrote, 'I felt at times, last year, a sense of repression from him which was painful' (p. 83). This sense of repression arose from Shakespeare's repression of what Dowden called 'his metaphysical mood and his passionate mood'; that is of course the Hamlet and the Romeo in him. In June, he was talking of finishing his book in terms of being 'delivered from Shakespeare', who was 'alien to my most vital self', adding 'I find certain needs not satisfied by Shakespeare [. . .] I instinctively, in self-defence, put some of myself into Shakespeare' (p. 99).

It becomes more and more evident that Dowden fashioned his extraordinary book in order to save Shakespeare from himself. That he was convinced of the worldliness of Shakespeare, of a spiritual myopia in his life and in his works. That he felt he owed it to – to what? – to the British Empire? – to make out the best possible case for a genius whom he considered to be crippled by visionary deficiency. So he invented an image of Shakespeare as one who was primarily a blend of his own Romeo and Hamlet, who was aware that if he allowed too free a rein to his capacity for intense love or intense thought he would snuff himself out, as his heroes did. Shakespeare's respect for action, achievement, efficiency and success in the histories is regarded as manufactured and factitious, a salute to qualities which he recognised as essential for survival, though in truth he despised them.

The weakness of Dowden's construct becomes apparent in his presentation of the spiritual side of Shakespeare. You are promised that, once Shakespeare is materially safe, you will see the real visionary Shakespeare appear; but nothing happens. It is all 'Watch this space!' The account of the tragedies and the romances as regards Shakespeare's exploration of what Dowden calls 'the deeper mysteries of being' is very disappointing. Only the failure of Brutus and Cordelia, the idealist victims, stands out. Dowden could not locate the spirituality which he felt bound to advertise.

But could that enthusiasm for pragmatic values which pervades Dowden's book, and which disgusted Yeats, have been faked? Dowden finds himself landed with a worldly Shakespeare whose pragmatism he found distasteful. Yet the book, as I have illustrated, is noisy in its acclamation of the virtue of pragmatism, or devotion to fact. But his acclamation *is* noise, political noise. Besides trying, rather unsuccessfully, to show that this worldly pragmatism was not the be-all and the end-all of Shakespeare, Dowden has a political duty to put the practical, bourgeois, Anglo-Saxon worship of success in the best light possible – even if later it must be seen to be overthrown. Insofar as pragmatism adheres to Shakespeare (and Dowden fears it may be ineradicable), it must be praised. For the sake of Great Britain, Shakespeare must be praised. The cause of unionism demands that even Shakespeare's visionary inadequacies should be shown in a good light. In any case, what are recognised as and accepted by Dowden as Anglo-Saxon characteristics have to be hailed as virtues.

So the enthusiasm for a tough pragmatism in the first half of the book, an enthusiasm which the second half undermines, has a political basis. But I believe it also has a strange psychological basis.

Although I find a fundamental insincerity in both halves of Dowden's book – in that half which praises Shakespeare for his toughness, and in that half which claims that Shakespeare was basically a transcendental visionary – I also find a core of sincerity in the book. It relates to Dowden's covert sympathy for failure in the plays; precisely the sympathy which Yeats (understandably) denied him. There is evidence in Dowden's writings that he knew only too well the seductive temptation to yield, to succumb, to be conquered, to fail. The evidence is chiefly in his poetry, which frequently images the pleasures of being dominated, being mothered, even ravished, as in the extraordinary unmasculine poem, 'Exchange of Sex'. This was written to Elizabeth West, and it comes from the collection, *A Women's Reliquary*, which Elizabeth West, as Dowden's widow, arranged to have published by the Cuala Press in 1913, immediately after Dowden's death. She added an amusing 'publisher's note' cancelling out Dowden's little fairy-tale about the origin of the poems, which was intended to disguise the fact that he was the author.[27]

EXCHANGE OF SEX

In some strange world, ere stars were old,
    Or here ere ocean whelm'd a land,
You were a bearded sea-king bold,
    I a white maiden on the strand.

Strong arms compell'd her to your bark,
    Light borne for all your ring-wrought gear;
You swept the waves from dawn to dark,
    While pride was trembling through her fear.

She half remembers in a dream
    Grey towers of her sea-eagle's nest;
Sunshine and storm, the gloom, the gleam,
    Warmth, might, male gladness on her breast.

You had your will, and very life
    Of yours was then her cherish'd store;
Can you recall when I was wife,
    And thoughts of yours grew babes I bore?

So now if sweet authority
    Touches, though in a different sex,
Your love, and I approve it, why
    Should instincts from the prime perplex?

With images like these in mind, one reads with different eyes perhaps the rather perfunctory bestseller, the *Shakspere* 'primer' of 1877, which Dowden carved out of his big book. The femininity of the failure Richard II is emphasised. He is 'deficient in all that is sterling and real in manhood'. We read not only of the 'masculine force' of Petruchio, but also of the 'cruel masculine force of Shylock'. And we remember that strange question, 'Who would not willingly be Cordelia?' She was hanged by the masculine force of Edmund.

If Dowden knew in himself gender-confusion, if he was given to masochistic fantasies of lying open to masculine force, is it not possible that he would compensate in the vociferous allegiance to a resolute masculinity in his writings? It seems that he visualised Shakespeare inventing a strong, masculine, no-nonsense success figure in his plays – Richard III, Fortinbras, Bolingbroke, Henry V – to compensate for the debilitating perils of the Romeo and the Hamlet within him. So is it not possible that the undoubted admiration for this strong, masculine figure in Dowden's criticism is generated by a similar compensation in his own life? 'I instinctively, in self-defence, put some of myself into Shakespeare.'

Arnold had suggested that the superior sensitivity and spirituality of the Celtic race had something feminine in it. Let us suppose that Dowden saw a little of what Arnold saw more and Yeats saw much more, the so-called Celticism in Shakespeare; and, instead of greeting it and acclaiming it, he was ashamed of it, and made Shakespeare ashamed of it because it imperilled the masculine values of English power, ashamed of it because he recognised its kinship with his own fantasy life of yielding to domination.

To sum up, then, we have Dowden worried about the Anglo-Saxon materialism of Shakespeare and his lack of transcendent vision. He does his best to alleviate this toughness by suggesting that actually Shakespeare was struggling to subdue the spirituality and the passion within him, acknowledging that wealth-creation was a primary requisite in human life. This ploy enabled Dowden to indulge in a good deal of political propaganda for Anglo-Saxon values. But there are deeper levels at which we may understand why Dowden offers us a Shakespeare who creates an anti-self. Dowden too was in the business of creating an anti-self. In spite of his conviction that Shakespeare was a worldly materialist, he recognised in him, not transcendent vision, but a deep sensitivity for the vanquished, for the underdog, and with that sensitivity he had voluptuous kinship. 'Who would not willingly be Cordelia?' For personal reasons and for political reasons it was essential for Dowden to underplay these emotions. What struck Yeats and most other readers of *Shakspere: His Mind and Art* as the dominating tone of the book, an aggressive praise for uncompromising masculine toughness, is doubly undermined.

Dowden's own attitude to the stereotype of the hard-fisted canny materialistic, Anglo-Saxon Shakespeare, which his book did so much to confirm and propagate, was deeply ambivalent. But this image was nevertheless the Shakespeare that was debated and fought over in Ireland. The rejection of Shakespeare, because he was so English; the acceptance of Shakespeare, because he was so English, both were founded on stereotypes: on stereotypes of Shakespeare, stereotypes of national character, even stereotypes of masculinity and femininity. It seems incredible how little real reading of Shakespeare went on. It is marvellous that Yeats, who you might say traded in stereotypes, was given a sudden recognition that the mundanity of Shakespeare, which he had swallowed hook, line and sinker, and on which he had based whole theories of the Renaissance – was a mare's nest. If Yeats's insistence on the Celticism of Shakespeare was a lot of nonsense deriving from Arnold, he read Shakespeare more perceptively than any other Irishman of his day, including Bernard Shaw and Edward Dowden. Yet the strange thing is that Yeats's conviction that he had recognised in Shakespeare a deep sympathy for those who fail in this world which the insensitive unionist Dowden was unaware of was erroneous. Dowden knew about this also. Had Dowden been less anxious about the cause of unionism and about his own masculinity, we might not have found their views of Shakespeare so opposed.

Notes

1 Frank Raymond Leavis, *Revaluation: Tradition and Development in English Poetry* (London: Chatto and Windus, 1936), p. 42.

2 In a seminar paper by Terence Hawkes, 'Putting on Some English'. Compare the conclusion of the same author's 'Take Me to Your Leda', *Shakespeare Survey*, 40, 1988, 31–2.

3 Alan Sinfield in *Political Shakespeare: New Essays in Cultural Materialism*, ed. by Jonathan Dollimore and Alan Sinfield (Manchester: Manchester University Press, 1985), pp 130–81; Terence Hawkes, *That Shakespeherian Rag: Essays on a Critical Process* (London: Methuen, 1986); Terry Eagleton, *Literary Theory: An Introduction* (Oxford: Blackwell, 1983), p. 11.

4 *Ben Jonson*, ed. Herford and Simpson, 11 vols (Oxford: Clarendon Press, 1947) VIII, p. 583.

5 John Mitchel, *Jail Journal* (Dublin: M. H. Gill, n.d.), p. 10.

6 Although his awareness of a 'bitter irony' in the presentation of the patriotism in *Henry V* (no doubt influenced by Yeats) is generations ahead of similar awareness in English critics.

7 John Eglinton [pseud.], *A Memoir of AE: George William Russell* (London: Macmillan, 1937), p. 23; p. 267.

8 Henry Summerfield, *That Myriad Minded Man: A Biography of George William Russell, 1867–1935* (Gerrards Cross: Colin Smythe, 1975), p. 170.

9 *AE: The Living Torch*, ed. by Monk Gibbon (London, Macmillan, 1937), pp 112–13.

10 John Eglinton, W. B. Yeats; A. E.; W. Larminie, *Literary Ideals in Ireland* (London, 1899), p. 73; see also W. B. Yeats, *Essays and Introductions* (London: Macmillan, 1961), p. 192.

11 George Moore, *Confessions of a Young Man*, ed. by S. Dick (Montreal: McGill-Queen's University Press, 1972), p. 66.

12 Ibid., p. 99; p. 90.

13 Ibid., p. 166.

14 A. E., D. P. Moran, George Moore, Douglas Hyde, Standish O'Grady, and W. B. Yeats, *Ideals in Ireland*, ed. by Lady Gregory (London: At the Unicorn, 1901), p. 19.

15 D. P. Moran, *The Philosophy of Irish Ireland* (Dublin: James Duffy, n.d.). Subsequent references are given within the text. See also Matthew Creasy's chapter below, pp 81–2.

16 Thomas MacDonagh, *Literature in Ireland: Studies Irish and Anglo-Irish* (Dublin: Talbot Press, 1916; repr. Tyone, Nenagh: Relay Books, 1996).

17 Matthew Arnold, *Complete Prose Works*, ed. by R. H. Super, Ann Arbor (Michigan: University of Michigan Press, 1962), p. 341.

18 Arnold derived this, like so much else in his essay, from his main source, Renan's 'Poesies des Races Celtiques'. See an excellent discussion by David Cairns and Shaun Richards in chapter 3 ('An Essentially Feminine Race') of *Writing Ireland* (Manchester: Manchester University Press, 1988).

19 *Essays and Introductions*, pp 104–8.

20 Marcus Tullius Cicero, *Letters to Atticus*, ed. by R. Shackleton Bailey (Cambridge: Cambridge University Press, 1965), I, 18, ii, 96. I am most grateful to Stephen Ryle for the help he has given me on this saying.

21 Edward Dowden, *Shakspere: A Critical Study of His Mind and Art* (London: Henry S. King, 1875). Subsequent references will be given within the text.

22 Edward Dowden, 'The Interpretation of Literature', in *Transcripts and Studies* (London: Kegan Paul, Trench, Trubner, 2nd edn 1896), p. 252.

23 *Letters of Edward Dowden and His Correspondents*, ed. by Elizabeth D. Dowden and Hilda M. Dowden (London: Dent, 1914), p. 69.

24 Compare *Fragments from Old Letters: E. D. to E. D. W.* (London: Dent, 1914), p. 84.

25 Dowden, *Letters*, pp 69–70.

26 *Fragments from Old Letters*, p. 9.

27 On the date and circumstances of publication (and Yeats's annoyance that his sisters should have undertaken to publish such feeble work) see William M. Murphy, *Prodigal Father: The Life of John Butler Yeats* (Ithaca: Cornell University Press, 1978), pp 407–8. I am grateful to Terence Brown for this reference.

CHAPTER 2

The 'Wild' and the 'Useful'

Shakespeare, Dowden and Some Yeatsian Antinomies

Brian Cosgrove

Readers of Yeats will be familiar with the late poem, 'Lapis Lazuli', and the way in which the poem's argument on behalf of a paradoxical tragic gaiety is substantiated by sustained and explicit reference some of the best-known tragic figures in Shakespeare's plays: Hamlet, Lear, Ophelia and Cordelia (ll. 10–11, 16, 21).[1] And the general importance of Shakespeare as an influence on Yeats is evident in his famous statement in 'A General Introduction for My Works' (1937) where he claims that he owes his 'soul' to 'Shakespeare, to Spenser, and to Blake, [. . .] and to the English language in which I think, speak, and write'.[2] It is perhaps significant that it is Shakespeare's name which heads the list.

Yeats was introduced to Shakespeare by his father, who read excerpts from the plays to him as a child.[3] Of even greater significance was his father's introduction of Yeats to Shakespeare on stage, when in the mid-1870s he brought the young Yeats to see Sir Henry Irving as Hamlet, a performance sufficiently memorable to be recalled many years afterwards in Yeats's late poem, 'A Nativity' (ll. 7–8): 'What brushes fly and moth aside? | Irving and his plume of pride' (p. 388). It seems clear that Yeats identified with Hamlet (as played by Irving), as is apparent in a remark in 1914 in *Reveries over Childhood and Youth*: 'For many years Hamlet was an image of heroic self-possession for the poses of youth and childhood to copy, *a combatant of the battle within myself*'.[4]

Roy Foster discerns a similar 'emotional identification' with Hamlet on the part of Yeats, but does not seem fully to agree with Jonathan Allison that it was Yeats's 'first encounter with Irving's Hamlet as a boy' that was the crucial determinant in 'his understanding of Shakespearean character'.[5] Foster thinks the beginning of Yeats's 'obsession' is to be dated from 6 March 1900, when 'he went to [F. R.] Benson's uncut *Hamlet* with AG [Lady Gregory]'.[6] But in any case Foster is aware of the importance of *Hamlet* for Yeats, and he quotes the following from a letter of Yeats to the actor John Martin Harvey, or

Martin-Harvey (25 October 1909): 'A performance of *Hamlet* is always to me what a High Mass is to a good Catholic. It is my supreme religious event.'[7]

Yeats, in whom subjective concerns habitually antecede more general formulations or commitments, may have initially viewed Shakespeare and specifically *Hamlet* from a perspective dictated by his own personal needs; but he did come to engage with Shakespeare in more general terms throughout his formative years. He 'sought every opportunity to see Shakespeare performed in London, and he visited the Stratford Memorial Theatre in 1901, 1902, 1904, 1905, 1908, and 1909. He read Shakespeare avidly'.[8] And while he feared that Shakespeare – as he put it in *The Secret Rose* (1897) – might become 'one of our superstitions', Yeats the dramatist 'was to return again and again to Shakespeare's plays and characters for fresh understanding of his own thought and art'.[9]

On Baile's Strand may be cited as one play where the influence of Shakespeare on Yeats is very much in evidence, and Leonard Nathan suggests that 'the Cuchulain of the earlier part of the play is the offspring of [Walter] Pater's interpretation of Richard II'.[10] Ruth Nevo goes further and argues more generally that Cuchulain, a figure that accompanies Yeats's creative life 'from beginning to end [. . .] in a peculiarly obsessive way', and recurs again and again in his drama, originates 'in Shakespeare'; she further suggests that we should see Cuchulain 'in the mirror of Shakespeare's Hamlet'. She adds that 'Shakespeare's dramatisations of Lear's self-division are transformed into the symbolic Fool and Blind Man' in *On Baile's Strand*.[11]

We may take as a given, then, the very real connections between Yeats and Shakespeare. What this essay specifically undertakes, however, is an examination not just of what Shakespeare came to signify for Yeats, but also the extent to which Yeats sought to enlist Shakespeare on the side of an emergent nationalism. It is understandable that, given the recent developments in Irish cultural studies, there should be a particular interest, for Irish critics especially, in analysing the ways in which Irish writers such as Yeats should have appropriated Shakespeare and adapted him to an Irish framework. There are, however, dangers in reducing a matter as complex as Yeats's attitude to and use of Shakespeare to a preordained cultural argument. In foregrounding the multivalency of Shakespeare in Yeats's thinking, then, it is, in large part, the purpose of this essay to highlight such dangers. I begin with the treatment of Yeats, Shakespeare (and Edward Dowden) as that is found in Declan Kiberd's challenging, thought-provoking and influential study, *Inventing Ireland*.

One of the many vivid sequences in Kiberd's work deals with Yeats's reading of *Richard II*. In Kiberd's view, *Richard II* was, for Yeats, 'the story of England despoiling Ireland.' Yeats's Shakespeare, then, was a crypto-Celtic one, 'who loved Richard's doomed complexity and despised the usurper [Bolingbroke]'s basely political wiles.'[12] While taking issue with Kiberd's version of Yeats's response, my purpose here is not so much to contest it as to place Yeats's approach to Shakespeare – binaristic in structure – in a broader context of Yeatsian antitheses (or antinomies); thereby offering a perspective which might allow us to see the England/Ireland opposition, in the context of Yeats's work, as a part (and perhaps a subordinate part) of a larger or more wide-ranging series of antithetical prototypes.

Yeats's view of Richard II, we should note, is in fact placed in opposition not to Bolingbroke (later Henry IV) but rather to Henry V (the Prince Hal of the *Henry IV* plays); the contrary evaluations being provided in a comparatively short piece written after Yeats's visit to Shakespeare's birthplace in May 1901, simply called 'At Stratford-on-Avon', and subsequently published in *Ideas of Good and Evil* (1903). As the references in the essay make clear, one of Yeats's primary disagreements was with Edward Dowden, who interpreted the polarity between Richard II and Henry V exclusively in the latter's favour. In Dowden's *Shakspere* (first published in 1877), Henry is Shakespeare's 'ideal of active, practical, heroic manhood', while Richard is quite simply 'deficient in all that is sterling and real in manhood'.[13] In fairness, we should acknowledge that Dowden allows to Richard 'a certain regal charm',[14] just as, in his earlier *Shakspere: A Critical Study of His Mind and Art*, Dowden had conceded that Richard 'has an indescribable charm of person and presence'.[15] But whereas Henry V 'exhibits the utmost greatness which the *active* nature can attain', the 'self-indulgent' Richard remains 'incapable of strenuous *action*'.[16] Richard, in Dowden's view, belongs to the company of 'the sentimentalist, the dreamer and the dilettante'.[17]

In his essay 'At Stratford-on-Avon', Yeats clearly undertakes a transvaluation of the two figures, and, in his reversal of Dowden's judgement, prioritises Richard. Thus Henry V is described by Yeats (in words that seem to echo part of Andrew Marvell's assessment of Oliver Cromwell in his notoriously ambivalent 'Horatian Ode') as one who is 'as remorseless and undistinguished as some natural force' (p. 108);[18] whereas, Yeats insists, Richard is presented in predominantly sympathetic terms, Shakespeare 'understanding indeed how ill-fitted he was to be king, at a certain moment in history', but understanding also 'that he was lovable and full of a capricious fancy [. . .]' (p. 105). Richard, however, 'the vessel of porcelain', gives way to 'the vessel of clay', Henry V, who is 'the reverse of all that Richard was', Henry having 'the gross vices, the coarse nerves, of one who is to rule among a violent people' (p. 108). And in an antithesis between poetry and rhetoric which every reader familiar with his work will instantly recognise as typical of Yeats, Henry's 'resounding rhetoric' is contrasted with 'that lyricism which rose out of Richard's mind like the jet of a fountain' (p. 108).

It is, as I hope the subsequent argument makes clear, an entirely legitimate exercise to concentrate solely on Yeats's comments on the history tetralogy

Richard II to *Henry V* in an attempt to gauge his more general evaluation of Shakespeare. Thus it is clear from the essay 'At Stratford-on-Avon' that Yeats is concerned, as he says, not just with the contrast between two individual Shakespearean characters, but with the larger matter of 'an antithesis [. . .] between two types', *as these are seen to be represented by* Richard II (wrongly dismissed in previous criticism as 'sentimental', 'weak', 'selfish', and 'insincere'), and by Henry V (thoughtlessly acclaimed as 'Shakespeare's only hero'; pp 103–4). Moreover, as a later passage in the essay suggests, Yeats saw these anti-types as recurrent in Shakespeare: thus Richard is that 'unripened Hamlet', as Henry is 'that ripened Fortinbras' (p. 108: extrapolating from Yeats's views, we might describe Antony as that virile Richard, and see in Octavius, later Augustus Caesar, another version of Henry V). Yeats makes these comments as he speculates that there may be one dominant 'myth' for every man, and in the case of Shakespeare the dominant myth is described in typically antithetical terms. The myth involves, on the one side, 'a wise man who was blind from very wisdom', the blindness symbolising a refusal of the phenomenal world (we think of Hamlet in particular, burdened as he was by a degree of awareness that made a proactive engagement with the 'real' world seem futile, but also of Richard and Antony); and, on the other, 'an empty man who thrust him from his place, and saw all that could be seen from very emptiness' (Henry V, Fortinbras, Octavius, whose inner 'emptiness' opens them to the pragmatic claims of immediate reality: p. 107).

Citing this passage, Declan Kiberd astutely relates it to the clash in Yeats's own 'epic cycle of dramas' between Cuchulain, the 'wise man blind from very wisdom', and Conchobhar, who assumes the role of the 'empty man'.[19] The context of Kiberd's statement suggests that Yeats is involved in an act of appropriation whereby the subaltern writer, adapting from the imperialist tradition to his own purposes Shakespeare's Richard and Bolingbroke (or Henry V), re-imagines/re-creates them: a perspective that focuses on one specific kind of binarism. What I wish to do here, however, is to keep at the centre of our critical attention the typical, or, more precisely, the prototypical antitheses which govern Yeats's thinking, and to see these as not necessarily tied to any narrow political agenda. This brings us back to the central issues at stake in this essay: that is, the possibility of a nationalistic investment by Yeats in his Shakespeare criticism, and whether or not the important or central antithesis is that between England and Ireland (or, to extend the range of reference somewhat, between Yeats's Ireland and Dowden's Britain).

To deal first with the latter: it is undoubtedly the case that one basis for the quarrel between Dowden and Yeats derived from Dowden's Unionism. And with that in mind, it is inevitable that we should pay particular attention to Dowden's praise for Henry V's ability to unite 'in loyal service the jarring nationalities of his father's time – Englishmen, Scotchmen, Welshmen,

Irishmen', all of whom are 'at Henry's side at Agincourt'.[20] Roy Foster, too, would situate Yeats's quarrel with Dowden in precisely this context, noting for example how, as early as 1886, Yeats in a lengthy essay on Samuel Ferguson included 'an explicit attack on Dowden and the spirit of West-Britonism in Ireland'.[21] There is, however, more to the disagreement between the two men than politics of that kind, as is clear from the sequence on Dowden in Yeats's *Reveries over Childhood and Youth*. The initial quarrel, we should first note, was not between W. B. Yeats and Dowden, but between Dowden and Yeats's father (John B. Yeats). Thus, according to his son, John B. Yeats felt that Dowden 'believed too much in the intellect' at the expense of the emotions; moreover, in a further antithesis which becomes central to Yeats's critique both of Dowden and of Dowden's version of Shakespeare, Yeats attributes to his father a preference for those 'who talk and write to discover truth', over those who do so 'for popular instruction':[22] a contrast, one might suggest, between those who seek truth as an end in itself, and those who would subordinate truth to a pragmatic or utilitarian end.

More to the point, the suggestion on Yeats's part (prompted by his father's comments) is that Dowden failed to nourish his own creativity.[23] In Roy Foster's summary, Dowden in *Reveries* is 'finally drawn as a portrait of artistic limitation and bourgeois respectability'.[24] In Yeats's view, Dowden might have been a poet, but chose instead the lower, safer path to professional success. We might, then, at the risk of some simplification, see Dowden as one who might have had some of the qualities of a Richard II, but chose (in bourgeois respectability and professional success), a path which made him, if not a Henry V, then one who might claim some kinship with the spirit of pragmatism associated with Henry and related Shakespearean prototypes.

The general point is that the differences with Dowden reach well beyond politics to embrace richer and more diverse polarities. We can discern a similar widening of focus when we turn to the Stratford-on-Avon essay and to Yeats's comments there on, specifically, the state of Shakespeare criticism. It is true that, in one telling phrase, Yeats relates what he calls the 'apotheosis' of Henry V in Shakespeare criticism to 'imperialistic enthusiasm' (p. 104), and that phrase might be said to glance at Britain's imperialistic dealings with Ireland; but it remains one note (and perhaps a subordinate one) among many. Prior to that, indeed, Yeats suggests that the debunking of Richard II and the elevation of Henry V to heroic status 'began among the German critics' (not the British or the 'West Briton'; p. 104). True, again, that in a passage quoted by Declan Kiberd, Yeats attributes Dowden's views of Richard and Henry to a pro-English bias: 'He [Dowden] lived in Ireland, where everything has failed, and he meditated upon the perfection of character which had, he thought, made England successful' (p. 104). But, in what follows, this ready-to-hand contrast between Ireland and England yields to a more significant antithesis between what Dowden wrongly 'thought' had made England great, and what had in fact made England so. For Dowden forgot, says Yeats, that England 'was made by her adventurers, by her people of wildness and imagination and eccentricity' (p. 104); and perhaps at this point we should recall Yeats's early and persistent interest in the imaginative and eccentric William Blake. A further sentence implies that Henry V was neither 'the model Shakespeare held up before England', nor even 'the typical Anglo-Saxon' (p. 104). Thus the antithesis that begins to emerge as primary in Yeats's thinking, is not that between England and Ireland, but between one version of England and another.

If we turn to some of the opening remarks in the essay 'At Stratford-on-Avon' we may begin to discern the broad outlines of the antithetical categories which provide the context for Yeats's subsequent observations. The early reference to George Eliot in the essay may seem odd, but not if we recall (from the account given in *Reveries*) how it was Dowden who first urged Yeats to read George Eliot, and how Yeats was repelled by her because she 'seemed to have a distrust or a distaste for all in life that gives one a springing foot'.[25] I take it that George Eliot is being dismissed in this way because she is (in Yeats's view) emphatically *not* one of 'the people of wildness and imagination' who have contributed to England's true greatness. In the Stratford-on-Avon essay the major accusation levelled against both George Eliot and the Shakespeare critics who emerged in the late nineteenth century is given in a single, loaded word: utilitarianism. Such utilitarianism, according to Yeats, gives rise to the view that 'nothing about a man seems important except his *utility* to the State, and nothing so *useful* to the State as the actions whose effect can be weighed by reason' (italics added). Clearly adumbrated here are the characteristics of Henry V (as evaluated by Yeats; in addition, the reference to reason points back to John B. Yeats's criticism of Dowden as one who believed in the intellect at the expense of the emotions); while on the other hand, as Yeats proceeds to add: 'The deeds of Coriolanus, Hamlet, Timon, Richard II had no obvious use [. . .]'. In the same vein, Yeats insists that Shakespeare 'had no nice sense of utilities, no ready balance to measure deeds [. . .]' (p. 106).

Correlative with utilitarianism, in Yeats's view, is an unacceptable moralism – hence, in the opening remarks in the Stratford-on-Avon essay the distaste for 'the Accusation of Sin' – as found in George Eliot; and opposed to both is the quality that Yeats called 'wildness'. The antithesis is memorably articulated in a famous comment Yeats made on Spenser's *Faerie Queene* in an essay on Spenser which (dating from October 1902) belongs to the same period as 'At Stratford-on-Avon'. Spenser, in Yeats's view, inherited a richly imaginative world, but subordinated it to a utilitarian moralism:

He wrote of knights and ladies, wild creatures imagined by the aristocratic poets of the twelfth century, and perhaps chiefly by English poets who had still the French tongue; but he fastened them with allegorical nails to a big barn-door of common sense, of merely practical virtue.

In the remainder of the passage, Yeats sees the change as part of an historical shift which brought an emergent middle class to power, and created the cultural conditions which allowed for the taming of a previous wildness and freedom:

> Allegory itself had risen into general importance with the rise of the merchant class in the thirteenth and fourteenth centuries; and it was natural when that class was about for the first time to shape an age in its image, that the last epic poet of the old order should mix its art with his own, long-descended, irresponsible, happy art. (p. 367)

Allegory may make use of the extravagant or fanciful imagery of imaginative or 'visionary' poets, but in what becomes an increasingly didactic mode, such imagery is subordinated to a dominant moral purpose. Hence Yeats's impatience with Spenser's *The Faerie Queene*, as a primer of 'merely practical virtue' (p. 367).

When it comes to *Richard II*, Yeats, not surprisingly, readily appropriates from his predecessor Walter Pater the description of Richard as a 'wild creature' (Pater's precise wording was 'the graceful, wild creature'), noting in the same context that Richard is 'full of capricious fancy' (p. 105).[26] Wildness, the refusal of orthodoxy and pragmatic common sense, takes, we may recall, many forms in Yeats's own work: from the declaration he places on his own 'boyish lips' in the 'Introductory Rhymes' to *Responsibilities* ('Only the wasteful virtues earn the sun'), to the *sprezzatura* of those who in their 'delirium' died for Ireland in 'September 1913' ('They weighed so lightly what they gave'), to the characters of 'Crazy Jane' in *Words for Music Perhaps* and 'The Wild Old Wicked Man' in *Last Poems*.

There is, we should be aware, a further significant reference to the antithetical category of utilitarianism in the essay on Stratford-on-Avon. Yeats asserts that Shakespeare 'meditated as Solomon, not as Bentham meditated, upon blind ambitions, untoward accidents, and capricious passions, and the world was almost as empty in his eyes as it must be in the eyes of God' (pp. 106–7). When Yeats refers here to Solomon, he is thinking of the tradition that attributes *The Book of Ecclesiastes*, with its emphasis on the vanity of life and the transience of human existence, to Solomon (even though modern scholars now dispute Solomon's authorship). The contrast, then, is between a thinker such as Solomon, who saw life as essentially empty (thereby signalling a possible withdrawal from such a life), and the antithetical philosopher, the British utilitarian Jeremy Bentham, whose horizon was limited to a consideration of life as a potential source of pleasure and utility, both of which, in addition, could be measured in quantitative terms. On the other side, Solomon's vision amounts to a qualitative judgement.

The invocation of what Yeats calls the 'empty' world of Solomon points to what might be termed 'negative transcendence': if life has nothing to offer, then we must turn from such nothingness to some alternative (perhaps, since this is after all Yeats, subjective vision), even if such an alternative is not at this point positively formulated. Moreover, this allusion to Solomon precedes the reference in the Stratford-on-Avon essay to 'the wise man who was blind from very wisdom' (p. 107), where the blindness, as I suggested earlier, amounts to a symbolic turning away from the phenomenal world (thereby, we add, validating the reality of the 'wisdom' attributed to the wise man), and the reliance instead on inner vision. This, of course, is a trope that is central to the Romantic tradition, and to a traditional way of interpreting such a visionary poet as the blind Milton. The 'empty' world of Solomon's vision seems, moreover, to anticipate the coming 'Into the desolation of reality' in the late poem 'Meru' (in *A Full Moon in March*). But the reference to Bentham also relates in a highly specific way to a passage on Dowden in *The Trembling of the Veil*, where it is claimed that Dowden 'turned Shakespeare into a British Benthamite'.[27] I would suggest here that given the elaborate implications for Yeats's thought of the significance of utilitarianism, something we have just been exploring, we should give more emphasis to the second B-word than the first; which is to say that Yeats recoiled specifically from British utilitarianism rather than from Britishness (or Englishness) in general. It is after all note-worthy that in his remarks on Spenser Yeats attributes the wild imaginings 'chiefly' to the late medieval *English* poets, thereby in the wild (visionary)/utilitarian antithesis placing such English poets on the side of the angels.

Taking our cue from the historical shift indicated in that passage on *The Faerie Queene*, we should, finally, locate Yeats's opposition between wildness and utility in the historical framework he himself provides. In the Stratford-on-Avon essay, 'the practical ideals of the modern age' are very deliberately contrasted with the 'courtly and saintly ideals of the Middle Ages' (p. 106). In a similar way, a little earlier, Richard is somewhat controversially related to the figures of 'artist or saint'. Shakespeare (and indeed Spenser) are for Yeats historically located at a point in time when 'Merry England was fading', but had not entirely disappeared (p. 106). In *The Trembling of the Veil*, Yeats relates this chronology to the master-schema of the Phases of the Moon, placing Shakespeare at the cusp of change:

> Somewhere about 1450, though later in some parts of Europe by a hundred years or so, and in some earlier, men attained to personality in great numbers, 'Unity of being,' and became like 'a perfectly proportioned human body' [. . .] What afterwards showed for rifts and cracks were there already, but imperious impulse held

all together. Then the scattering came, the seeding of the poppy, bursting of pea-pod, and for a time personality seemed but the stronger for it. [Thus] Shakespeare's people make all things serve their passion.

The Middle Ages, he later adds, is close to the full moon of the fifteenth phase, when the 'subjective mind' predominates; and to the sixteenth, seventeenth and eighteenth phases we may, says Yeats, 'attribute the men of Shakespeare, of Titian, of Strozzi, and of Van Dyck [. . .]'.[28]

Shakespeare and his character creations, then, are provided in Yeats's mythic schema with a context which certainly includes but, I want to argue, goes beyond any simple opposition between Ireland and England. As I stated earlier, near the beginning we should be wary of any presupposition that Yeats in his writings will necessarily validate our own assumptions regarding his possible interpretation of Shakespeare in broadly nationalist terms. Indeed, we should be cautious in making any such suppositions in advance of what should be an objective investigation of a writer's views on any topic. As critics who accept a *parti pris* position, we may end up indulging in a merely circular argument; and we do well to bear in mind the general warning implicit in a comment made some years ago by Frank Lentricchia: 'Tell me your theory and I'll tell you in advance what you'll say about any work of literature [. . .]'.[29] The remark suggests not just the conservative (or uncritically self-reinforcing) nature of any given critical theoretical approach, but also its possible reductivism. In our eagerness to utilise English literary texts to illuminate Irish history and culture, we should be careful not to ignore those aspects of the texts we deal with which, in their expansive complexity, do not fit a preconceived template that threatens to turn Procrustean.

The problem is compounded when a subsequent critic takes the paraphrase provided by an ideologically similar predecessor as a valid summary of the original text, the result being a further authorisation of a critical argument that may or may not be entirely just. One incidental but nonetheless revealing example may suffice. In Andrew Gibson's memorable study of Joyce (2002),[30] Gibson, dealing it must be said only in passing with Yeats's attitude to Shakespeare (his main interest being in Joyce's), provides a summary of Yeats's views which is in fact Declan Kiberd's interpretation of those views: 'For Yeats, the problem with Dowden was that he just recycled "the received categories of English thought"' (p. 63). The quotation within the quotation here, however, is not what *Yeats* says about Dowden (as one might be led to suppose), but *Declan Kiberd's paraphrase of Yeats*. On the same page, Gibson likewise states: 'Yeats argued that Dowden wrote "as would any Englishman of Shakespeare or Shelley"'. But again, as Gibson's own footnote makes clear, it was Kiberd who said this, and the 'argument' attributed in the main text to Yeats is nowhere to be found in Yeats's own work. Gibson, fine critic though he is, is using the quotations which suit his pre-supposed argument. When he states in the same context that 'Dowden was indomitably English-oriented, a defender of middle-class, utilitarian, Victorian English assumptions', he seems not to give sufficient weight to the epithets other than 'English' in his precisely worded summary. And that has been a major part of the preceding argument in this essay: what Yeats reacts against in Dowden is not only the latter's English bias but his uncritical acceptance of an entire spectrum of values which were anathema to Yeats. Such a spectrum subsumes, it is true, certain aspects of Englishness, but includes a lot more besides.

Notes

1   *The Collected Poems of W. B. Yeats* (1933; repr. Dublin: Gill & Macmillan, 1988), pp 338–9. Subsequent references will be given within the text.

2   W. B. Yeats, *Essays and Introductions* (London: Macmillan, 1961), p. 519. Subsequent references will be given within the text.

3   A convenient summary of Shakespeare's influence on Yeats is provided in Sam McCready, *A William Butler Yeats Encyclopedia* (Westport, Connecticut: Greenwood Press, 1997), p. 354. For a more sustained treatment, see Rupin W. Desai, *Yeats's Shakespeare* (Evanston: Northwestern University Press, 1971).

4   Quoted by Jonathan Allison, 'W. B. Yeats and Shakespearean Character', in *Shakespeare and Ireland: History, Politics, Culture*, ed. by Mark Thornton Burnett and Ramona Wray (Basingstoke: Macmillan, 1997), p. 116, emphasis added. 'Predictably', Allison adds, 'Hamlet became a touchstone by which Yeats measured others' (p. 117).

5   R. F. Foster, *W. B. Yeats: A Life. I: The Apprentice Mage 1865–1914* (Oxford: Oxford University Press, 1997), p. 413; Allison, 'W. B. Yeats and Shakespearean Character', p. 129.

6   Foster, *Yeats*, p. 606.

7   Ibid., p. 413.

8   McCready, *A William Butler Yeats Encyclopedia*, p. 354.

9   Leonard E. Nathan, *The Tragic Drama of William Butler Yeats: Figures in a Dance* (New York/London: Columbia University Press, 1965), p. 7; p. 8. Nathan may be overstating the case, however, when he refers to Yeats's conviction that the Noh Theatre 'was far less alien to him than was the drama of Shakespeare [. . .]' (p. 166).

10   Ibid., p. 118.

11   Ruth Nevo, 'Yeats, Shakespeare and Ireland', in *Literature and Nationalism*, ed. by Vincent Newey and Ann Thompson (Liverpool: Liverpool University Press, 1991), p. 183; p. 186; p. 192.

12   Declan Kiberd, *Inventing Ireland: The Literature of the Modern Nation* (London: Jonathan Cape, 1995), p. 269.

13   Edward Dowden, *Shakspere* (1877; repr. London: Macmillan, 1893), p. 100; p. 89.

14   Dowden, *Shakspere*, p. 89; Dowden, *Shakspere: A Critical Study of His Mind and Art* (London: Henry S. King, 1875), p. 195.

15   *Shakspere: A Critical Study of His Mind and Art*, p. 195.

16 *Shakspere*, p. 89; emphasis added.

17 *Shakspere: A Critical Study of His Mind and Art*, p. 202.

18 For Andrew Marvell's sense of Cromwell as a natural force, see 'An Horatian Ode upon Cromwell's Return from Ireland', ll. 13–16, 21–6.

19 Kiberd, *Inventing Ireland*, p. 269.

20 *Shakspere*, pp 100–1.

21 Foster, *Yeats*, p. 52.

22 W. B. Yeats, *Autobiographies* (London: Macmillan, 1955), p. 88.

23 Ibid.

24 Foster, *Yeats*, p. 530.

25 *Autobiographies*, p. 88.

26 Leonard E. Nathan is among those who have noted that 'Yeats tended to rely for his view of Shakespeare on the opinions of Walter Pater, especially those found in Pater's essay, "Shakespeare's English Kings", from which Yeats borrowed for his own essay on Shakespeare's drama, "At Stratford-on-Avon" (1901)'. Nathan also notes, however, significant differences in emphasis in Yeats: see Nathan, *The Tragic Drama*, pp 104–5.

27 Yeats, *Autobiographies*, p. 235.

28 Ibid., p. 291; p. 292.

29 *Lingua Franca* (Sept./Oct., 1996), p. 64.

30 Andrew Gibson, *Joyce's Revenge: History, Politics and Aesthetics in 'Ulysses'* (Oxford: Oxford University Press, 2002).

CHAPTER 3

'Bhíos ag Stratford ar an abhainn'

Shakespeare, Douglas Hyde, 1916

Andrew Murphy

The first of May, 1916, was officially designated as 'Shakespeare May Day' and various events were organised around this time to celebrate the tercentenary of the playwright's death. The Shakespeare Tercentenary Committee arranged to convene on May Day itself, at the Mansion House in London. Admission was by invitation only and the Prime Minister was scheduled to address the gathering.[1] As part of the proceedings, the Honorary Secretary of the Tercentenary Committee, Israel Gollancz, Professor of English at King's College London, publicly unveiled his edited volume *A Book of Homage to Shakespeare*, published by Humphrey Milford for Oxford University Press. The *Times* described the book as 'A sumptuous volume', which 'may be said to record, in a peculiarly catholic way, what after three hundred years the best literary representatives of British and allied culture are saying about Shakespeare'.[2] The project had been initiated in July 1914, a peculiarly inauspicious time for embarking on such a venture. As Coppélia Kahn has noted, the first planning meeting was convened 'about a month after the assassination of Archduke Franz Ferdinand at Sarajevo, a few weeks before Britain declared war on the Central Powers'.[3] Just as the project was being formulated, then, as Gollancz himself observes, 'the dream of the world's brotherhood to be demonstrated by its common and united commemorations of Shakespeare, with many another fond illusion, was rudely shattered.'[4]

Feeling, however, that 'not even under present conditions should the Shakespeare Tercentenary be allowed to pass unobserved', Gollancz pressed on with the venture.[5] The finished volume, as unveiled at the Mansion House, included items from 166 'Homagers' (as Gollancz styles his contributors), with many more left unpublished for want of space. Gollancz received contributions from far and wide and the book included texts in Greek, Latin, Hebrew, Sanskrit, Bengalee, Urdu, Burmese, Arabic and Bechuana. He also sought out contributors closer to home. Among those Gollancz wrote to soliciting a piece for inclusion in the volume was George Russell (AE). Russell declined the invitation, however, observing that 'I am one of the worst critics in the world. I could perhaps write about small people. I could not write about big people. To write about Shakespeare seems to me like writing about the Earth or anything else huge and secret'. 'I have never tried to make clear to myself what I think about Shakespeare,' he concluded, '& doubt if I could'.[6] Gollancz did succeed in securing a contribution from the 'Rt. Hon. Mr Justice Madden, LL.D., Litt.D., Vice-Chancellor of Dublin University', writer of the authoritative legal textbook *Madden on the Registration of Deeds* (1901) and, more appositely, author of *The Diary of Master William Silence: A Study of Shakespeare and Elizabethan Sport*.[7] Madden's contribution consists of a rather anodyne meditation on Shakespeare and Stanyhurst's *Description of Ireland* and his positioning in relation to the political issues of the day may be guessed from the fact that he notes in his piece that 'To-day an earnest and active Dublin branch of the Empire Shakespeare Society celebrates the tercentenary of the Master's death'.[8]

An Irish contributor of a rather different stripe was Douglas Hyde who, in response to Gollancz's invitation to participate in the volume, proposed sending an Irish language poem of 'some five and twenty verses'.[9] In some respects Hyde seems rather an odd person for Gollancz to have approached in connection with the book. Doubtless he would have been known in London academic circles for his work as a folklorist (and for his contributions to Yeats' work in this area) and possibly also as Professor of Modern Irish at University College Dublin.[10] But Hyde's most prominent public role was as founder and President of the Gaelic League, and his avowed programme for the League was – as summarised in the title of a speech delivered at the National Literary Society in Dublin in 1892 – 'The Necessity for De-Anglicising Ireland'. For this reason, he seems a rather unlikely contributor to a volume celebrating Britain's national poet, published in time of war. At the same time, however, it should be noted that Hyde's understanding of just what 'De-Anglicising' actually meant was rather complex and it was interestingly intertwined with his sense of where Ireland stood in relation to English canonical writers, including, notably, William Shakespeare. In his 1892 speech, Hyde mapped out the aims of the 'De-Anglicising' project, in cultural – and specifically literary – terms. He argued in favour of the necessity for encouraging the use of Anglo-Irish literature instead of English books, especially of English periodicals. 'We must set our face sternly against penny dreadfuls, shilling shockers, and still more, the garbage of vulgar English weeklies like *Bow Bells* and the *Police Intelligencer*. Every house should have a copy of Moore and Davis.'[11]

What Hyde is objecting to here is the Irish embracing what he considers to be low-grade English popular culture, particularly, we might say, the cheap newspapers and disposable fiction that often tended to be favoured by the newly literate working-class British public in the wake of the 1870 Education Act (which, ultimately, had the effect of making school attendance both universal and compulsory, thus broadening the reading public).[12] His attack on this form of English culture develops an argument he had first made in 'A Plea for the Irish Language', published in the *Dublin University Review* in August 1886. In this article, Hyde writes:

> If by ceasing to speak Irish our peasantry could learn to appreciate Shakespeare and Milton, to study Wordsworth or Tennyson, then I would certainly say adieu to it. But this is not the case. They lay aside a language which for all ordinary purposes of every day life is much more forcible than any with which I am acquainted, and they replace it by another which they learn badly and speak with an atrocious accent, interlarding it with barbarisms and vulgarity.[13]

Hyde combined the two elements of his argument in an interview given to the San Francisco *Leader* in February 1906, where he observed that:

> Our people, when they threw away their own native literature and language, did not turn to Shakespeare, or Tennyson, or Matthew Arnold. They turned to the cheapest English weeklies and the insipid papers that are really sucking the brains out of the people, and this to them represents 'the great English literature'.[14]

The project of 'De-Anglicising' Ireland does not, then, for Hyde, represent a blanket rejection of *all* English culture. He wants his fellow-countrymen to abjure the worst of English literature and to embrace what he considers to be the best of traditional Irish culture, which he identifies as 'the literature of the poets, the literature of the saints and shanacies, the old songs, the old folk tales, the old histories full of old ideas and enthusiasms'.[15] Quite where the Irish might stand in relation to works of English high culture, such as Shakespeare, remains unexplored in his prose writings.[16] We might say, however, that Hyde does glance at this question in his contribution to the Gollancz volume. Furthermore, his tercentenary poem itself nicely illustrates the complexity of Hyde's positioning in relation to the high cultural products of a neighbouring country which he saw as historically being hostile to Ireland's best interests.

Gollancz responded to Hyde's offer of an Irish poem for the tercentenary volume with the comment 'Heartiest thanks: whatever you deem fitting & best will be most welcome'.[17] It would seem that Gollancz then asked, by telegram, that the Irish text be supplemented by an English translation. Hyde responded by asking Gollancz why a translation was required, inquiring whether the editor wanted it for his 'own information or to print'. 'I should not like to give a translation unless all the other tributes in non-English tongues are translated also', he continued. 'It would look very disparaging to Irish!'[18]

He did, in fact, send on a translation the very next day, but stressed that he hoped Gollancz would not print it 'unless you are giving translations of the other non-English contributions'.[19] The editor was, in fact, aiming to provide translations for most of the foreign-language texts and he intended to publish Hyde's Irish and English versions in parallel.

Gollancz must surely have been surprised by what he read in the translation of 'An Rud Tharla do Ghaedheal ag Stratford ar an Abhainn', as Hyde's poem was called.[20] The conceit of the poem is that an Irishman sails to England and finds himself on the Avon, in Stratford.[21] Here he falls into a trance and he experiences a vision in which a procession of characters from Shakespeare's plays appears to him. In the wake of his experience, he tells the story of his vision to an Chraoibhín (Hyde),[22] who is responsible for rendering the tale as a poem. The basic outline of the story is uncontroversial; the problem, from the perspective of the English editor of the *Book of Homage*, lies in the robust and uncompromising views of England and the English expressed by the journeying Irishman. The point of the poem is, essentially, that a wholly justified hatred of England is assuaged while the Irishman undergoes his Shakespearean experience. The supreme power of Shakespeare is to make the Irishman forget English treachery and aggression. In the second and third stanzas of the poem, Hyde writes:

> Ní h-áil liom Sacsana. Do thuill
> Ó'n nGaedheal, an tír sin mallacht trom,
> Feuch! Níor chuimhnigh mé air sin
> Agus mé ag Stratford ar an abhainn.
>
> Bhí fuath do'n Ghall im'chroidhe go buan
> An drong le cluain d'fhág mé go lom.
> D'imtigh, arís, an fuath sin uaim
> Agus mé ag Stratford ar an abhainn.[23]

The translation of these stanzas supplied to Gollancz runs as follows:

> I like not England. That country has earned
> From the Gael a heavy malediction.
> But see! I did not remember that
> And I at Stratford on the Avon.
>
> Hatred of the Gall was constant in my heart
> The people who with deceit left me naked,
> But that hatred went away again,
> And I at Stratford on the Avon.[24]

The twenty-fourth stanza of the poem is equally forthright in the views it offers of England and the English:

> A Albion do sgrios mo shinnsir,
>   A Albion na bhfocal sleamhain,
> Má bhuaileann námhaid ar do dhorus
>   Tóg é chum Stratford ar an abhainn.[25]

translated by Hyde as:

> O Albion, deceitful sinful guileful
>   Hypocritical destructive lying slippery,
> If an enemy knock at thy door,
>   — Take him to Stratford on the Avon.[26]

It is, of course, inconceivable that Gollancz could have published such damning criticisms of his own native country, particularly in time of war (notwithstanding the fact that he was himself, as Coppélia Kahn points out, an interestingly 'hybrid' figure).[27] He contacted Hyde and asked that all three stanzas of the translation be changed and also requested that he make alterations to the prose preface to the poem, where Hyde had written of his Munsterman that 'do baineadh a gcuid talmhan ó n-a shinnsearaibh, gur crochadh mórán díobh agus gur díbreadh tar lear mórán eile' (in his own translation: 'from whose ancestors the government had taken their share of land, so that many of them were hanged and many more were banished across the sea').[28] Hyde agreed to make the requested changes in the translation, though he did so with some reluctance. In an undated letter to Gollancz, he writes:

> You have been so kind and have taken such an awful lot of trouble over the Homage book that of course no one could find it in their heart to hold out against anything you desire. Only I would submit that if vv 2 & 3 go the whole raison d'être of the thing goes with them! After all, Ireland is not England, & if she does homage to Shakespeare it must be more or less in her own way!

> Yes, of course I'll change v. [25], as it might as you say, be wrenched from its context. Would this do you. 'O Albion who destroyedst my ancestors, O Albion of the smooth words' - and goodness knows that's letting 'la perfide' down easily![29]

In fact, stanza 25 was moderated still further in the final published text, becoming the wholly innocuous 'O Albion, | If an enemy knock at thy door, | Take him to Stratford on the Avon!'[30] Stanzas 2 and 3 were also tempered considerably[31] and the translation of the preface was significantly condensed, so that the Munsterman became one 'who had sorely suffered, he and his folk'.[32]

While Hyde agreed to all of Gollancz's changes to the translation, the Irish text of the poem was included in the *Homage* volume in its original, unamended form.[33] Hyde's poem thus lives a curiously double life, showing two different faces to the world. The English text is compliant and accommodating. Reproduced in a self-consciously 'Empire led' volume it offers nothing to the English-language reader that serves to challenge imperial orthodoxy. Yet, lurking side by side with this benignly acquiescent – and, indeed, quiescent – text is a very different piece of work, which offers a sharp interrogation of the nationalistic and imperialist foundations on which the tribute volume is based. This text's message is encoded in a language that the metropolitan centre cannot understand. Hyde might be said to be operating here as a kind of inverse Caliban. The profit of the language that has been imposed on him is not the ability to curse, but rather a kind of placid urbanity. Behind that urbanity, however, lies a wholly different discourse, severely critical of the master narrative of imperial hegemony, but presented in a language that is directed back to his native culture and not outward to the culture of empire.[34] In a fascinating analysis of the contributions of two of the other writers included in the *Homage* volume – the black South African Solomon Tshekisho Plaatje, who provided a text in Setswana, and Maung Tin of Burma – Coppélia Kahn makes a somewhat similar point about their fruitfully ambiguous self-positioning: 'The tributes of Plaatje and Tin [. . .] display a certain insouciance toward the coloniser: though the writers are conscious of their "difference" from him, they are primarily concerned with getting back to what *they* see as "originary", or simply significant, in their *own* cultures.'[35]

In their biography of Hyde, Janet and Gareth Dunleavy have noted that he was, throughout his career, adept 'at concealing his own confrontational intentions behind a benign exterior'.[36] In a sense, this neatly sums up his method of approach in dealing with Gollancz. Not long before he was asked to contribute to the *Homage* volume, however, Hyde's default policy of tempering confrontation with benignity had failed him in his work with the Gaelic League. Hyde had always sought to maintain an apolitical profile for the League, though in practice – especially given the context of the times – the League's cultural activities inevitably had a strong political dimension. Much of the time, Hyde found himself playing a double game in his role as president of the organisation. His general approach is nicely indicated in an incident detailed by Donal McCartney:

> Hyde saw that certain passages in what he described as an excellent pamphlet written by a priest for the League could be regarded as sectarian. So he suggested [privately] that the pamphlet be printed at the expense of the League but without its stamp. It would do as much good without the League's *imprimatur* as with it, and the League would avoid hurting the feelings of more sensitive Protestants

[. . .] A diplomatic Hyde was able to make the best of both worlds for the sake of the language.[37]

In time, however, Hyde's sleight-of-hand temporising would fail him. In 1914, the British Government's proposal to grant 'Home Rule' to Ireland was suspended owing to the outbreak of the war. This served to reinforce a shift towards militancy among some Irish activists. The League was seen as potentially offering a useful vehicle for advancing the radical cause and Hyde's policy of presenting the League as an apolitical organisation (even granted that this was little more than an expedient fiction) was strongly challenged. At the *Ard-Fheis* of the organisation in August 1915, a motion was put forward calling for the League to add to its objectives that of working to free Ireland from foreign rule. When the motion was passed by a substantial majority, Hyde immediately left the meeting and subsequently resigned his presidency of the organisation.[38]

Hyde's methods were out of step with the times and this was graphically brought home to him just at the point when the Gollancz volume appeared in print. The three hundredth anniversary of Shakespeare's death coincided with Easter Sunday in 1916. The organisers of the tercentenary celebrations were anxious to avoid any suggestion that they might be drawing a link between the poet and the risen deity, which is why May Day was settled on as the central date for organisational purposes.[39] The Dean of Westminster, Herbert Ryle, wrote to the *Times* specifically to make clear that there were no plans to commemorate Shakespeare at the Abbey on Easter Sunday: 'A statement in your columns on January 29 has unfortunately produced the impression that the Dean and Chapter of Westminster Abbey intend to commemorate Shakespeare on Easter Sunday, April 23. I need hardly say that we have no such intention.'[40] By contrast, the propaganda value of the Easter symbolism of sacrifice, renewal and rebirth were readily embraced by Irish militants who launched an uprising on Easter Monday. Hyde was appalled by the events in Dublin (which he witnessed at first hand) and, some months after the uprising, he wrote that the 'League had been steered on the rocks by fools' and that the outlook in Ireland was 'as black as can be'.[41]

The uprising had some local Shakespearean consequences in that the *Irish Times* had to cancel a special tercentenary supplement, which it had planned for the Monday.[42] But events in Dublin interwove themselves with the tercentenary project in other ways as well. The Rev. Fred Askew and Francis Colmer, 'late exhibitioner of Exeter College, Oxford', both published volumes which sought to abstract from Shakespeare words of comfort and encouragement for the British public in time of war. Both volumes make use of Shakespeare to comment on recent events in Ireland. The second quotation presented by Askew is taken from *Macbeth* and is included under the heading 'IRELAND – THE LAND OF LOYALTY AND THE LAND OF REVOLT':

As whence the sun 'gins his reflection
Shipwrecking storms and direful thunders break,
So from that spring whence comfort seem'd to come
Discomfort swells.[43]

Askew also takes up the case of Roger Casement, a former British diplomat who had collaborated with the Germans in attempting to smuggle arms into Ireland in advance of the uprising. He was executed in London in August 1916. Roger Sawyer has observed that hatred of Casement 'reached a peak of intensity which has seldom been equalled in England'.[44] Under the heading 'ROGER CASEMENT HANGED AT PENTONVILLE', Askew quotes again from *Macbeth*, this time from Angus' account of the death of Cawdor:

He labour'd in his country's wreck . . .
But treasons capital, confess'd and proved,
Have overthrown him.[45]

References to the situation in Ireland recur throughout the volume, including a rather striking quotation reproduced under the heading 'THE SINN FÉIN STAB IN THE BACK AND BRITISH LENIENCY':

Though with their high wrongs I am struck to the quick
Yet with my nobler reason 'gainst my fury
Do I take part.[46]

This quotation is from Prospero, in the final act of *The Tempest*, when he reconciles himself with his enemies. It seems singularly inappropriate when applied to the aftermath of the uprising, given the British decision to execute fifteen of the rebel leaders (a course of action which served to generate sympathy for the militants' cause).[47] There are threats, too, in Askew's compendium: under 'TO THE SINN FÉIN LEADERS', he includes Stephano's warning to Trinculo: 'If you prove a mutineer – the next tree!' (as is often the case when Shakespeare is quoted for polemical ends, the actual context of the quote is completely ignored).[48]

Colmer's volume is far less haunted by events in Ireland, but he does include an extended section, headed 'Merely Players' (pp 127–57), in which he draws on Shakespeare's words to provide pen pictures or to comment on notable public figures of the day. The first of the 'players' treated by Colmer to have a connection with events in Ireland is Sir Edward Carson. Colmer's view of the unionist leader is positive, but his admiration seems tempered a little by a certain anxiety, driven, perhaps, by the threat implied by Carson's role in raising the Ulster Volunteer Force (dedicated to resisting Home Rule by force, if necessary). Colmer offers three quotations, taken from *The Tempest*,

2 Henry VI and *Henry VIII* respectively: 'I want that glib and oily art | To speak and purpose not; since what I well intend, | I'll do't before I speak'; 'Whiles I in Ireland nourish a mighty band'; 'I swear he is true-hearted, and a soul | None better in my kingdom.'[49] George Bernard Shaw also features in Colmer's gallery of players, mostly to be castigated as a self-publicist: 'His own trumpet, his own chronicle' (*Troilus and Cressida*), 'One whom the music of his own vain tongue | Doth ravish like enchanting harmony' (*Love's Labour's Lost*), but also to be credited with a certain core patriotic feeling: 'Yet I love my country, and am not | One that rejoices in the common wrack, | As common bruit doth put it' (*Timon of Athens*).[50] Finally, under a subsection headed 'The Foe', Colmer comes to Roger Casement, for whom just a single, short quotation is provided, from *King Lear*: 'A most toad-spotted traitor.'[51]

What we find in the Askew and Colmer volumes is, in essence, an inversion of what we witnessed in Hyde's contribution to the *Book of Homage*. Where Hyde uses Shakespeare to offer – at least in the Irish language version of his poem – a critique of the English project in Ireland, Askew and Colmer take Shakespeare's words and use them to voice a critique of Irish resistance to that project. Shakespeare, then, standing at the intersection of conflicting nationalist ideologies, becomes, in his tercentenary year, a kind of Janus figure, recruited to face both ways, across the divide. There is, in a sense, something fitting about this, given that – as many of the essays in this collection indicate – what Shakespeare offers the Irish writer is always a fractured legacy.

Notes

I first came across a reference to Hyde's poem and the variations between the text and its translation in Richard Foulkes's masterful study *Performing Shakespeare in the Age of Empire* (Cambridge: Cambridge University Press, 2002), pp 197–8. I am grateful to Heather Wolfe, Curator of Manuscripts at the Folger Shakespeare Library, for chasing out the manuscript material for me in advance of a visit to the Library. My thanks also to Janet Clare and Stephen O'Neill for providing the occasion for this piece.

1   Details taken from the pamphlet *Shakespeare Tercentenary Observance* ([London: George W. Jones], 1916) and from 'Shakespeare Celebration', *Times*, 13 Apr. 1916, p. 5.

2   'A Book of Homage', *The Times*, 2 May 1916, p. 6.

3   Coppélia Kahn, 'Remembering Shakespeare Imperially: The 1916 Tercentenary', *Shakespeare Quarterly* 52: 4 (2001), 456–78 (p. 456).

4   Israel Gollancz, *A Book of Homage to Shakespeare* (London: Humphrey Milford/Oxford University Press, 1916), p. vii.

5   Ibid.

6   Folger Shakespeare Library MS W.a.80 (29)., George Russell, letter to Israel Gollancz, 18 Jan. 1916.

7   Contents page of Gollancz, *Book of Homage.* For general details of Madden's career and publications see Daire Hogan's entry in the *Dictionary of National Biography (DNB)* <http://www. oxforddnb.com/view/article/47199> [accessed 16 Apr. 2007].

8   Gollancz, *Book of Homage*, p. 274.

9   Folger Shakespeare Library MS W.a.79 (59), Douglas Hyde (n.d.) to Israel Gollancz.

10   On Hyde's contributions to Yeats' *Fairy and Folk Tales of the Irish Peasantry,* see Janet Egleson Dunleavy and Gareth W. Dunleavy, *Douglas Hyde: A Maker of Modern Ireland* (Berkeley: University of California Press, 1991), p. 131.

11   Douglas Hyde, 'The Necessity for De-Anglicising Ireland', in *Language, Lore and Lyrics: Essays and Lectures,* ed. by Breandán Ó Conaire (Dublin: Irish Academic Press, 1986), p. 169.

12   One of the most notable figures to capitalise on the emergence of a greatly expanded reading public in the wake of the 1870 act was Alfred Harmsworth (Viscount Northcliffe), who, early in his career as a publisher, observed that 'The Board Schools [. . .] are turning out hundreds of thousands of boys and girls annually who are anxious to read' and that 'they will read anything which is simple and is sufficiently interesting' – Max Pemberton, *Lord Northcliffe: A Memoir* (London: Hodder & Stoughton, n.d.), p. 29; pp. 29–30. By the final decade of the nineteenth century, Harmsworth's combined stable of publications was achieving total sales of 2,000,000 – the largest of any such publishing concern in the world.

13   Hyde, 'A Plea for the Irish Language', in *Language, Lore and Lyrics*, p. 77.

14   Hyde, 'The Great Work of the Gaelic League', in *Language, Lore and Lyrics*, p. 194.

15   Ibid., p. 194.

16   Hyde himself was a member of the Shakespeare Club while a student at Trinity College Dublin, and a copy of the complete works was included among the books in his library at the time of his death – see Dunleavy and Dunleavy, *Douglas Hyde,* p. 120; p. 435. In February 1889 he took part in a reading of *Twelfth Night* at the Shakespeare Club – see Dominic Daly, *The Young Douglas Hyde: The Dawn of the Irish Revolution and Renaissance 1874–1893* (Dublin: Irish University Press, 1974), p. 96.

17   This is written on Hyde's own letter to Gollancz, Folger MS W.a.79 (59).

18   The Folger does not hold Gollancz's own side of the correspondence for the *Homage* volume. Princeton University Library does have a significant amount of Gollancz correspondence, but the online catalogue does not indicate that it holds any letters addressed to Hyde. My assumption that Gollancz telegraphed Hyde to ask for a translation is based on the opening sentence of a card sent by Hyde to Gollancz on 18 March 1916: 'I have just got your wire', which he follows up by asking why Gollancz requires a translation – Folger MS W.a.79 (60).

19   Folger MS W.a.79 (61), Letter from Hyde to Gollancz, 19 Mar. 1916.

20   Hyde's own translation of the title is 'How it fared with a Gael at Stratford-on-Avon'. Gollancz, *Book of Homage*, p. 275.

21 All of Hyde's original ms translations of the poem are taken from Folger MS Y.d.85 (29). His original Irish text is not included with the Folger manuscripts (presumably it would have been sent to the printers); all quotations from the Irish are therefore taken from the text as published.

22 Hyde's pen name was, in its full form, 'An Craoibhín Aoibhinn' – 'the delightful little branch'.

23 Gollancz, *Book of Homage*, p. 276.

24 Y.d.85 (29), p. 3. Throughout much of the MS, Hyde had originally written 'Stratford on the river' ('abhainn' in Irish being 'river'), but he has struck out the word and substituted 'Avon'. In quoting from the translation, I use the later substitution.

25 Gollancz, *Book of Homage*, p. 279.

26 MS Y.d.85 (29), p. 9.

27 Gollancz was the son of a rabbi who came to England from Poland. His brother was Professor of Hebrew at University College, London and Gollancz himself was very closely involved in the Jewish community in Britain. See Kahn, 'Remembering Shakespeare', p. 478.

28 Gollancz, *Book of Homage*, p. 275; MS Y.d.85 (29), p. 1.

29 Folger MS W.a.79 (62), Undated letter from Hyde to Gollancz.

30 Gollancz, *Book of Homage*, p. 279.

31 Stanzas 2 and 3 became, in the final form:

> England was not like of me,
> But I remembered this not,
>> I at Stratford on the Avon.

> I brooded on my ills,
> But all this went away
>> At Stratford on the Avon.

Werner Habicht, in his very interesting 'Shakespeare Celebrations in Time of War', *Shakespeare Quarterly* 52: 4 (2001), 441–55, comments that, in the wake of the changes, 'some of the original four-line stanzas appeared suspiciously short in the printed translation' (p. 451). However, the attenuation of the stanzas is not quite as noticeable as it might have been, as there are other moments in the poem where Hyde renders his standard four line Irish verses in three lines of English. A good example is his stanza on *Romeo and Juliet*, which, in Irish, reads:

> Agus tháinigh Rómeo le na ghrádh,
>> Beirt áluinn aoibhinn óg, dar liom,
> Agus an bráthair rinne an crádh;
>> Bhíos ag Stratford ar an abhainn.

Hyde's original translation of this stanza is: 'And Romeo came with his love, | A couple beautiful ~~lovely~~ delightful young, me thought, | And the friar who did the harm, | I was at &c', but, in the printed text, this is (without explanation) reduced to the rather telegraphic: 'Romeo with his love | And the Friar: | I was at Stratford on the Avon'.

32 Gollancz, *Book of Homage*, p. 275.

33 Hyde does seem to have tinkered with the Irish version of the prose preface. His original and amended English translations of the preface do not quite square with the Irish text as published. The original translation mentions the Munsterman's 'great grandfather who died in prison' and 'his father who fled with him to the New Island'. A footnote from 'prison' reads 'Probably in '98' and a footnote from 'Island' reads 'ie America. Probably in Fenian times', both notes being signed 'Translator'. None of this material is included in the published Irish text, though there is no indication that these were changes requested by Gollancz.

34 I would, however, want to resist the temptation to place too much weight on the dual nature of the text. It is important to remember that the *Homage* volume had a very limited circulation: the printrun was just 1,250 copies, of which only 1,000 were offered for sale (at a price of one guinea each). It may well be that, at the time, 'Rud Tharla' was never actually read by anyone with a command of the Irish language.

35 Kahn, 'Remembering Shakespeare', p. 476, italics in original.

36 Dunleavy and Dunleavy, *Douglas Hyde*, p. 4.

37 Donal McCartney, 'Hyde, D. P. Moran, and Irish Ireland', in *Leaders and Men of the Easter Rising: Dublin 1916*, ed. by F. X. Martin (London: Methuen, 1967), pp 45–6.

38 In fact, Hyde later came to feel that what had happened within the League may, in the end, have been for the best. Gareth W. Dunleavy quotes from an unpublished text by Hyde in which he writes: 'I am not at all sure that the League did not do the right thing for the language in practically throwing me over. I did not see this at the time, however, for I did not foresee the utter and swift débâcle of the Irish Parliamentary Party and the apotheosis of Sinn Féin. The only reason I had for keeping politics out was the desire to offend nobody and get help from every party, which I did. But when Sinn Féin swallowed up all parties except the Unionists this was no longer necessary' – Gareth W. Dunleavy, *Douglas Hyde* (Lewisburg: Bucknell University Press, 1974), pp 38–9.

39 An additional reason for moving the date forward was the fact that 3 May New Style was the equivalent of 23 Apr. Old Style – see *The Times*, 29 Jan. 1916, p. 5.

40 *Times*, 29 Feb. 1916, p. 7.

41 Dunleavy, *Douglas Hyde*, p. 51, quoting a letter from Hyde to John Quinn.

42 See Richard Foulkes, *Performing Shakespeare in the Age of Empire* (Cambridge: Cambridge University Press, 2002), p. 198.

43 Fred Askew, *Shakespeare Tercentenary Souvenir: England's Thoughts in Shakespeare's Words* (Lowestoft: Flood & Son, 1916), p. 5.

44 Roger Sawyer, *Casement: The Flawed Hero* (London: Routledge, 1984), p. 142.

45 Askew, *Shakespeare Tercentenary*, p. 5. Casement is a recurring target. On page 23, under a heading consisting simply of his name, Askew includes Hamlet's 'Bloody, bawdy villain! | Remorseless, treacherous, lecherous, kindless villain! | O vengeance!'

46 Ibid., p. 8.

47 Under 'THE BOMBARDMENT OF DUBLIN' – a reference to the shelling of the city centre by the British warship the 'Helga' – Askew includes Claudius' 'Diseases desperate grown, | By desperate appliances are relieved' – p. 36.

48 Askew, *Shakespeare Tercentenary*, p. 11.

49 Francis Colmer, *Shakespeare in Time of War: Excerpts from the Plays Arranged with Topical Allusion* (New York: E. P. Dutton, 1916), p. 130.

50 Ibid., p. 141; p. 142.

51 Ibid., p. 156.

CHAPTER 4

Shakespeare as Gaeilge

Tadhg Ó Dúshláine

Shakespeare is now regarded as a world writer, whose poems and plays have been translated into numerous languages, including Irish. Over the last one hundred years or so, a sizable body of Shakespeare's work has been translated into the Irish language. Yet, this material has not featured in discussion of Shakespeare's reception in Ireland, which has tended to be Anglophone in its focus on English language responses in the work of Irish writers such as Yeats, Joyce, Shaw and others, as if Shakespeare had not been given a Gaelic accent. Viewed in relation to such canonical Irish writers, the category of Shakespeare *as Gaeilge* raises the question: why would anyone want to read Shakespeare in Irish when he can be read in the original? And its corollary: has Shakespeare 'as Gaeilge' any merit? This essay seeks to explore these and related questions by assessing Gaelic translations of Shakespeare and discussing the debates among Irish language writers about their relative value. Additionally, it argues for the inclusion of Irish language materials in the debate about Shakespeare in Ireland, especially given the ongoing fascination of creative writers in Irish with Shakespeare's work, as outlined below. What emerges are contrasting responses to Shakespeare by Irish language writers, whereby he is associated with Britishness, Empire and thus an anathema to Irish-language interests, or embraced as a classic writer indicative of and associated with a Western literary tradition and thus a powerful resource to be used by Irish language writers and *in* Irish.

In an Irish context, of course, translating Shakespeare was bound up with Ireland's colonial status and an association in some quarters of Shakespeare with Britishness and Empire. Accordingly, to interpret Irish translations of Shakespeare is to engage in debates about the uses of literature and, more generally, cultural nationalism. But the politics of Irish literature has meant an inaccurate historical division into the exclusive categories of Gaelic and Anglo-Irish: the one offensive to those who write in Irish, the other to those who write in English. Thematically and stylistically, Irish literature, be it in Irish or in English, is one. Certainly this has been the case since the literary revival in the 1880s, when Irish literature set out deliberately and self-consciously to conform to European models; some would contend that this occurred earlier, even as early as the seventeenth century, following the defeat of Gaelic Ireland at the Battle of Kinsale in 1601. The paradox of that defeat was that it allowed the Irish to access all that was best in late Renaissance and Baroque literature, on the proviso that the literature of the nearest neighbour, which included Shakespeare, be excluded, publicly at least, for Shakespeare was the genius of England, and England, in such reductive logic, was the source of all ills. While this myth has its origins in the Reformation politics of seventeenth-century Ireland, it persisted in certain official quarters. Up until the 1960s, for instance, a designated poem on the Leaving Certificate syllabus by Seán Ó Ríordáin claimed that to reach the promised land of the Gaeltacht, the Irish race must break free of the straddle of English civilisation: Shelley, Keats and Shakespeare – those very same canonical texts of the syllabus for State examinations.[1] And, the dangerous myopia contained in such sentiments, written by Ó Ríordáin in the 1950s, was never explicitly questioned in any of the extensive commentaries on the poem. Notwithstanding the cultural nationalist implications of the poem, Ó Ríordain's private diary, which mentions Shakespeare some fifty-five times, suggests a more nuanced response:

Fathaigh domhanda, abair, ab ea Homer, Virgil, Plato, Dante, Shakespeare.

('Homer, Virgil, Plato, Dante, Shakespeare, were, say, world giants'.)

Níl aon amhras ina thaobh. Bheith im scríobhnóir mór a theastuigheann uaim. Scríobnóir mór! Chomh mór le Shakespeare an eadh? Agus níl fhios agam ciaca teanga nar ceart dom scríobhadh.

('There is no doubt about it. I want to be a great writer. A great writer! As great as Shakespeare, is it? And I don't know which language I should write in'.)[2]

While the issue of what is the most apposite linguistic medium remains unresolved, Shakespeare is nonetheless a measure of greatness for Ó Ríordáin. Similarly, the private journal of Micheál Mac Aodha, a Connemara man who spent most of his working life as a school principal in County Meath, endorses Shakespeare as the measure of the human condition:

'Tá an saol as alt,' mar a dúirt Hamlet, Prionsa na Danmhairge. Tagaim leis tréis ar tharla sa scoil inniu. Beirt chailíní as rang na cúigiú bliana a bhí ag plioncadh a chéile

('"The times are out of joint", as Hamlet, Prince of Denmark, said. I agree with him after what happened in school today. Two fifth year girls belting each other.')

And, elsewhere in his diary, Mac Aodha draws upon Shakespeare to critique contemporary national politics:

> Tá imní ar an Tánaiste nach chun leasa a pháirtí a pháirt sa gComhrialtas. Nach breá an scéal atá aige! Bíonn an páirtí mór amplach. Bhí riamh agus cé a thógfadh sin orthu? Cá bhfuil an páirtí nach ndéanfadh amhlaidh? Ní dheachaidh sin amú ar an mBard. Nár léigh tú *Coriolanus*?[3]

> ('The Tánaiste is afraid that participation in Coalition is detrimental to his party. Isn't that a great excuse he has! The big party is always voracious. They always were and who would blame them? Where's the party that wouldn't be so. That wasn't lost on the Bard. Have you not read *Coriolanus*?')

Why *Coriolanus*? It would appear that the popularity of this particular play, not considered one of Shakespeare's finest historical adaptations, despite T. S. Eliot's assessment,[4] has something to do with a certain anxiety of influence regarding Shakespeare, as the translator's note in the 1938 Irish language edition indicates:

> [. . .]dráma an-bhreá mar a bpléann Shakespeare, os comhair ár súl, ceist atá chomh beo agus chomh bríomhar inniu agus a bhí lena linn féin .i. an cheist idir an daonlathas agus an deachtóireacht.

> ('[. . .] a fine play in which Shakespeare discusses, before our eyes, a question that is as alive and controversial today as it was in his own time i.e. the conflict between democracy and dictatorship')[5]

Private endorsement of this kind is one thing, but public acknowledgement another. There is a sense in which Shakespeare may not have been entirely palatable in Ireland in view of the portrayal of the Irish in the plays: the choice of character and cultural trait would not have endeared him to the educated Irish abroad in the early seventeenth century, who may well have been introduced to his work by their English recusant colleagues in Spain, France and the then Spanish Netherlands. They would surely have been angered by those correspondences and illustrations recorded by David Comyn, Plunkett Barton and others: the 'group of three weird women [. . .] a familiar feature of Gaelic folklore' in *Macbeth*; Hamlet's swearing by St Patrick; references to 'rug-headed' and 'shag-haired' kernes, in *Richard II* and *Henry VI, Part 2* respectively; the allusion to 'barnacles' in *The Tempest*; the 'aquavitae' bottle in *The Merry Wives of Windsor*; and that 'line of apparent gibberish' in *Henry V*.[6] These constructions and stereotypical references are precisely those highlighted by English historians of the Elizabethan period, such as Campion, Moryson,

Davies, Spenser and Stanihurst. Geoffrey Keating, in his *History of Ireland*, from the 1630s, vehemently refutes this portrayal of the Irish and while he does not mention Shakespeare by name, the theatrical imagery he uses to dismiss Campion is indicative of a general familiarity with the contemporary English stage:

Gur cosúla é le cluicheoir a bheadh ag reic scéal scigiúil ar scafall ná le stairí.

('He is like a player who would be recounting jeering stories on a platform rather than an historian'.)

And, his condemnation of Stanihurst reverberates with Hamlet's expression of disgust at Osric's sycophancy: 'Gurb é fuath na nÉireannach céad bhallán do tharraing' ('That hatred of the Irish was the first dug he drew').[7] The revivalists of the post-Famine Ireland of the 1880s regarded Keating as the Irish Herodotus and Douglas Hyde, whose philosophy did much to shape that of the Gaelic League, echoes Keating in his influential pamphlet 'On the Necessity of De-Anglicising Ireland' of 1892, a philosophy articulated more stridently in Diarmuid Ó Súilleabháin's pamphlet *Towards Ireland Britless* (1973). Hyde's philosophy was to shape the critical outlook of the Gaelic revivalists and, in some instances, relegate Shakespeare in the interests of amplifying the case for Irish literature. Thus in his *Gaelic Literature Surveyed* (1929), Aodh de Blácam, describing the Ossianic lays compiled in Ostend and Leuven in 1626 and 1627 for Captain Sorley MacDonnell, stresses how Irish literature is on a par with the classics of the Western literary tradition:

Such was the book that an Irish soldier craved in the days when Shakespeare and Spencer [*sic*] were but lately dead and when Milton had not arisen. (p. 84)

Likewise, of the tragic tale of Deirdre, best known as the dramatic version re-cast by Synge as *Deirdre of the Sorrows*, de Blacam says: 'This is a story that a Sophocles or a Shakespeare would be proud to tell' (pp 190–1). De Blacam evokes two literary giants as the paragons of excellence while at the same time enhancing the Gaelic text. A similar move is evident in Daniel Corkery's *The Hidden Ireland*, where lauding the poetry of Aogán Ó Rathaille, he suggests 'It seems we are hearing a voice that out-Lears Lear's (p. 179). Corkery's claim about Ó Rathaille's, as in de Blacam's comment on Deirdre, puts Shakespeare in the role of a literary forefather that must be outdone or even surpassed.

This romantic evaluation of Irish literature indulged in by Corkery and de Blacam, together with that of David Comyn and Plunkett Barton, can be traced to Matthew Arnold's *Study of Celtic Literature* (1891), where the uncom-plimentary epithet of 'wild' that Victorian historians applied to the Irish is replaced by the equally problematic term 'natural magic'. Incensed as nationalists were by references to the 'mere' and the 'wild' Irish, Arnold's thesis was nonetheless music to their ears:

> If I were asked where English poetry got these things, its turn for style, its turn for melancholy, and its turn for natural magic, for catching and rendering the charm of nature in a wonderfully near and vivid way, I should answer, with some doubt, that it got its turn for style from a Celtic source; with less doubt, that it got its melancholy from a Celtic source; with no doubt at all, that from a Celtic source it got nearly all its natural magic.[8]

And, by way of illustration, Arnold refers to the 'sheer, inimitable Celtic note in passages like this':

> The moon shines bright. In such a night as this,
> When the sweet wind did gently kiss the trees,
> And they did make no noise, in such a night
> Troilus, methinks, mounted the Trojan walls –
>
>   . . . in such a night
> Did Thisbe fearfully o'erstrip the dew –
>
>   . . . in such a night
> Stood Dido, with a willow in her hand,
> Upon the wild sea-banks, and waved her love
> To come again to Carthage.[9]

All of this created something of a dilemma for the Gaelic Leaguers: put simply, should they gratefully accept the kudos for the putative Irish contribution to much that was good in Shakespeare, or should they attempt to retake the lot *as Gaeilge*? Of course opinions varied between those who, on the one hand, regarded Irish translations of Shakespeare in the broader context of European languages' responses to Shakespeare and, on the other, the traditionalists who regarded English language classics as detrimental to the cause of the national language. Thus, while the former conceive of Shakespeare as a writer of universal appeal and as a fluid cultural resource, for the latter he triggers associations with Britishness, Empire and thus an anathema to the cause of the Irish language. Gaelic writers did actively debate the value of translating Shakespeare into Irish and cited comparative European examples. For instance, Uilliam Mac Giolla Bríde, writing from Paris in 1911, describes in glowing terms a French version of *Hamlet* and makes the point that the modern German and French versions were more accessible to their audiences than the original English was to audiences at home:

Is é seo an rud atá i m'aigne anois: nach féidir Shakespeare a léiriú i mBéarla chomh maith agus is féidir sin a dhéanadh 'sna teangachaibh eile. Ní teanga bheo ach teanga mharbh atá 'san dteanga sin mar atá sí aige. Teanga bheo atá cosúil léithi an Ghermáinis atá dhá labhairt indiu agus teanga neamhchosamhal í ach teanga bheó atá 'sa bhFrainncis. Ní féidir na drámanna a aistriughadh go droch Bhéarla na haimsire seo. *Sacrilége* a bheidheadh ann, chun úsáid a dhéanadh de fhocal as an Fhrainncise. Ós mar sin atá an scéal, má's do- thuigsionach Shakespeare do na Sasanaibh atá ann indiu, ní so- thuigsionaighe a bheidh sé aca 'san am atá le teacht. Rud aisteach! Beidh file náisiúnach ann agus a dhrámanna dá léiriughadh ag gach aon náisiún acht a náisiún féin. An mbeidh Shakespeare ann riamh i nGaedhilge? Níl a fhios agam.

('This is what occurs to me now: that Shakespeare can't be produced as well in English as in other languages. Shakespeare's English is a dead and not a living language. German, as spoken today is similar to Shakespeare's English and French as spoken today is unlike it. The plays cannot be translated to the bad English of today. That would be sacrilege. Since Shakespeare is unintelligible to English people today, he won't be any more intelligible to them in the future. Most strange! There will be a national poet whose plays will be produced by every nation but his own. Will Shakespeare ever be as Gaeilge? I don't know').[10]

Such speculation as to Shakespeare's future *as Gaeilge* continued and some- one writing under the pseudonymn 'Dubhán Alla' (or 'Spiderman'), voices the hard-line Gaelic League approach to the question:

SÉICSPÍR I nGAEDHILG

Chím go bhfuil Fergus Ó Nualláin ag casadh le Gaedhilg do chur ar dhráma de dhrámannaibh Shéicspír. Isé mo chomhairle dó gan bac leis. Tá an iomarca den Bhéarla againn. Isé an Béarla atá ag marbhadh ár dteangain féin. Pé nídh dhéanfaimíd, beidh rian an Bhéarla ar ár gcaint agus ár smaointibh.

('I see that Fergus Ó Nualláin is planning to translate one of Shakespeare's plays. My advice to him is not to bother . . . We have too much English. English is killing our own language. Whatever we do, the influence of English will be on our speech and on our thoughts).[11]

The hostility to the English language evidenced here was one that left a long legacy, as Ó Ríordáin's poem cited earlier suggests. But such cultural nation- alism did not determine responses to Shakespeare and, in an enlightened reply the following month, Mac Giolla Bríde contends that such a rejection of Shakespeare is based on a misunderstanding of the value of the classics being made available in translation:

GAEDHILGE AR SÉICSPÍR

. . . is léar nach dtuigeann 'An Dubán Alla' cad is aistriughadh ann. Dá ndéanadh ní bheadh sé ag trácht ar Francis nó Gearmánais mar adhbhar aistrighidh. 'Tífeadh sé gur éigin eolas ó dhúthchas ar an teanga táthar aistriughadh chomh maith leis an Ghaedhilge. Tá an méid seo riachtanach, gan an dúthchas ní fiú faic an saothar. Rud eile nach haon bhac ar dhuine an Ghaedhilg is feárr mar aon leis an Beurla is feárr bheith mar a chéile aige, ach ní mór an saothar céadna leis an Ghaedhilg a sgríobh gheibh an Beurloir leis an Beurla a sgríobh.

('Tis obvious that 'Spiderman' doesn't understand what translation is. If he did he wouldn't be talking about French or German as material for translation. He'd understand that it's necessary to have a native grasp of the language being translated as well as Irish. This is essential: without a native grasp of the language the work is worth nothing. Even if one be equally competent in Irish and English, one must still exercise the same diligence writing Irish as the English person does when writing English').

This corrective develops into an argument about the nuances of translation, as the author contemplates how to convey Shakespeare's language in Irish:

Cuir i gcás go bhfuilthir ag cur Gaedhilge ar an Beurla seo: 'If it were done when 'tis done, then 'twere well it were done quickly.' Ní hé an Ghaedhilg air a rádh: 'Dá mbeadh sé déanta nuair tá sé déanta, ba mhaith déanta in am é.' Se mheasaimse bfhearr mar Gaedhilg air: 'Mara bheadh den ghníomh ach an gníomh a dhéanadh ba mhaith déanta an gníomh.' Nó arís: 'He would not play false yet would wrongly win.' Níor mhaith liom mar Ghaedhilge: 'Ní imreochadh sé go fealltach, ach bhainfeadh sé go h-eugcóra.' Bfhearr aistriughadh mar seo: 'Ní chuirfeadh sé an cluiche le caime, ach bhainfeadh sé an geall gan géilstean.

Dar liom-sa go bhfuil Séicspír an-fhoirstinneach mar adhbhar aistriughadh. Tá sé mar úghdar déaghchainteach, déisbheulach glic 'na chuid cainte, agus is beag a bhaineas le cúrsa an duine ná dearn sé tagairt dó.

Níl sé 'na chleachtadh ag luch labhartha na Gaedhilge cúrsaí léigheanta an t-saoghail a chur tré na chéile as Gaedhilg. Níl, leis, bun ar bith léighinn ag fás i nGaedhilge na haimsire seo, ach is féidir tús a chur ar an obair ar an dóigh atá ceapaidh ag Feargus Ó Nualáin. An Ghaedhilge bhíos ar an páipéirí agus ins na leabhraibh ní minic a bhíonn sé os cionn na bpáisdí.

Má éirigheann le Feargus Gaedhilg mhaith a chur ar dráma de chuid Sheicspír is céim suas ar an teanga é. Ar chor a bith béidh sligh ag achan duine barramhail a thabhairt. Ar chor ar bith béidh sligh ag achan duine barramhail a thabhairt, is 'tífidh an saoghal ceocu bhuaidh nó mhill sé ar an Beurla.

(Take, for example, translating the following English into Irish: 'If it were done when 'tis done, then 'twere well it were done quickly.' The Irish for that is not to say: 'Dá mbeadh sé déanta nuair tá sé déanta, ba mhaith déanta in am é.' I think better Irish for that would be: 'Mara mbeadh den ghníomh ach an gníomh a dhéanamh, ba mhaith déanta an gníomh.' Or again: 'He would not play false yet would wrongly win.' I wouldn't like as Irish: 'Ní imreodh sé go fealltach, ach bhainfeadh sé go héagórach.' It would be better translated as follows: 'Ní chuirfeadh sé an cluiche le caime, ach bhainfeadh sé an geall gan ghéílleadh.'

It is my opinion that Shakespeare is very suitable for translation. He is an eloquent, clever author and there is little of the human condition that he does not treat. It is not the custom of Irish speakers to deal with intellectual matters in Irish. Nor is there any learning apparent in present day Irish, but a start can be made in the way Fergus Ó Nualláin suggests. Written Irish, in books and newspapers is often childish. If Fergus succeeds in providing a good translation of one of Shakespeare's plays it will be an asset to the language. In any case everyone will be able to judge for themselves whether he enhances or destroys the original.)[12]

The argument here is a laudable one: to revive, by means of exemplary translation, the capability of the Irish language to deal with the complexities of the human condition, a capability which, for socio-political reasons, had been on the wane in Gaelic literature since the seventeenth century, when the decline of Gaelic Ireland saw a considerable retraction in the use of the language on a learned level.

The claim that translating Shakespeare might enhance the Irish language is apparent in the work of other Irish-language writers and scholars but especially in the full Irish translation of *Macbeth*, by J. L. O'Sullivan of Bantry in 1925. 'I have taken upon myself the task of translating Shakespeare's *Tragedy of Macbeth* into Irish', writes O'Sullivan in the preface,

with the diffidence born of a study of the Irish language extending over very many years, and of an appreciation of the unscalable heights attained by the greatest of foreign dramatists: The great continental nations, Germany, France, Italy, have long ago realised to the full the educative value of making available for their peoples, through translation, the classic literatures of foreign countries. At the particular stage which has now been reached in the cultivation and spread of our own language, I feel that the value of this phase of literary development – the translation of foreign classics – cannot well be overestimated.[13]

Despite O'Sullivan's claims as to the cultural significance of his edition, the quality of it was castigated by the reviewer in the *Catholic Bulletin*: 'is cuibhrighe do-gheibhim mé féin d'á rádh nach Craithsleágh an leabhrín seo, ná mór mó, mar eagluighim, Gaedhilge' ('I feel obliged to say that this little booklet is neither Shakespeare, nor, even more so, I'm afraid, Irish'). To the reviewer, this particular *Macbeth as Gaeilge* could not match the tragic pathos of the Shakespearean text:

> Maidir leis na h-áitibh mhóra, troma, daimhne, féidhmeamhla, cliútacha – na háite doghní Macbeth in a Mhacbeth – ní mór atá le rádh fútha ach nach bhfuilid ann chor ar bith.

> ('As regards those great, profound, substantial, essential, famous passages – those passages that make Macbeth Macbeth – not much can be said about them other than that they're not there at all'.)

The problem with O'Sullivan's translation from the outset would appear to emanate from the misunderstanding of the project, as outlined in his preface: despite the antipathy of the less-enlightened language enthusiasts, Shakespeare was never a foreign classic to the Irish. For all O'Sullivan's claims, the attempt to use such material for the promotion of the Irish language proved ineffectual. Nonetheless, his edition of *Macbeth* constitutes an intriguing instance of cross-cultural contact and an early contribution to Shakespeare's considerable afterlife in other languages.[14]

If O'Sullivan's *Macbeth* was deemed unsatisfactory in its rendering of Shakespearean language, other Irish translations faired better, especially where the translation brought to the Shakespeare play some aspects of Gaelic literature and culture. This brings us to the second question posed at the outset: do the efforts of Irish translators have any merit? I think that the potential of the Shakespearean text can be enriched and exploited by what critics now call decontextualisation and even recontextualisation. An appreciation of the richness of the Irish tradition of the keen and the lament pervades Msgr Pádraig De Brún's translation of the lament for Fidele from *Cymbeline* (a piece also translated, coincidently or otherwise by his niece, Máire Mhac an tSaoi, in her collection *Margadh na Saoire*). There is somewhat more of classical restraint and dignity about the former, as a comparison of the opening verses demonstrate:

> Ní baol duit feasta teas ón ngréin,
> Ná stoirm ná síon ar aon chor;
> Taoi réidh anois le dua is le péin
> Tá sáimhe agat is luach do shaothair:
> An t-óglach breá 's an cailín glé,
> Mar lucht na rámhainne téid go cré.[15]

Fear no more the heat o' the sun,
Nor the furious winter's rages;
Thou thy worldly task hast done,
Home art gone, and ta'en thy wages:
Golden lads and girls all must,
As chimney-sweepers, come to dust.

De Brún's colleague in Maynooth, Gerald O'Nolan, Professor of Irish, and an uncle of Flann O'Brien's, uses Shakespeare to illustrate the methodological approach necessary for translation. In his *Studies in Modern Irish* (1921), O'Nolan discusses in considerable detail the nuances of translation concerning certain passages from *Julius Caesar*. He emphasises the principle that one must not be too literal in translation and illustrates the point with the well know example of Anthony's speech:

Friends, Romans, Countrymen! lend me your ears;
I come to bury Caesar, not to praise him.
(A chairde mo chroí, éistigí liom go fóill –
Romhánaigh sibh-se, 's de threibh mo thíre dúchais;
Ní hamhlaidh 'thána-sa ag moladh Chaesair –
Ar a adhlacadh is ea atá mo thriall.)

O'Nolan observes that 'It is difficult to get a single term to render "honourable"' in the line 'And Brutus is an honourable man!' and, continuing the principle of avoiding literalism in translating a text, suggests 'Mar fear ceart, uasal is ea an Brútus san'.[16]

Perhaps one of the most successful of all these attempts to recontextualise Shakespeare was that of the celebrated lexicographer Seán Óg Ó Caomhánach, during his interment in the Curragh from 1922–3 for Republican activities.[17] Both the author's predicament and his translation skills bring added meaning to the text. On 10 January 1923, Ó Caomhánach wrote in his diary:

Ag léamh *Amhlaoibh* dom tharla ar an bhfocal 'crants'. Sin ceann des na focalaibh do chuireas go dtín Athair Ó Duinnín blianta ó shoin – ná raibh san bhfoclóir. Tá sé coiteann againn i nGaeilge. B'ait liom an uair sin é ach anois cím gurb í an bhrí chéanna atá ag Shakespeare leis atá againne. Agus ní focal coiteann i mBéarla anois é.

('Reading *Hamlet* I came across the word 'crants'. That's one of the words I sent to Father Dineen years ago – which wasn't in the dictionary. 'Tis common with us in Irish. I thought it odd at the time but now I see that it has the same meaning in Shakespeare as it has with us. And it isn't a common word in English now'.)

Ó Caomhánach's observation about word borrowings, with its suggestion of cultural exchange between Irish and English, is an interesting instance of how Shakespeare becomes or is perhaps made a familiar or contemporary of the individual interpreter when related to a specific context. A few days later, Ó Caomhánach returns to Shakespeare in his diary, where Hamlet's best-known and most meditative soliloquy takes on a powerful, imminent resonance for him:

> Do léas i Hamlet inniu 'a bheith nó gan a bheith – sin í an cheist'. Sid é as Gaeilge agat é.
>
> ('I read "To be or not to be that is the question" in *Hamlet* today. Here it is in Irish').
>
> A bheith, nó gan a bheith – sin í an cheist:
> Cé acu is uaisle don mheanmain a fhulaing
> Urchair agus saigheada mí-áidh diabhalta
> Nó arm do ghlacadh in aghaidh bóchna clampair
> Agus lena bhfreasúra deireadh a chur leo –
> Bás – codladh – faic eile:
> Agus trí chodladh a rá críochnaíonn
> Daigh chroí agus míle creathnú aiceanta
> Is dual don gceat – is críoch é.
> Is mian díograiseach – bás – codladh –
> Codladh! Taibhreamh b'fhéidir. Á, sin í an fhadhb. . .

This is an extraordinary piece, not just of translation but of meditation, where the pathos and the urgency of the vocabulary, combined with the knowledge of Ó Caomhánach's imprisonment, enhance the impact of his citation of *Hamlet*. Ó Caomhánach was obviously satisfied with his efforts at translation and adds, addressing the reader:

> Conas tá san, a léitheóir? Níl am agam ar fhilleadh air. Ní léifead arís é fiú amháin chun a cheartaithe. Ar nós Amhlaoibh, ná fuil ag triall ar mo bhás? Nách iomdha rud a bheadh bailithe brúite isteach im bheatha agam dá ndeininn dícheall? Ach an tsiléig, cladhaire na beatha, mheall sí mé agus anois táim féin 'san bás ar chomh-náth (sin focal breá) le chéile, agus mo chreat córach, agus m'fholt dubh agus smior mo chnámh, sid é an claochló a bheas ortha de réir an fhile – Níl rud in aon chor ar bith san tsaol so.

> ('How's that, dear reader? I haven't time to return to it. I won't read it again, even to correct it. Like Hamlet am I not going to my death? Are there not many things I would have achieved in my life, had I tried? But negligence, the thief of life, seduced me and now death and myself are intertwined (that's a great word), and my fine body, my black hair and the marrow of my bones, will be changed as the poet says – There's nothing at all at all in this life'.)

'Like Hamlet am I not going to my death?': for Ó Caomhánach, reading the play in internment provokes an identification with the occasional nihilism of Shakespeare's psychologically complex character.

As with Ó Caomhánach, the same rich folk tradition informs the feminist perspective from which Nuala Ní Dhomhnaill exploits the potential of Shakespeare in Irish, allowing her to put her own indelible stamp on the original. Significantly, Ní Dhomhnaill's emphasis on gender issues and politics in her poetry frees the potential of Shakespeare *as Gaeilge* from preoccupations with language and the validity of translation. Ní Dhomhnaill's playful feminist readings of Shakespearean texts and motifs can be understood in the context of revisions of Shakespeare by women writers.[18] But, in view of the Irish setting, Ní Dhomhnaill's poems can also be considered as post-colonial takes on Shakespeare in the sense that they seek to move beyond the 'old' issues and dichotomies. In 'Mo ghrá-sa (idir lúibíní)', for example, Ní Dhomhnaill rescues the dark lady of Shakespeare's Sonnets from the male moralising of the *vanitas* tradition:

MY OWN LOVE (IN BRACKETS)

My own love –
he's no sloe-blossom
in a garden
(nor on any tree)

and if he's anything to do
with daisies
it's from his ears they'll grow
(when he's eight foot under). . .

A similar playful, feminist revision is evident in 'An Bhabóg Briste' ('The Broken Doll'), where Ní Dhomhnaill uses her wealth of Irish folk allusion to add to the pathos of Ophelia's death:

Oh small doll in the well, broken,
thrown by a child easily ambling
downhill, to his mother's skirts.
He got a fright in the lonesome dusk
when toadstool caps jumped to his mouth
when the foxgloves nodded towards him
when he heard an owl hoot in an oaktree.
His small soul nearly left him when
a stoat passed, a fat rabbit in her teeth
(its guts spilling out around the place)
and the bat flew through the air. . .

Nuala Ní Dhomhnaill is one of those contemporary Irish language poets who have not felt the obligation to either explain or excuse their fascination with the classics of world literature. Neither does she afford the Shakespearean canon any of its traditional male respect. Nowhere is this more evident than in 'Clann Horatio' ('Horatio's Children'), a satire on male chauvinism, dedicated 'Dos na hIntleachtóirí inár measc' ('To the Intellectuals among us'), with its dramatic dialogue, full of local colour and devilment, anchored in its Shakespearean title and conclusion:

'You're suspicious'
says your man to me.
I admitted I was
and even added that I never go out at night
without a *kitchen devil*
deep in my pocket.

Kitchen devil?
'Erra, you know
those kitchen knives that are great
for cleaning vegetables and peeling potatoes,
though that's not why I carry it,
but because of the black handle'.

'The black handle?'
'Erra, did you never hear tell
of the knife with the black handle.
The only protection against phantoms at night –
stick it in and leave it there.

There was a man in Dunquin
not too long ago
(I won't say who)
and there wasn't a morning
that someone passing wouldn't find his knife
stuck in a furze bush'.

Your man scrutinized me well.
He's still looking
not knowing what to think,
or whether I'm serious or not.

> Erra, am n't I always serious
> and like my country folk
> though we believe none of this
> we still don't deny anything
> because there is more on earth and in heaven
> than is know to you, children of Horatio.[19]

There is an interesting continuity between Ní Dhomhnaill's poem and the writings of Ó Caomhánach discussed earlier, for despite the differences of historical context and form, both seize on and expand Hamlet's scepticism. Of course, as the final stanza of 'Clann Horatio' indicates, the tone of Ní Dhomhnaill's poem is mischievous but it nonetheless shares with Ó Caomhánach a sense of how *Hamlet* can be used to speak to and for contemporary requirements, especially with its closing suggestion that all humans might play a minor role in life as Horatio does in Hamlet's world.

In discussing Irish-language translations and references to Shakespeare, this essay has sought to demonstrate the contribution to the study of Shakespeare by Irish writers, *as Gaeilge*. When dealing with the reception of Shakespeare in Ireland, there has been a tendency to overlook questions of language and translation, those very questions which have preoccupied and, in some instances, constrained writers in Irish until the 1960s. The generation of writers that have come to prominence since afford evidence of a post-colonial response or, perhaps more accurately in the context of the global issues of our times, post-post-colonial responses to Shakespeare, rather than a narrow or cultural nationalist preoccupation with questions of language translation and politics evident in some of the earlier texts discussed. It has been note by Harold Bloom that various cultures have appreciated Shakespeare in translation, and such is Shakespeare's genius that the plays arguably do transcend linguistic differences. But, of course it has always been the case that Shakespeare's plays have been accommodated and embraced in specific contexts, be they national, cultural or historical: the work of Ó Caomhánach and Ní Dhomhnaill is a good instance of Shakespeare being made contemporary in an Irish-language context. No Irish speaker is unable to access Shakespeare in the original, but an appreciation of Irish translations is important if we are to consider the forms of cultural exchange in Irish history with other languages and national literatures, including English.

Notes

1 Seán Ó Ríordáin, 'Fill Arís', in *Brosna* (Dublin: Sairséal and Dill: 1964), p. 41.

2 University College Dublin, Ó Ríordáin Archive.

3 Gearóid Ó Cleircín, 'Cín Lae Mhichíl Mhic Aodha' (unpublished doctoral thesis, NUI Maynooth, 2005).

4 Eliot remarks, '*Coriolanus* may be not as 'interesting' as *Hamlet*, but it is, with *Antony and Cleopatra*, Shakespeare's most assured artistic success'; see *The Sacred Wood: Essays on Poetry and Criticism* (London: Methuen, 1920), p. 99.

5 Michael Ó'Briain, *Coriolanus* (Dublin: An Gúm, 1938).

6 Plunkett D. Barton, *Links Between Ireland and Shakespeare* (Dublin: Maunsel, 1919).

7 Geoffrey Keating, *History of Ireland*, ed. by David Comyn, 3 vols (London: Irish Texts Soc. 1902–14), I, p. 63; p. 35.

8 Matthew Arnold, *The Study of Celtic Literature* (London: J. M. Dent, 1900), p. 104.

9 Ibid., p. 127.

10 *An Claidheamh Soluis*, 3 June 1911.

11 Ibid., 24 Nov. 1917. The planned translation by Ó Nualláin that 'Spiderman' refers to never materialised.

12 Ibid., 15 Dec. 1917.

13 *An Brón-chluiche Macbeit* (Dublin: Cahill & Co, 1925).

14 Despite a number of valiant attempts to translate Shakespeare into Irish, more often than not the attempted translations are undistinguished. Among such unsatisfactory efforts I would include: the eight sonnets translated by George Thomson in 1930; and the purple passages translated by Gearóid Ó Lochlainn from *Julius Caesar*, *Macbeth*, *Hamlet* and *As You Like It*, in 1943 and 1954.

15 Pádraig De Brún, in *Irisleabhar Mhá Nuad* (1924), 10.

16 Gerard O'Nolan, *Studies in Modern Irish, Part III* (Dublin: Educational Company, 1921), pp 103–4; 122–3.

17 'Shakespeare a Tháinig go hÉirinn', in *Bliainiris* 2003, ed. by Liam Mac Cóil agus Ruairí Ó hUiginn (Rath Cairn, Co. Meath: Carbad, 2003), pp 188–97.

18 See for example *Transforming Shakespeare: Contemporary Women's Re-Visions in Literature and Performance*, ed. by Marianne Novy (New York: Palgrave, 1999) and Julie Sanders, *Novel Shakespeares: Twentieth Century Women Novelists and Appropriation* (Manchester: Manchester University Press, 2001).

19 The first two poems are translated by Michael Hartnett, in Nuala Ní Dhomhnaill, *Selected Poems* (Dublin: Raven Arts Press, 1988). The translation of 'Clann Horatio' is my own.

CHAPTER 5

'Hamlet Among the Celts'

Shakespeare and Irish Ireland

Matthew Creasy

Walter Raleigh had little patience with Shakespeare amateurs. In *Shakespeare* (1904), his contribution to The English Men of Letters series, he dryly noted:

> There is no writer who has been so laden with the impertinences of prosaic enthusiasm and learned triviality. There is no book, except the Bible, which has been so misread, so misapplied, or made the subject of so many idle paradoxes and ingenuities.[1]

This desire to defend Shakespeare against 'impertinences' may come laden with political implications. Terence Hawkes and Coppélia Kahn locate Raleigh at the heart of twentieth-century English cultural nationalism.[2] For Andrew Gibson, *Shakespeare* does not just attempt to preserve the status and dignity of the English national poet, it seeks to preserve England's national identity and justify her right to Empire.[3] From this perspective, the 'learned triviality' of Leopold Bloom in *Ulysses* might seem like a Fenian assault upon English values (Joyce, after all, owned a copy of Raleigh's book).[4] 'Misapplied' quotations from Shakespeare provide him with a ready source of private jokes. The phrase, 'glimpses of the moon' evokes for Hamlet the nightscape in which his father's ghost appears (1.4.34), but Leopold Bloom uses it for a pun about women's buttocks: 'Or their skirt behind, placket unhooked. Glimpses of the moon' (v.4.54–5).[5] Similarly, when Bloom quips, 'For this relief much thanks. In *Hamlet*, that is' (13.938–41), the sexual release he feels after masturbating over Gerty Macdowell's knickers is far from Francisco's nervous anxiety at the beginning of the play. Ireland's relationship to the British Empire lends a particular edge to these 'idle paradoxes'. Such misreadings and misapplications belong to the 'radical criticism of Shakespeare' that Declan Kiberd discerns 'concealed within works of art' in Ireland at the beginning of the twentieth century.[6]

Kiberd draws up stark, partisan lines for Irish writers during this period, paraphrasing Frantz Fanon: 'the language of the enemy comes freighted with historic meaning, every utterance being either an order or a threat or an insult.'[7] Bloom's bawdy imagination is, then, Joyce's 'Celtic revenge' upon his imperial oppressors.[8] Stephen Dedalus's theory of *Hamlet* constitutes a salvo in the violent, Freudian conflict described by Christina Britzolakis:

> *Ulysses* turns *Hamlet* into a Shakespearian rag, obsessively unmaking, remaking and democratizing the language of this paternal text. For Joyce, to wreck the inherited structures of the oppressor's language was the only way of forging an authentically Irish literary Modernism that would not cut off the travails of an Irish state in the making from the larger global stage of imperial crisis.[9]

On this reading, Joyce and Raleigh appear on different sides of the barricades. But such rigid dichotomies can also obscure appreciation of the complex, divided loyalties that Shakespeare elicits. Given Joyce's aesthetic commitment to avoiding direct political pronouncement, it could be claimed that Bloom's Shakespearean misquotations are meant to indict this character's vulgarity. This would make Shakespeare a literary ideal, rather than the target of political opprobrium.

Joyce is usually the exceptional case in Irish literature and politics, but I shall demonstrate that this particular ambiguity is representative of a wider state of affairs. This essay re-addresses Shakespeare's reception in Ireland in the years before independence by examining a series of Shakespearean parodies published in *The Leader*. It might be thought that the explicit political agenda of this Irish nationalist journal would produce a violent rejection of Shakespeare and everything he represents, but close examination reveals a more complex situation. I shall argue that Shakespeare's status in Ireland was not simply a matter of 'wreck[ing] inherited structures' and that we need a more flexible critical vocabulary to describe it.

The complexity of Shakespeare's reception in Ireland partly reflects the diverse political and social interests at this time. Kiberd's *Inventing Ireland* makes clear that his work was significant in different ways to Irish writers from Anglo-Irish and Unionist backgrounds, as well as nationalists and Irish Catholics.[10] Raleigh's Shakespeare is inseparable from his imperialist sympathies, according to Gibson and Hawkes. So too accounts of Shakespeare by Irish writers have been closely linked to Irish politics. The dreamy 'Celtic' figures of Richard II and Hamlet that W. B. Yeats idealises in his essay 'At Stratford-on-Avon' are widely recognised as a form of rejoinder to Professor Edward Dowden's pragmatic, Benthamite account of Shakespeare and a rejection of his Unionist affiliations.[11] In turn, Len Platt argues that Stephen Dedalus's emphasis upon Shakespeare's preoccupation with sexual betrayal and paternity embodies an antipathy towards Anglo-Irish aesthetics.[12]

To these Irish versions of Shakespeare can be added 'Hamlet Among the Celts' by 'A. M. W.' from *The Leader*, the journal of D. P. Moran's Irish Ireland movement. This satirical sketch depicts Hamlet observing various social groups and classes within Ireland. It does not attempt to accommodate Hamlet to a set of Irish values. Rather, it presents him as standing in judgement upon Ireland. It is explicitly, even crudely political in its satire, which is inseparable from the political and cultural agenda laid down by Moran in *The Philosophy of Irish Ireland* (1904), a series of articles originally published by Father Tom Findlay's *New Ireland Review* during 1898.

Moran believed that the key to Irish independence lay in fostering national identity through cultural means. Like Douglas Hyde, founder of the Gaelic League, he perceived the Irish language as key to this. Moran was indebted to Hyde's approach in 'The Necessity for De-Anglicising Ireland' (1892) and his interest in Gaelic was awakened by an encounter with a London branch of the Gaelic League in 1896. Unlike Hyde, though, Moran came from an Irish-Catholic background and his position is further distinguished by its emphasis upon a swingeing self-criticism.

This is partly a question of degree. Hyde attributed the decline of indigenous national culture to a failure of Irish will: 'What the battleaxe of the Dane, the sword of the Norman, the wile of the Saxon were unable to perform, we have accomplished ourselves.'[13] Ireland should reject cultural forms alien to her true values. 'Penny dreadfuls, shilling shockers, and still more, the garbage of vulgar English weeklies like *Bow Bells* and the *Police Intelligence*' were the invidious means of spreading English imperial values within the Irish imagination.[14] Moran shared this desire to remove contaminating English influences, urging his contemporaries to be 'original Irish' and 'not imitation English'.[15] But he pursued Hyde's criticisms of contemporary Irish culture with greater rigour and zeal and he was sceptical about the value of the activities and output of writers and dramatists already involved with cultural nationalism. For Moran, the Protestant Anglo-Irish backgrounds of writers like Yeats and Lady Gregory compromised their nationalist credentials. He described the Irish Literary Revival as 'one of the most glaring frauds that the credulous Irish people ever swallowed' and repeatedly denounced the 'Celtic Note' as a commercial fabrication:

A certain number of Irish literary men have 'made a market' – just as stock-jobbers do in another commodity – in a certain vague thing, which is indistinctly known as the 'Celtic Note' in English literature, and they earn their fame and livelihood by supplying the demand which they have honourably and with much advertising created.[16]

Irish Ireland did not confine its wrath to Anglo-Irish writers. As Patrick Maume observes, Moran was also severe towards 'middle class snobs who aped English habits; the dictatorial neo-agrarianism of William O'Brien and his United Irish League; [and] the separatism of Arthur Griffith, which Moran dismissed as a fantasy of "Green Tin Pikers"'.[17] His targets are wide-ranging: 'Is the Irish Nation Dying?' lambasts an imagined array of self-proclaimed Irish patriots from pretentious students to 'the bank clerk in his knickers and brown boots'.[18]

Moran hoped to bring such figures to consciousness of their lapsed condition through *The Leader*, which he established in 1900 with Findlay's backing. It answers his call for a 'literature of national self-criticism'.[19] His first editorial lamented:

> The English Government does not make us drink too much, it does not compel us to buy British gutter literature, it does not ask us to believe that the present can be righted by eternally proving that we were cheated in the past; notwithstanding its persistent efforts it never had the power to compel us to drop our language. We did that ourselves.[20]

Moran's criticisms of Irish cultural tastes and the predominance of 'British gutter literature' are linked with an oppositional stance that placed him at loggerheads with other nationalists, who are criticised here for an excessive attachment to previous wrongs. This violence of feeling and recrimination reflects the persistent 'self-criticism' that distinguishes the Irish Ireland movement from other contemporary strands of Catholic Irish nationalism.[21]

'Hamlet Among the Celts' transforms the social divisions described by Moran into stereotypes. In three tableaux, 'Hamlet' overhears three different groups and comments on their behaviour. Clod, Patch and Lump ('A Huxter, a Coachman and a Police Pensioner') discuss racing tips and compare their losses; McGinty and Breen ('Young Tradesmen') recall carousing in music-halls and at the billiards table; and finally, Block and Mallet ('Two grave respectable-looking gentlemen') review the delights of Blackpool and 'coon' minstrel bands.[22] The satire encompasses Ireland's rising Catholic middle classes, as well as proletarian figures. As 'Celts', these characters represent the indigenous Irish racial type, but this term is pejorative. They are mapped onto the fallen Irish nationhood outlined by Moran. They have become debased by anglicised activities such as drink and racing and reduced to 'imitation English' through their taste for music-hall ditties.

Although 'Hamlet Among the Celts' does not observe the plot of *Hamlet*, it is pointedly Shakespearean. This Hamlet's tendency to soliloquy evokes Shakespeare's play and his speech is punctuated by further allusions. He refers to McGinty and Breen as:

> Two sparrows of humanity
> Who skim the social purlieus in our midst
> With avaricious bills in quest of chaff
> And husks and offal. Their little life
> Is symbolled by a bet, a drink, a lark,
> A quarrel, or an argument inane.
> All thought, or mental insight to their souls
> Is boundless space unsearchable and dark.
> Their universe is bounded by a brick,
> And there, no chance or revolution works.
> Their past or present centres in a job,
> And their horizon of the future spreads
> No further than a Saturday.[23]

The description of the men as 'two sparrows of humanity' recalls the 'special Providence in the fall of a sparrow' (V.2.200) described by Shakespeare's Hamlet. The observation that 'their universe is bounded by a brick' echoes his declaration that he 'could be bounded in a nutshell, and count myself a King of infinite space; were it not that I have bad dreams' (II.2.252–4). Similarly, the reference to 'their little life' is an obvious echo of Prospero's famous speech to Ferdinand in *The Tempest*:

> [. . .] We are such stuff
> As dreams are made on, and our little life
> Is rounded with a sleep. (IV.1.156–8)

These allusions create the possibility of sympathy towards McGinty and Breen as 'sparrows' or 'little' creatures, but parodic transformation forecloses this. Their parasitic 'avaricious' qualities are the focus (they steal 'chaff'), rather than their vulnerability and they have little chance of waking to any kind of afterlife since 'their universe is bounded by a brick'. Hamlet damns the Irish for their failings with the same severity as Moran. He is not the dreamy Celt idealised by Yeats. Instead Shakespearean allusion becomes the vehicle for Moran's peculiar brand of Irish politics.

'Hamlet Among the Celts' is not singular. The initials 'A. M. W.' contract 'A Man Who Was There', the pseudonym of John Swift. Between August 1903 and September 1906, Swift contributed weekly to *The Leader*, usually providing parodies in the form of prose, songs and dramatic sketches. These varied from individual songs less than one column in length, to extensive contributions to Christmas issues. On 3 December 1904, *The Leader* published a dramatic skit entitled, 'Our Evergreen Pantomime' by Swift, a parody of Yeats's 'The Lake Isle of Innisfree' with accompanying cartoon and two further columns of parodic songs.

As his obituarist noted, Shakespearean parody was Swift's speciality.[24] In 'The Bigots of the Wood', he pastiches the mechanicals' rehearsal in *A Midsummer Night's Dream*. It depicts a group of 'bigots' rehearsing 'The Triumph of the "Saved"' somewhere near Castle Saunderson on 'Samhain'. ('Saved' was Moran's nickname for evangelical Protestant Unionists.) This involves reworking famous speeches from Shakespeare. 'Bottom' echoes his counterpart in the *Dream* ('my chief humour is for a tyrant. I could play 'Ercles rarely' (1.2.24–5):

> Myself will personate Ascendancy.
> A mild and pious gentleman, oppressed
> By persecutors of enslaving Rome.[25]

Swift here satirises self-pitying upper middle-class members of the Anglo-Irish ascendancy who consider themselves affronted by Irish Catholics (a recurrent target of Moran's ire). The rehearsals are interrupted by Puck, who revenges himself upon their religious intolerance by giving Bottom a donkey's head. When 'A Minor Poet', 'Bubble', enters, he takes the transformed Bottom for a 'satyr', recalling Titania's infatuation. He delivers a wishful speech, based on Hamlet's first soliloquy:

> Oh, that this too, too solid flesh would melt,
> Thaw and resolve itself into a fay,
> That I could play with satyrs through the night.
> And track those mystic wonders through the wood.
> Oh, rare adventure of great Celtic note;
> Oh, mystery poetic.[26]

This preoccupation with 'satyrs' and 'fay' marks Bubble as a proponent of Moran's hated 'Celtic note'. His sympathy for the transformed 'bigot', Bottom, links the Literary Revivalists' fondness for supernatural stories about Irish faery to their Anglo-Irish background and Irish Unionist prejudice.

'Some Rathmines Goblins' makes a similar point by depicting 'a "Saved" Seer' who goes 'spook-hunting' in 'a certain lonely grove around Rathmines'.[27] Once again, a taste for faery and the supernatural mark this character as a Literary Revivalist and the stereotyped label 'saved' makes the accusation of Protestant bigotry explicit. Inevitably, the '"Saved" Seer' encounters something he takes for a ghost:

> 'Got him at last,' exclaimed the 'Saved' seer, exultingly, 'a ghost, or I'm no judge
> of horseflesh'. Then, remembering that ghosts should be addressed in a pro-
> per, awesome, melodramatic manner, he threw himself into the most correct,

tragical attitude, as practised in the Gaiety on such solemn occasions, and said impressively:

> Oh, angels good, and ministers of grace,
> Defend and guard me in this haunted place;
> Be thou a healthy soul, or goblin damned,
> With holy airs, or hellish sulphur crammed,
> I'll speak to thee, though I be courting woe,
> And try thy hidden destiny to know.
> Oh, tell me being who has passed the goal,
> The secret troubles of thy living soul.

To this the figure replied solemnly:

> I am a Popish spirit, and my plight
> Is now to walk the dark and dreary night,
> And be debarred from life's eternal day
> Till all my earthly dross is purged away;
> Till dogma's fetters, from my soul are clear
> Beneath the moon I'll have to wander here.

Once again, Shakespeare is made into the vehicle for political satire. These speeches clearly parody Hamlet's encounter with the ghost of his father. The joke is that this ghost confirms 'the "Saved" seer's Protestant bigotry' by referring to Catholicism ('I am a Popish spirit') and 'dogma's fetters'. The same scene from *Hamlet* haunts *Ulysses* too. But Swift here offers in explicit form the critique of Anglo-Irish values that Len Platt reads as implicit in Joyce's writing.

Three more supernatural encounters follow: the seer interprets a vision of sun, moon and stars as pagan spirits unencumbered by 'orthodoxy'; he runs across the ghost of Bung, a native Irish alcoholic; and he meets a goblin who reveals that his present form is punishment for being a 'bigot sour' during his lifetime. This final vision revolts the seer. Having been content to find his religious prejudices confirmed by these supernatural visions, he is dismayed by this 'fleshless libel upon Rathmines immortality' which challenges his own sense of religious complacency. Quoting from *Measure for Measure* he describes this last vision as 'a Rathmines bigot, and only a common ghost, instead of a "delighted spirit bathing in fiery floods"'.[28] Shakespeare's words are intended to convey the elevated status of the kind of spirits valued by the seer, but he takes Claudio's words out of context, eliding a line break. Horrified by apprehension of his own death, Claudio worries that it will be the fate of 'the [delighted] spirit | to bathe in fiery floods' (III.I.I2I–2).[29]

'Delighted' here is an archaic form, meaning 'Endowed or attended with delight' (*OED* Sense 2. (obs.)), and it contrasts with the 'fiery floods' in the burning lakes of hell. In contrast, 'the "Saved" seer' is disappointed that the goblin is not a higher being having a jolly time in the afterlife.

Although he should not be conflated with Moran, Swift's contributions are clearly faithful to *The Philosophy of Irish Ireland*. They may not seem like a direct form of response, but Swift's original choice of pseudonym ('A Man Who Was There') indicates the degree to which his contributions react to recent events in Ireland and topics discussed in *The Leader*. From March 1904 to March 1905, for example, Michael O'Riordan published a series of articles criticising the progressive Unionist politics of Horace Plunkett's *Ireland in the New Century*, and prompting the Revivalist poet AE to contribute articles and letters during September and October 1904, defending Plunkett.[30] So Swift's creations respond directly to Irish Ireland's unease about these links between the Literary Revival and Unionism. Similarly, his mockery of the supernatural coincides with the recent publication of Lady Gregory's *Poets and Dreamers* and the rehearsal in 'The Bigots of the Wood' alludes to the Irish National Theatre Society's preparations for the opening of the Abbey Theatre in December 1904.

Swift also responded to contemporary productions of Shakespeare. In April 1904, he satirised Irish amateur theatricals in a piece which begins with a mock-review of a production of *As You Like It* at Blackrock College:

> Needless to say, the whole thing was a triumph of histrionic art. The two young gentlemen who played Rosalind and Orlando appear to have utterly outclassed Ellen Terry and Henry Irving in the same roles, while the youth who personated the melancholy Jacques delivered his philosophic reflections with an elocutionary power and beauty hardly equalled by the late Barry Sullivan in his palmiest days.[31]

The opening of this pastiche explains that it was inspired by 'reading a puff in Pink' – the Dublin edition of the *Evening Telegraph*, published on pink paper. Although the *Evening Telegraph* does not refer to any performances at Blackrock College during April 1904, 'As You Like It' coincides with Herbert Beerbohm Tree's season of Shakespearean plays at the Theatre Royal and a production of *Hamlet* by St Mary's College at Rathmines Town Hall.

Swift attacks firstly the aspirations of middle-class Catholic parents. (Moran frequently criticised Catholic private schools for imitating their English counterparts.)[32] Their taste for Shakespearean theatricals is treated as symptomatic of capitulation to English values. But the hyperbole of 'As You Like It' ('a triumph of histrionic art') also echoes and mocks the language of the *Evening Telegraph*'s theatre critic, who praises the appearance of Miss Viola Tree (the director's daughter) in *Twelfth Night*:

Divinely tall and most divinely fair, with a beautiful voice, well modulated and a manner charming in its utter absence of straining after effects where they are most likely to tempt one so young and inexperienced, she yet showed that she had the fullest appreciation of the part she had to play.[33]

The boys of St Mary's College receive similar eulogies:

They attained a remarkable degree of efficiency, their facility of expression, correctness of elocution, and gracefulness of movement drawing the frequent applause of the crowded house. [. . .] The Hamlet of Master Musgrave was a great success, the varying humours of Shakespeare's great creation being interpreted by the youthful artist in a really remarkable manner.[34]

What looks like exaggeration in 'As You Like It' is strikingly close to these superlatives ('divinely [. . .] most divinely [. . .] remarkable [. . .] really remarkable'). Pastiche of such obsequiousness turns a localised dig against the pretensions of Catholic schools into a broader point about English hegemony in Ireland. The object of Swift's satire encompasses the domination of Dublin's theatrical scene by visiting English performers and its acceptance by the press.[35]

The title of Shakespeare's play jokes about the kind of entertainment favoured by contemporary Elizabethan and Jacobean audiences. In Swift's hands, 'As You Like It' indicts the debased tastes of Irish audiences. This echoes other contributors to *The Leader*, who complained about the lack of 'a drama of our own' and lamented the popularity of 'the "Latest London Success" [. . .] some tawdry burlesque, some stupid comedy or some unwholesome melodrama'.[36] Swift concludes with a pastiche of Amiens's song from the close of Act II of Shakespeare's play:

The Irish Irelander might leave the place singing softly to himself–

> Blow blow thou winter's wind,
> Thou art not so unkind to this neglected isle
> As many native folk who glory in the yoke
> Of foreign borrowed style.[37]

Like Hamlet in 'Hamlet Among the Celts', the 'Irish Irelander' observes the follies of 'native folk' from a position of ideological and aesthetic superiority, condemning the contamination of 'foreign' cultures.

And yet, even while damning 'foreign borrowed style', the pastiche remains strongly indebted to a 'foreign' author, since it replicates Shakespeare's first two lines and his rhyme scheme. The form of Swift's satire seems at odds with its contents. This may be a problem intrinsic to parody itself. As Simon Dentith observes, even where parody makes fun of a source text, it confirms that the source is important enough to be worth mocking. Parody has an intrinsic double value: benevolent parodies cannot help drawing out some ridiculous aspect to their source texts and hostile parody has, 'the paradoxical effect of preserving the very text that it seeks to destroy'.[38] If Swift's parodies aim to desecrate Shakespeare, they also confirm his importance and help to reinforce his cultural standing.

It is not clear, though, that Swift's target *is* Shakespeare. The plays he chooses usually function as the vehicle of satire upon other topics: 'Hamlet Among the Celts' targets the 'Celts' and not 'Hamlet'; 'The Bigots of the Wood' attacks the self-complacence and hypocrisy of Protestant Unionism, not *A Midsummer Night's Dream*; and 'Some Rathmines Goblins' makes fun of Revivalist spiritualism rather than *Hamlet*. In these parodies 'polemic [is] directed to the world rather than the preceding text' (in this case, Shakespeare).[39] Far from being the object of criticism, Shakespeare is often the means by which this criticism is effected. In 'Some Rathmines Goblins', the '"saved" Seer' is damned by his misquotation from *Measure for Measure* and in 'Hamlet Among the Celts', the role of Hamlet is evoked in order to establish a moral vantage point from which to criticise the 'Celts'. Instead of exemplifying the literature of colonial oppression, Shakespeare figures as a literary ideal. If anything, he represents the standards from which Ireland is understood to have fallen.

A fundamental conservatism about cultural matters underlies Swift's parodies, but he is not idiosyncratic in this. When *The Leader* complained that 'dramatic taste' had reached 'a low ebb', it protested that:

> 'The Shop Girl' and 'The Belle of New York' with their indifferent music and their indifferent plots will draw better houses than 'Twelfth Night' or 'The Tempest'.[40]

Even while calling for an indigenous Irish theatre, Shakespeare remains a touchstone. This is similar to Douglas Hyde's position, as described by Andrew Murphy in this volume.[41] Hyde's conservatism, his distaste for 'penny dreadfuls, shilling shockers' and 'vulgar English weeklies' is inseparable from a desire for Ireland to embrace Shakespeare's example. Paradoxically, Irish nationalist programmes for de-Anglicisation tend to exclude the English national poet from their remit.[42]

Shakespeare is so often a tool for Swift's critical ire that this apparent contradiction with the de-Anglicising agenda of Irish Ireland exceeds the structural ambivalence common to all parody. The existence of a deeper internal conflict in works like his pastiche of Amiens' song is confirmed by English influences and affinities within the particular form of Swift's parodies. The seer's speech in 'Some Rathmines Goblins' ('Oh, angels good, and ministers of grace | Defend and guard me in this haunted place') follows Hamlet's words very closely:

> Angels and ministers of grace defend us!
> Be thou a spirit of health or goblin damned,
> Bring with thee airs from heaven or blasts from hell,
> Be thy intents wicked or charitable,
> Thou com'st in such a questionable shape
> That I will speak to thee. (1.4.18–23)

Swift retains the drift of Hamlet's stated intention to speak to the ghost and much of the same vocabulary. Shakespeare's blank verse is, however, regularised into rhyming couplets ('grace' | 'place') of an easy monosyllabic fullness that smoothes out Hamlet's consternation, making space for comic effect. The 'figure's reply ('I am a Popish spirit') parodies the words of the ghost of Hamlet's father ('I am thy father's spirit | Doomed for a certain term to walk the night' (1.5.9–10) in the same way.

These new versions of Shakespeare are strongly akin to John Poole's *Hamlet Travestie* (1812), where the ghost of Hamlet's father delivers his speech in the form of a ballad sung to the tune of 'Giles Scroggins Ghost':

> Behold in me your father's sprite. Ri tol tiddy lol de ray,
> Doom'd for a term to walk the night. Tiddy, tiddy, &c.
> You'll scarce believe me when I say,
> That I'm bound to fast in fires all day,
> Till my crimes are burnt and purg'd away. Ri tol tiddy, &c.[43]

Like Swift, Poole regularises the rhythm and introduces a consistent rhyme scheme, rendering the diction banal and comically incongruous ('sprite') to the original subject matter. This play is one of the earliest recognised Shakespeare burlesques, a genre from the theatrical mainstream that enjoyed the height of its popularity in London during the 1860s. Swift's techniques, then, are not revolutionary.

Such clear similarities betray the links between Swift's parodies and older, attested forms of having fun with Shakespeare. 'As You Like It' shifts from mimicking the banal exaggerations of contemporary critics into more a conventional form of burlesque, by parodying Jacques's speech from *As You Like It* (11.7.139–66):

> All this land's a stage,
> And all the shoneens in it merely players;
> They have their exits and their entrances;
> And one snob in his time plays many parts,
> His acts being seven ages.[44]

Substituting 'land' for 'world' deliberately narrows the focus of this speech, from the human condition to the local social and political situation in Ireland. This burlesque version of the 'Seven Ages' catalogues different varieties of 'shoneen' (someone with (usually Anglo-Irish) pretensions to gentility). The scope of its social criticism echoes 'Hamlet Among the Celts' as it ranges from 'Johnny habit' at the music hall to 'the Justice, the shoneen Jay Pee' and ambitious administrators in the colonial administration at Dublin Castle.

This echoes some of the oldest Shakespeare burlesques, which originate in occasional parodies, popularised on broadsheets. Re-workings of the 'Seven Ages' speech date back to the eighteenth century, and remained popular throughout the nineteenth.[45] (William Hamilton lists twenty-three versions written between 1803 and 1885, from 'The Seven Drinks of Man' to 'All the World's a Newspaper'.)[46] Hamlet's soliloquy was another favoured target, inspiring 'A Pugilistic Soliloquy' ('To box or not to box?') and four different versions of 'A Bachelor's Soliloquy', beginning 'to wed or not to wed'.[47] As well as theatrical burlesque, then, Swift's methods belong to a long tradition of Shakespeare parody.

Elsewhere in *The Leader*, 'The Irish Hamlet' adopts this form to mock Pan-Celticism:

> Pan-Celt or Irish Gael; that is the question:–
> Whether 'tis nobler in the Gael to suffer
> The shifts and shallows of my lord's affection,
> Or to take arms against the Lia Cineil
> And by dislocation end them.[48]

This was probably written by 'Imaal' (the pen name of J. J. O'Toole), who contributed a satirical account of a Welsh 'Pan-Celtic' recital at the Antient Concert Rooms in Dublin to the same edition.[49] But Swift uses the same approach in 'The Bigots of the Wood', substituting effete reference to 'a fay' for Hamlet's 'dew' ('Oh, that this too, too solid flesh would melt, | Thaw and resolve itself into a fay') in order to satirise the Revivalist's obsession with Irish faery.

Shakespearean parody in *The Leader* was clearly very similar to the kind of item that was a stock in trade of English satirical papers. The connotations of this similarity are problematic. Even Swift's trick of introducing reference to contemporary Irish politics belongs to this less radical, English tradition. For comic weeklies such as *Punch* regularly held competitions for the best Shakespeare parody on a topic from current affairs.[50] Although his use of Moran's stereotypes lends Swift's productions a peculiarly Irish Ireland flavour, he retains the same methods. Contrary to its declared political agenda of eradicating English influence upon Irish cultural life, *The Leader* may even find itself modelled upon *Punch*.

This is damning because *Punch* was such a significant source of stereotyped images of the Irish.[51] 'Imaal' referred to these same stereotypes in May 1904, complaining about crude representations of the Irish as Fenian terrorists characterised by 'a huge and hideous upper-lip' and armed with 'blunder-busses'.[52] *The Leader* saw its role as redressing such slander. One reader wrote in to *The Leader* praising Swift's comic songs: 'If Englishmen are so ready to caricature the Irish, I don't see why we should not do the same.'[53] This commends Swift's use of stereotypes, such as 'John Bull', against 'Englishmen', but the syntactical ambiguity is telling. It raises the prospect that Swift reproduces 'the same' caricatures of Irishness as his English counterparts. 'Hamlet Among the Celts' ascribes a gross brogue to lower-class characters such as Breen, who describes his previous night: 'I went an' got dhrunk wud a few chaps of the Navy. Ah, looka, we had great gas.'[54] Moran observed:

> There is something essentially mean about the corrupt English of the Irish peasant, particularly when put into cold print; it passes the power of man to write literature in it.[55]

This seems to be Swift's satirical intent: Breen's brogue is a mirror up to nature, meant to remind Irish readers of the corrupting English forces present in the language they speak. The problem is that such tactics also replicate and perpetuate the kind of stereotyping of which 'Imaal' complained.

Writing about the rebels of 1916 and their attitude towards Shakespeare, Richard English discerns a 'tension' between 'Catholic Ireland's Anglophobic marginality' and 'its Anglocentric attachment to Britishness'.[56] These Shakespearean parodies embody a similar tension. Swift transformed his source material into a channel for Moran's brand of nationalism, but the form and content are both, in different ways, at odds with that agenda. The absence of critical reflection upon this indicates that this was not a matter of conscious policy.

Part of Joyce's achievement in *Ulysses* is his ability to turn similarly conflicting and conflicted feelings into imaginative richness. He was well aware that Bloom's bawdy allusions are not far removed from Hamlet's own propensity for inappropriate sexual reference ('Do you think I meant country matters?' (III.2.111), his sexual puns may be celebratory rather than derogatory. Stephen Dedalus identifies with Hamlet as a model of the persecuted artist and the moody, brooding intellectual, but this affinity is divided. He also identifies Hamlet with the imperial violence of the Boer War ('Khaki Hamlets don't hesitate to shoot' (9.132)). Later on, however, Old Gummy Granny appears to Stephen as both Kathleen Ní Houlihan ('Strangers in my house, bad manners to them!') and as the Ghost of Hamlet's father ('Hamlet, revenge!'). He refuses to comply with her demand for violent action, identifying her as 'the old sow that eats her farrow' (15.4578–88). The Rathmines Seer's ghostly visions of the 'Popish spirit' in *The Leader* invoke *Hamlet* to indict anti-Catholic prejudice. But Joyce's allusions damn the violent impulses of Catholic nationalists too, inviting comparison with their imperialist oppressors.

Stephen Dedalus proves to be a better pacifist than Shakespeare's Hamlet. Borrowing from *Macbeth*, Stephen describes Act V of *Hamlet* as 'a blood-boltered shambles' (9.134–5). For Declan Kiberd such allusive transformations constitute political acts. According to one post-colonial model, subject nations must, like Caliban, appropriate and reinvent the language of their oppressors. For Kiberd this is an Oedipal process – a matter of defeating or overcoming 'Father Shakespeare'. It involves 'laying violent hands on Shakespeare' and 'offer[ing] the act of reading as a rehearsal for or version of revolution'.[57] But 'violent hands' were antipathetic to Stephen Dedalus and to Joyce. This is where the vocabulary of much current criticism needs to expand. As well as appropriation, violence and wrecking, Shakespearean ghosts haunt *Ulysses* and *The Leader* in such ways that make terms such as tribute, travesty, influence, burlesque and resource apposite too.[58] Kiberd is right about the political sensitivities of Shakespeare's work for Irish writers at the beginning of the twentieth century. But the imaginative transformation of Hamlet into 'a Celt' was deeply problematic. In this respect, the divided impulses and conflicted cultural loyalties of Stephen Dedalus are exemplary.

Notes

I am grateful to Janet Clare, Stephen O'Neill and Matthew Campbell for helpful comments on an earlier draft of this essay.

1   Walter Raleigh, *Shakespeare* (London: Macmillan, 1911), p. 3.

2   Terence Hawkes, 'Swisser Swatter: Making a Man of English Letters', in *That Shakespeherian Rag: Essays on a Critical Process* (London: Methuen, 1986), pp 51–72; Coppélia Kahn, 'Remembering Shakespeare Imperially: The 1916 Tercentenary', *Shakespeare Quarterly* 52: 4 (2001), 456–78.

3   Andrew Gibson, *Joyce's Revenge* (Oxford: Oxford University Press, 2000), pp 60–80. Kahn makes similar claims regarding Raleigh's involvement in the 1916 tercentenary celebrations also discussed by Andrew Murphy in this volume.

4   Michael Gillespie, *James Joyce's Trieste Library* (Austin: Harry Ransom Humanities Research Center, 1986), p. 193.

5   James Joyce, *Ulysses*, ed. by Hans Walter Gabler et al. (London: Random House, 1993).

6   Declan Kiberd, *Inventing Ireland: The Literature of the Modern Nation* (London: Vintage, 1996), p. 281.

7   Ibid., p. 276.

8 Gibson argues *passim* that this phrase of John Eglinton's epitomises *Ulysses*.

9 Christina Britzolakis, 'Speaking Daggers: T. S. Eliot, James Joyce and *Hamlet*', in *New Essays on 'Hamlet'*, ed. by Mark Burnett and John Manning (New York: AMS Press, 1994), p. 241.

10 Kiberd, *Inventing Ireland*, pp 268–80.

11 See above, pp 40–9; ibid., pp 269–70; Jonathan Allison, 'W. B. Yeats and Shakespearean Character', in *Shakespeare and Ireland: History, Politics, Culture*, ed. by Mark Thornton Burnett and Ramona Wray (London: Macmillan, 1997), pp 114–35; Ruth Nevo, 'Yeats, Shakespeare and Ireland', in *Literature and Nationalism*, ed. by Vincent Newey and Ann Thompson (Liverpool: Liverpool University Press, 1991), pp 182–97.

12 Len Platt, *Joyce and the Anglo-Irish: A Study of Joyce and the Literary Revival* (Amsterdam: Rodopi, 1998), pp 73–86.

13 Douglas Hyde, 'The Necessity for De-Anglicising Ireland' (1892), in *The Revival of Irish Literature and Other Addresses* ed. by Sir Charles Gavan Duffy et al. (London: T. Fisher Unwin, 1894), p. 128.

14 Ibid., p. 159.

15 D. P. Moran, 'The Future of the Irish Nation', in *The Philosophy of Irish Ireland* (Dublin: James Duffy, 1905), p. 26.

16 Ibid., pp. 21–2.

17 Patrick Maume, *The Rise and Fall of Irish Ireland: D. P. Moran & Daniel Corkery* (Coleraine: University of Ulster Press, 1996), p. 3.

18 D. P. Moran, 'Is the Irish Nation Dying?', in *The Philosophy of Irish Ireland*, pp 4–7.

19 D.P. Moran, 'The Gaelic Revival', in *The Philosophy of Irish Ireland*, p. 79.

20 *The Leader*, 1 Sept. 1900, p. 5.

21 Moran denied this was 'a wholesale denunciation of the people'. Instead, he claimed to attack false ideas of Irishness and criticise Irish Catholics for failing to live up to their responsibilities ('Is the Irish Nation Dying?', p. 7).

22 A. M. W. [John Swift], 'Hamlet Among the Celts', *The Leader*, 2 July 1904, pp 300–2.

23 Ibid., p. 301.

24 *The Leader*, 27 Jan. 1927, p. 606.

25 A. M. W., 'Some Bigots of the Wood', *The Leader*, 29 Oct. 1904, p. 152.

26 Ibid., pp 152–3.

27 A. M. W., 'Some Rathmines Goblins', *The Leader*, 24 Sept. 1904, pp 70–1.

29 Wells and Taylor amend the word to 'dilated' but here I am following the text of *The Riverside Shakespeare*, ed. by G. Blakemore Evans (Boston: Houghton Mifflin, 1974).

30 These articles were later collected as *Catholicity and Progress in Ireland* (London: K. Paul, Trench, Trübner, 1906).

31 A. M. W., 'As You Like It', *The Leader*, 23 Apr. 1904, p. 137.

32 Willard Potts, *Joyce and the Two Irelands* (Austin: University of Texas Press, 2000), pp 38–9.

33 'The Entertainments: Theatre Royal: Mr Tree's Company', *Evening Telegraph*, Dublin, 18 Apr. 1904, p. 3.

34 'Dramatic Entertainment in the Rathmines Town Hall', *Evening Telegraph*, Dublin: Special Edition, 12 Apr. 1904, p. 2.

35 Disparaging reference to the 'melodramatic' posturing of actors at the Gaiety Theatre in 'Some Rathmines Goblins' makes a similar point. For contrasting views on the state of Irish theatre at this time see, Stephen Watt, *Joyce, O'Casey, and the Irish Popular Theatre* (Syracuse: Syracuse University Press, 1991) and Christopher Morash, *A History of Irish Theatre 1601–2000* (Cambridge: Cambridge University Press, 2002).

36 'Imported Amusements', *The Leader*, 15 Sept. 1900, p. 41; 'British Plays in Ireland' *The Leader*, 13 Oct. 1900, p. 108.

37 'As You Like It', p. 138.

38 Simon Dentith, *Parody* (London: Routledge, 2000), p. 36.

39 Ibid., p. 18.

40 'British Plays in Ireland', p. 108.

41 See Andrew Murphy's chapter in this volume, especially pp 52–6.

42 See Philip Edwards's chapter, p. 25 and Andrew Murphy's chapter, p. 52.

43 John Poole, *Hamlet Travestie* (1812), in *Nineteenth-Century Shakespeare Burlesques*, ed. by Stanley Wells (London: Diploma, 1977), I, 16.

44 'As You Like It', p. 138.

45 See, MS Johnson Ballads 2834 and Harding B.25 (1463) in the broadsheet ballad collections at the Bodleian Library, Oxford University.

46 Walter Hamilton, *Parodies of the Works of English and American Authors* (London: Reeves & Turner, 1885), II, pp 169–75; pp 195–6.

47 Ibid., pp. 149; 158–61. See also, Beate Müller, '"Hamlet at the Dentist's": Parodies of Shakespeare', in *Parody: Dimensions and Perspectives*, ed. by Beate Müller (Amsterdam: Rodopi, 1997), pp 144–52.

48 'Neo-Pan-Gaelic-Celt', 'The Irish Hamlet', *The Leader*, 31 Aug. 1901, p. 10.

49 'Imaal' [J. J. O'Toole], 'Some Pan-Celtic Comicalities', *The Leader*, 31 Aug. 1901, pp 11–12. Regarding O'Toole's contributions as 'Imaal', see Maume, *The Rise and Fall of Irish Ireland*, pp. 15–16.

50 Müller, 'Hamlet at the Dentist's', p. 131. In 1883, for example, *The Weekly Dispatch* awarded Mr Jesse H. Wheeler a prize of two guineas for his parody of Hamlet's soliloquy referring to the Suez Canal: see Hamilton, *Parodies*, II, p. 149.

51 L. P. Curtis, *Apes and Angels: The Irishman in Victorian Caricature*, rev. edn (Washington: Smithsonian, 1997).

52 'Imaal', 'Different Kinds of Celt', *The Leader*, 7 May 1904, p. 171.

53 'Rock', 'Letter to the Editor', *The Leader*, 2 Apr. 1904, p. 93.

54 'Hamlet Among the Celts', p. 301.

55 D. P. Moran, 'The Battle of Two Civilisations', in *The Philosophy of Irish Ireland*, p. 104.

56 Richard English, 'Shakespeare and the Definition of the Irish Nation', in *Shakespeare and Ireland: History, Politics, Culture*, ed. by Mark Thornton Burnett and Ramona Wray (London: Macmillan, 1997), pp 136–8.

57 Kiberd, *Inventing Ireland*, p. 280.

58 I draw here upon Adrian Poole's *Shakespeare and the Victorians* (London: Arden, 2004), p. 2.

CHAPTER 6

Shakespeare and Company

Hamlet in Kildare Street

Declan Kiberd

On a walk home from Belvedere College one afternoon, James Joyce was asked by his classmate Albrecht Connolly to admit that Shakespeare was the greatest poet. He refused. Connolly, a far more robust boy, began to twist Joyce's arm and to frog-march his victim along the footpath for quite a distance, in hopes of extracting the concession. Joyce was in tears but did not submit.[1] In *A Portrait of the Artist as a Young Man*, that scene was recast with the young Stephen Dedalus's refusal to admit that 'Byron was no good';[2] but the real-life version shows Joyce in a more immodest light. He really did see Shakespeare as his antagonist, someone whose greatest work might some day be trumped. If both the *Odyssey* and *New Testament* contained immense artistic potentials, as yet unfulfilled, then how much more true might that be of a great but flawed work like *Hamlet*.

After all, that very notion of a gap between the potential of an idea and its working-out in action was one of the play's innermost themes:

> Sure, he that made us with such large discourse,
> Looking before and after, gave us not
> That capability and god-like reason
> To fust in us unused.

> (IV.4.27–30)

The problem – for Shakespeare almost as much as for Hamlet – was that the multiple possibilities opened up by his story became more an end in themselves than the basis for a clear action. This is why T. S. Eliot would find the weakness of the play in its summoning up of an emotion in excess of the facts as they appear.[3] For Joyce, *Hamlet* the play as well as Hamlet the character was a dire warning that interior monologue may displace action rather than enable it. There may be no resolution in the world of *nacheinander*, just one sorry thing after another. A man can lose the power of action in the sheer energy of the resolve, for the relation between an idea and an act is always uneasy.[4] Goethe put this well when he said: 'Few people have the understanding and simultaneously the ability to act. Understanding extends, but also immobilises; action immobilizes, but it also restricts.'[5]

Stephen Dedalus at the outset of *Ulysses* appears in mourning clothes, like Hamlet, at the start of things – that black suit ridiculed by Malachi Mulligan because it makes Stephen look like a priest. Both men insist, however, on the depth of that psychic wound which justifies such clothing. Hamlet says: 'But I have that within which passeth show – | These but the trappings and the suits of woe' (1.2.85–6). Like Stephen, he knows that in a world which judges by appearances, it is important to 'dress the character': Hamlet has his Wittenberg style as Stephen his Latin Quarter hat. Yet both men are also troubled by how little their clothes manage to say. The sadness remains unexpressed in words or 'inky cloaks', and certainly unresolved. Polonius illustrates the underlying problem, with his glib assurance to his son that 'the apparel oft proclaims the man' (1.3.72), a too-easy equation between avowal and feeling. Polonius is a shallow, courtly soul who judges only by appearances. The cloud pointed out to him by Hamlet is variously seen by him as like a camel, a weasel or a whale, depending on what his superior deems it at any moment to be: but the little cloud seen by Stephen and Leopold Bloom at the start of 16 June, although it appears at different locations, is clearly one and the same entity, not to be reduced to simile or metaphor. Yet that Dublin skyscape through which it moves does evoke memories of the pillar of cloud in the desert which drew the people of Israel on.

At the beginning of both works Hamlet and Stephen lack advancement and suffer from bad dreams. When Stephen sleeps in Sandycove Tower, which Haines likens to Elsinore 'that beetles o'er his base into the sea', he suffers unquiet slumber, being haunted by the spirit of his dead mother. His response to a ghost is less ambiguous than Hamlet's: 'Ghoul [. . .] Chewer of corpses [. . .] Let me be! Let me live!'[6] He does, nonetheless, share Hamlet's doubts about the revenger's role. Confronted by the Englishman, Haines, who epitomises the forces which have undone Ireland, he refuses Mulligan's invitation to avenge himself, recognising that the guilt-ridden usurper too has broken dreams: 'There's nothing wrong with him, except at night' (p. 7). Stephen prefers to keep free of all the grudges of a nightmarish past: 'You will not be master of others or their slave' (p. 56). In fact, he refuses to identify himself with any role, for a role would be a dreadful simplification. To entrap the self in a role would be to know again the humiliation reported in *A Portrait of the Artist as a Young Man* of having to hold down an abject and unworthy part.

In the past, Stephen had had some involvement with the actors of Yeats's emerging national theatre ('But I would not accounted be | One of the mumming company');[7] but he knows that Hamlet was too shrewd ever to take a part, contenting himself merely with writing or directing them. *Hamlet* is in fact an early warning system for Stephen that the intellectual may be one who can play every part except his own. Hamlet's sense of the theatrical quality of everyday life allows him to feign madness, puncture the facile acts of Rosencrantz, Guildenstern and Osric, coach the players in their parts, and teach Queen Gertrude how to assume virtues which she lacks. Obsessed with role-playing in a court of dissemblers, he is the modern discoverer of interior monologue as something that goes well beyond the stage soliloquy of earlier Renaissance drama – as Harold Bloom notes, he overhears or catches himself saying things and thinking things.[8]

What he overhears or hints at is precisely that part of him which 'passeth show', that element of himself which cannot be expressed in mere action and which no mere actor can represent. Those inner promptings ('that within') recall the monitions which revealed themselves to Homer's protagonists and to the Cuchulain of the Irish epic, to such a degree that Standish O'Grady argued that epic should never be played by mortal actors but should simply be left to the imagination. But tragic drama tries to break this interdiction. Invariably, it describes a protagonist whose self never quite fits the appointed role and whose self-awareness can never become fully incarnate in the action. The ghosts and spirits which appear from the past seem to epitomise that problem. They return precisely because of unfinished business, because they did not completely express themselves when alive. Yet they are crippled by their status as pure spirits, unable to do anything for themselves and able only to ask others to act on their behalf. For them, the ignominy of such powerlessness is akin to that of a Homer or a Shakespeare, or any other past master who necessarily leaves some of even his greatest work undone. As Leopold Bloom muses, in another context, in a late episode of *Ulysses*: 'You had to come back. To show the understudy in the title role how to' but the returnee always discovers that 'coming back was the worst thing you ever did because it went without saying you would feel out of place as things always moved with the times' (p. 757).

In that sense, fathers are always like ghosts. That is why Stephen identifies Shakespeare not with his greatest creation Prince Hamlet, but rather with the ghost of the dead king, whose (impossible) part he bravely played. By the time he wrote *Hamlet*, Shakespeare knew what the *Book of Common Prayer* proclaimed: it was no longer proper or even legal to talk *to* the dead. Now, one could only talk *about* them, in the third person.[9] Those spiritual forces which are suppressed in life will often reappear in art; and *Hamlet* certainly suggests that people, however sceptical, will continue to talk to the dead. Their attitude is rather like that taken by an Irish farmer towards the fairies in a local mound which his excavations inadvertently dug up: 'I don't believe in them – but they're there anyway.'[10] And the dead themselves may not even know that they are dead. To have lived is never quite enough, and so they talk on, hoping to achieve through their children what eluded them in life, a second chance. Such a second look at experience may be a blessing, transforming a person from one who is imprisoned by experience to a figure who is liberated by its inner meanings. But it can also be unnerving. Hamlet is never sure whether the ghost is honest; or even whether he is his father's son, for if Gertrude's love is fickle in the present, it may have been so in the past as well. Joyce also was tortured by this fear, the fear that only the mother truly knows her own children and that the doubts which trouble fathers may also assail offspring. Hamlet's inky cloak may in fact be designed to cover over his *lack* of inner feeling for the dead father, as well as masking his consequent hesitation over the need to avenge him.[11]

Whether Hamlet really sees a ghost or simply conjures up a spirit from a fevered mind is strictly irrelevant: for he talks to his dead father as surely as Stephen addresses his dead mother. A great deal of *Ulysses*, as of *Hamlet*, concerns the human commerce with the dead, but also with the act of dying, and even more with the state of being dead.[12] For all their powerlessness to act in the present – perhaps *because* of this very powerlessness – the spirits of the dead seem endlessly demanding, not to say peremptory. To a remarkable degree, the plot of *Hamlet* is dictated by the ghost. He sets the action up, directs his son on how to proceed, intervenes when the prince's resolve appears to weaken, prevents excessively rough handling of his former wife, and sees to it that there is a bloody catastrophe. Compared to all that, the son might seem rather derivative and pallid, a sort of cipher, but of course the ghost – and Shakespeare knew this – is really Hamlet's own interior monologue, embodying his dialogue with himself. So the hidden logic of the play (that the re-imagination of past lives comes to dominate all that is achieved in the present) is the principle which so impressed Joyce that he made it the very key to *Ulysses*.

Nor should that seem at all surprising. Joyce from childhood had been obsessed with the course of the past through the present. Like Hamlet and his creator Shakespeare, he was seeking to depict something that had never been quite so fully represented before. In order to do this, he had to enter unknown territory – 'that undiscovered country from whose bourn | No traveller returns' (III.1.81–2) – and to write out of unprecedented depths. Homer, Shakespeare and Joyce have their characters visit hell, as in all great epics; but, coming out of such lower depths, the act of writing, no less than the act of revenge, cannot be one man's only. As Karl Marx observed, whenever persons are about to do something radical or new, they nervously summon the spirits of the dead onstage and seek to portray themselves as secret sharers of past heroes. So the French revolutionaries of 1789, attempting to replace inherited rank with the meritocracy of careers open to talents, commissioned portraits of themselves clad in togas, as if they were restoring the democratic traditions of ancient Rome. In effect, they nerved themselves for the creation of something radical and new with the proposition that all it would entail was a restoration of something very familiar and very old. Analysing this phenomenon, Marx called it 'a nightmare weighing on the brain of the living', an astonishing anticipation of Joyce's Stephen, who calls history 'a nightmare from which I am trying to awake' (p. 42). Marx saw the need of the frightened revolutionary to connect the dead voices of the past to the as-yet unutterable, unrepresentable personae of the present, to 'that within which passeth show' (1.2.85).[13]

So the ghost speaks to Prince Hamlet as Homer speaks to Joyce. So the play-within-the-play is used by Hamlet, like the play-within-the-play that is the 'Circe' episode of *Ulysses*, to show just how much is yet left unsaid. The problem is obvious: how to complete an authentic action which expresses, rather than simplifying or falsifying, the inner self? Hamlet, at first sight, rejects the old plot of the prior play, a revenger's tragedy, because he is above and beyond such crude simplifications. What he wants is not revenge but wholeness and self-acceptance. The past text exists, but only as a scaffolding which must fall away, like those Roman costumes which must make way for the protagonists' own clothes.

At the age of thirty, after a protracted education as a courtier, scholar and soldier, Hamlet was about to come into his own, when he was unfortunate enough to meet a ghost. Henceforth, he could never fully become himself. Although the role of revenger was one to which he was ill-suited and ill-disposed, once that ghost had seized the centre-stage, Hamlet was destined to fill it, becoming in consequence a character obsessed with role-playing, able to play every part but his own. For Joyce, he became an example of what *not* to do, of how not to capitulate to the past. Marx believed that too often history was reduced to costume-drama, as revolutions lost their innovatory zeal and lapsed back into the farce of revivalism; and Hamlet certainly became in the end a prisoner of that costume drama which he himself had so early and so comprehensively mocked.

To know his deed, he has to postpone and finally cancel the moment when he might know himself. To murder the king, he must first abort his scarcely-born self. But even as he lies dying, that self has not gone away. The play-within-the play called life is over, but the troubled inner self remains; and the nearer it comes to the moment of truth, the harder it is to express that moment in words, the more time is 'lost' between episodes and the less expressible everything becomes:

> Had I but time – as this fell serjeant Death
> Is strict in his arrest – O, I could tell you –
> But let it be. Horatio, I am dead,
> Thou livs't.

> (v.2.88–90)

This is Shakespeare's own hint at the 'emotion in excess of the facts', to recall Eliot's words, which could never be completely uttered, at least not by him or by the players in his company. Perhaps, such feelings never could be fully expressed, but the speech remained a challenge for all subsequent writers. On the verge of death, Hamlet – like Conrad's Mr Kurtz three centuries later – found the experience almost unutterable. Odysseus, Jesus, Dante and Hamlet all descended into hell and reappeared in hopes of a reprieve, only to find at least some of their insights not negotiable in any human language. But writing is that undiscovered country from whose bourne some intrepid travellers do return, every few centuries, with the ability to articulate just a little more of what it is like to be in and out of the world. And, that may be why the young Joyce, who always knew his destiny, could not say what Albrecht Connolly asked him to.

Joyce recognised in Hamlet the problem of the neurotic modern intellectual, in whom the balance between inner and outer worlds has been lost. People, he understood, are happy only when for every force within them, there is an equivalent energy outside them. Stephen became an epitome of the same syndrome, for he was one in whom intellectual ability was so great as finally to immobilise him. If Prince Hamlet wondered whether the dead king had really been his father, that nagging doubt would explain why he appointed the court jester Yorick to that role, for 'he hath borne me on his back a thousand times' (V.1.180–1) as he made jokes to entertain the solitary child. In similar fashion, Stephen will 'appoint' Leopold Bloom to play the part of surrogate father, from whom he may learn how to act in a world which is quite flawed and uncertain in its meaning. By shifting his focus from Stephen to Bloom, Joyce moved from depicting the self to representing the institutions which frustrate its expression; but in between these manoeuvres he presents us with Bloom, the normalised Hamlet, the intellectual as Everyman.

This move is possible because of the ambiguity of Hamlet's age. He is thirty and so somewhere between what Joyce, referring to his two main characters, calls 'the boy of act one' and 'the mature man of act five' (p. 272). Romantic readers think of Hamlet as an unresolved youth, but by the standards of 1600 he was well on his way, more a Leopold than a Stephen. The skill with which Joyce eases Bloom into the role suggests the value of the second analogy. Bloom, like Hamlet, has lately 'forgone all custom of exercise' (IV.2.299), but resolves to put that right with Mr Sandow's body-building scheme. He is fat and scant of breath, but 'the shape is there still' (p. 212). He has a tendency to melancholy, but never fully gives into it, preferring to immerse himself in the real world of action. Like Hamlet, he stands in a graveyard and imagines what it must be like to be dead, quoting 'Alas, poor Yorick!'. But, most of all, Bloom's marital condition seems to repeat Hamlet's sexual difficulties with Ophelia.

If Bloom is a womanly man whose marriage has stalled, then Hamlet seems at least as effeminate. Sarah Bernhardt often played the part of Hamlet, as Mrs Bandman Palmer has once again done in Dublin of June 1904, prompting some apt thoughts in Bloom: 'Male impersonator. Perhaps he was a woman. Why Ophelia committed suicide' (p. 218). Bloom is well aware of his wife's sexual frustration, her desire for a lover 'the right height over me' (p. 923). Hamlet's own problems with women derived, in all likelihood, from the shattering of his faith in his own mother, after her over-hasty marriage to Claudius. Addicted to the theatrical, he feels nonetheless free to denounce it when he finds a pouting femininity performed by such soft and sensitive souls as Ophelia:

> I have heard of your paintings too, well enough; God has given you one face, and you make yourselves another. You jig, you amble, and you lisp, and nickname God's creatures, and make your wantonness your ignorance. Go to, I'll no more on't. It hath made me mad. (III.1.144–50).

Hamlet's obscene innuendoes to Ophelia are designed to bring out a more 'manly' side in her, which might complement the woman's part in him. But in this he fails. That androgyny which in Shakespeare's comedies made his women the heroines of each play here in the tragedies impels men to destruction. Hamlet is doomed to that very sensitivity which also brings down Lear (abjuring power) and even a killer like Macbeth (too full o' the milk of human kindness). Having idealised woman, he is revolted by her mere humanity. Having worshipped abstract ideals, he is disappointed to love simply mortal flesh:

> Get thee to a nunnery. Why wouldst thou be a breeder of sinners? I am myself indifferent honest, but yet I could accuse me of such things that it were better my mother had not borne me (III.1.122–5).

The fact that his dead father seems more concerned about his mother than his son seems to heighten the prince's loneliness and sense of betrayal by women. The thought that he may not really be the dead king's son is yet another reason to delay or even abandon the act of revenge. Equally deep is his resentment against a womanhood which expects men to strike macho poses which they may not truly believe in. Here, as much as anywhere, Hamlet anticipates the plight of Leopold Bloom:

> If thou dost marry, I'll give thee this plague for thy dowry: be thou as chaste as ice, as pure as snow, thou shalt not escape calumny. Get thee to a nunnery, go, farewell. Or if thou wilt needs marry, marry a fool; for wise men know well enough what monsters you make of them (III.1.137–42).

Hamlet was one of those unfortunate souls who wished to worship absolutely or not at all. Joyce shared this obsession with the dichotomy in western images of womanhood, between virgin and whore. For Shakespeare that ambiguity was summed up in the word 'nunnery', which could mean either a convent or a brothel.[14] Joyce once told his brother Stanislaus that Irishmen were interested in women only as street-walkers or as house-keepers[15] and having sampled the former in his adolescence, he fled the latter in his young manhood. He was never a believer in a spotless womanhood, seeing all too clearly how the double bind on Ophelia to play both virgin and trollop leads to her suicide. Joyce was obsessed with Act Four, Scene Five of *Hamlet*, in which Ophelia unleashed the obscene folk songs which were the predictable outcome of such repression. He knew by heart Queen Gertrude's later speech, in the seventh scene, on how the crazed girl strew flowers and then threw herself into the river. (A favourite party-piece with Willie Fallon was for Joyce to play Gertrude in the style of Biddy Mulligan, the Pride of Dublin's Coombe, while tossing cauliflowers and cabbages across the carpet.)[16] In *Ulysses*, Joyce attempted to reconcile the virgin/whore dichotomy in the figure of Gerty McDowell, who provides a false fusion, and later in the soliloquy of Molly Bloom, who seems a true balancing: but Joyce, through the ideas of Stephen, transferred his guilt about his dead unprayed-for mother onto Gertrude, depicted as a slave to her lusts.

Hamlet, like *Ulysses*, is not so much a celebration of a son's fidelity to his father as a lament for the lost integrity of the father-son relationship, which will never again achieve the unproblematic tenderness that is had in the *Odyssey*. That may be one reason why the references to *Hamlet* are manifest in *Ulysses*, while the citations of the *Odyssey* remain always implicit. Stephen's theory of Shakespeare manages, unknown to its sponsor, to highlight many analogies with Bloom's own life, from the moment when he was overborne in a field of feisty woman, through the period of 'assumed dongiovannism', down to the episode when he sent 'a lordling to woo for him by proxy' (p. 271; p. 243). But central to Stephen's conception is his rather self-flattering proposal that, in questions of paternity, the son holds the initiative.

Much as Joyce was free to convert *Hamlet* into a botched ur-text for *Ulysses*, Stephen contends that the son always has the power to reverse human chronology, so that his father, Simon Dedalus, will be found upon inspection to have 'my eyes'. Shakespeare's loss, says Stephen, is also his gain, because he is a son when he writes, but in addition someone aware, as Joyce was, that he too may be trumped, that 'futurity will forever father him'. Paternity is a legal fiction, because no man can be certain that his legal child derived from his seed; but it is also a fiction in a narrative sense because 'the corpse of John Shakespeare rests, disarmed of that mystical estate upon his son' (p. 266). Joyce, busy cannibalising so many previous epics, sensed that at some future time the same thing might de done to him. He may even have wished, sub-consciously, to speed up the process of his own reception by a futurity willing to father him, that futurity being embodied in the new democratic reader who knows how to interpret and recycle old texts.

Bloom, imagining himself in a bath, had thought of how he might contemplate his own penis, 'limp father of thousands' (p. 107): but Stephen in his library discourse implies as much of Shakespeare, who had become a father by the time he wrote the play. He had also lost his own son Hamnet, just as Bloom lost Rudy: 'He was not the father of his own son merely but, being no more a son, he was and felt himself the father of all his race, the father of his own grandfather, the father of his unborn grandson' (p. 267). Stephen believes that Shakespeare wrote *Hamlet* after his father's death, at that moment when a man realises that he is not going to live forever and when a son may come to seem more like a rival than an offspring. Stephen, having unconsciously read Bloom's life into Shakespeare's, now recklessly converts Shakespeare's attitude to sonship into little more than an anticipatory illumination of Stephen Dedalus's. The son is a new male, in such a scenario; 'his growth is his father's decline, his youth his father's envy, his friend his father's enemy'. There can be no love between fathers and sons in such a scheme, within which every son, having had a poor father, is compelled to reinvent him by the simple act of fathering himself. Not that this was anything new. It was a story at least as old as the *New Testament* itself: 'He who himself begot, middler the Holy Ghost, and Himself sent himself, Agenbuyer, between himself and others' (p. 253). Joyce knew that each new text redeems the past and makes the lines of the fore-text an incarnate fact.

Stephen uses Shakespeare in this way, like so many intellectuals of his age (not excluding Leopold Bloom), to resolve a real or imagined problem in his personal life: that of a feckless, improvident father. He can have no idea just how accurately prophetic of Bloom his complex portrait of Shakespeare actually is. There is in Stephen's discourse, as in all past epics, a utopian thrust into the future, a psychological surplus coming from his unconscious, which prepares him for the future meeting with Bloom. Already, he has dreamed of an eastern-looking man who will invite him into his home. Later, when their paths cross, they will both look into a mirror (that mirror which Hamlet said is held up to Nature) to see reflected back at them the face of Shakespeare, but a face whose features are paralysed, presumably by what Joyce has at this stage done to this father-figure too.

Crazy and monomaniacal though Stephen's theory of Shakespeare may be, it does contain the shape of his own destiny. Even as he disposes of one despised father, he begins the process of embracing an alternative, though not in a deliberated way. As the Player King had so sagely predicted in Shakespeare's play-within-a-play:

> But orderly to end where I begun,
> Our wills and faces do so contrary run
> That our devices still are overthrown;
> Our thoughts are ours, their ends none of our own.
>
> (III.2.201–4).

People, like the texts they produce, often subvert their own intended outcomes, as the unconscious undoes the will and brings all persons to a place in which they never expected to be. One way of explaining this would be to return to the *New Testament* in which Jesus said that, despite the randomness with which humanity governs its affairs, every hair on every human head is numbered by an external force. That text is much in Hamlet's mind after he returns from a death intended but somehow evaded. His statement that there is a special providence in the fall of a sparrow is a self-comparison with Jesus. There is a higher, if inscrutable, divine will, which may be at work behind the seeming folly of human affairs. Another way of accounting for this would be to see it as the unconscious, the uncharted inner depths being slowly and unpredictably excavated by literature and mapped onto the everyday mind. Either way, the overwrought intellectual, Hamlet or Stephen, must learn not to take on as a burden the woes of the entire world. Both men, marginal at best, have sought to give their marginality a transcendent importance by linking their personal problems to major public events. Hamlet plays at God by deciding whether the new king should live or die: but Stephen eventually learns that it is inside his own head, and nowhere else, that he must kill the priest or king.

The script of a life is never entirely self-assigned. Hamlet learns that it is sometimes better to act on instinct – 'praised be rashness' (v.2.7) – and ask questions later. Near the end of his life, he grows reckless in the knowledge that democratic death levels everything: 'A man may fish with a worm that hath eat of a king, and eat of the fish that hath fed that worm', with the consequence that 'a king may go a progress through the guts of a beggar' (IV.3.30–31). By a similar logic, in a graveyard one might find the noble dust of Alexander the Great 'stopping a bung-hole' (v.1.200). This was something Stephen Dedalus knew from the start: that matter exists only to be transformed into something more or less exalted than that with which it began: 'God becomes man becomes fish becomes barnacle goose becomes featherbed mountain' (p. 63). The neoplatonic lore, studied by Joyce in Marsh's Library, stated no less – man was 'In action how like an angel! In apprehension how like a god!' There could scarcely be a better description of the Bloom towards whom Stephen, even as he utters those lines, is moving. But the note of elegy is also present, for the same new Renaissance man is also 'this quintessence of dust' (II.2.301). Even in 1600 the greatest work produced by the era is a lament for a potential greatness, never fully sustained, never fully achieved.

Ulysses does keep faith with *Hamlet*'s deeper themes. Bloom, cuckolded like King Hamlet, seeks a son. Dressed in mourning, he enters the Holles Street Maternity Hospital 'ungyved', but with his 'beaver up' (p. 504), wearing the black suit as if lamenting his sundered marriage. The meeting between him and Stephen is entirely random, beyond any human control: but, of course, nothing is random when an epic Fate is at work behind the scenes. Stephen has the ability to think; Bloom has the inclination to act. The danger is that Stephen's consciousness is so gorgeous as to become an end in itself, unless it can be reclaimed for reality by a Bloom who offers a way of reconciling thought and deed.

Notes

1   Willie Fallon, *The Joyce We Knew*, ed. by Ulick O'Connor (Cork: Brandon Books, 1967), pp 46–7.

2   James Joyce, *A Portrait of the Artist as a Young Man*, ed. by Seamus Deane (Harmondsworth: Penguin, 1992), p. 86.

3   T. S. Eliot, *The Sacred Wood: Essays on Poetry and Criticism* (London: Methuen, 1920), p. 101.

4   On this see Harold Rosenborg, *Act and the Actor: Making the Self* (Chicago: University of Chicago Press, 1983), pp 74–103. I am much indebted to this.

5   Quoted by Alexander Welsh, *Hamlet in His Modern Guises* (Princeton: Princeton University Press, 2001), p. 150.

6   James Joyce, *Ulysses*, ed. by Declan Kiberd, Annotated Student's Edition (Harmondsworth: Penguin, 1992), p. 11. Subsequent references are given within the text.

7   James Joyce, *Critical Writings*, ed. by Ellsworth Mason and Richard Ellmann (New York: Viking Press, 1959), p. 150.

8   Harold Bloom, *Hamlet: Poem Unlimited* (New York: Riverhead, 2003), pp 118–19; see also Welsh, *Hamlet in His Modern Guises*, p. 64.

9   Eamon Duffy, *The Stripping of the Altars* (New Haven: Yale University Press, 1992), p. 475.

10 Seán O'Faoláin recounts a version of this conversation in the introduction to *The Irish* (Harmondsworth: Penguin, 1948).

11 See Bloom, *Hamlet: Poem Unlimited*, p. 8; and William Kerrigan, *Hamlet's Perfection* (Baltimore: Johns Hopkins University Press, 1994), p. 70.

12 C. S. Lewis, 'The Prince and the Poem', in *Hamlet*, ed. by O. J. Campbell, A. Rothschild and S. Vaughan (New York: Bantam, 1961), p. 248.

13 The preceding quotations of Marx are taken from his 'The Eighteenth Brumaire of Louis Bonaparte', *Surveys from Exile*, ed. by David Fernbach (Harmondsworth: Penguin, 1973), *passim*.

14 See Campbell, Introduction, *Hamlet*, p. 6.

15 Stanislaus Joyce, *My Brother's Keeper*, ed. by Richard Ellmann (London: Faber & Faber, 1958), p. 164.

16 See C. P. Curran, *James Joyce Remembered* (Oxford: Oxford University Press, 1958), p. 22.

CHAPTER 7

George Bernard Shaw and the Politics of Bardolatry

Cary DiPietro

PUPPET POLEMICS

In January of 1949, less than two years before his death in November 1950, George Bernard Shaw penned his last complete dramatic work, the puppet play *Shakes versus Shav*. The short piece, a mere one hundred lines commissioned for the Malvern Festival and performed at the Malvern Marionette Theatre later that year, stages an impossible confrontation between the two puppet figures William Shakes and Shav, or G. B. S., as the puppet calls himself using the pen-name Shaw adopted as a music and theatre critic much earlier in his career. The premise for the work was not his own, but had been initiated when the theatre's puppet master, Waldo Lanchester, sent Shaw figures of the two puppets with a request to supply a ten-minute drama for them. Lanchester must have realised that the finished piece would represent the culmination of a life-long one-way relationship in which Shaw cultivated a sense of rivalry and antagonism between himself and his literary predecessor, and he must have delighted in the resulting play, the title of which pointedly reflected Shaw's self-created *agon*. In the preface that accompanied the play's first print publication in 1949, Shaw himself wrote, 'This in all actuarial probability is my last play and the climax of my eminence, such as it is.'[1] After this observation follows a reflection upon his lifelong interest in Shakespeare: 'Nothing can extinguish my interest in Shakespear. It began when I was a small boy, and extends to Stratford-upon-Avon, where I have attended so many bardic festivals that I have come to regard it almost as a supplementary birthplace of my own' (p. 470). Such admissions of genuine admiration, which appear throughout Shaw's body of writing, occur in sharp contrast to the vituperative denigration and often comic invective that Shaw more commonly, and notoriously, directed towards Shakespeare. Shaw perpetuated a view of himself by turns throughout his career as Shakespeare's inheritor, reincarnation, demolisher and improver, and this is the note upon which the preface to the play then concludes: 'Enough too for my feeling that the real Shakespear might have been myself, and for the shallow mistaking of it for mere professional jealousy' (p. 471).

Shaw's is a playful, but very serious, iconoclasm. In the opening speech, Shakes, predictably in blank verse, declares that an 'infamous impostor. . .'

> . . . in an ecstasy of self-conceit
> Shortens my name to Shav, and dares pretend
> Here to reincarnate my very self (p. 473).

He then goes on to call Shav, just before the second puppet enters, a caitiff and a 'fiend of Ireland'. Their initial short banter very quickly devolves into a comic brawl in the style of Punch and Judy that sees Shakes first knocking Shav down to a count of nine ('Hackerty-backerty one, Hackerty-backerty two. . .'), after which '*Shav springs up and knocks Shakes down with a right to the chin*' ('Hackerty-backerty one . . . Hackerty-backerty ten. Out.'). After their brief physical encounter, the two continue to argue about whose drama packs the heavier punch, but this verbal banter takes second seat to the spectacle of puppetry; the two characters play the audience to short dramatic vignettes, one of which sees Walter Scott's Rob Roy besting Macbeth by cutting of his head, which Macbeth then picks up and tucks under his arm while he walks off to the tune of British Grenadiers. The playful encounter between Shakes and Shav ends, all too quickly, on a note of rapprochement. After Shakes references his own supposed dramatic swansong, *The Tempest* ('The great globe itself, / Yea, all which it inherit, shall dissolve. . .'), Shav offers his last words:

> Peace, jealous Bard:
> We both are mortal. For a moment suffer
> My glimmering light to shine (p. 477).

The idea of Shakespeare's jealousy of Shaw is humorously anachronistic. This was Shaw's joke to deflate the admitted 'self-conceit' of positioning himself as Shakespeare's rival, a vanity perhaps not unjustified for a non-agenarian with a dramatic canon nearly double in size to that of Shakespeare. Yet despite its dismissive humour, *Shakes versus Shav* is consistent with a life's worth of writing that, on the one hand, was informed and inspired by Shakespeare's writing, but in which, on the other hand, Shaw used Shakespeare as a critical counterpoint to advance his own artistic and political agendas. Also made in jest is Shaw's self-denigration, voiced early in the play by Shakes, as a 'fiend of Ireland'. The epithet is little more than a token nod to Shaw's place of birth, but the antagonism of an otherwise trivial joke still raises the spectre of a political crisis that loomed in the background of Shaw's more than five decades as a dramatist in the British theatre. Indeed, Shaw's relationship to his homeland was not unlike that of his relationship to Shakespeare, one of affection and admiration tinged with nostalgia, but marked by a desire to separate himself from the past and by deliberate disavowal, in the case of Ireland, of a 'romantic nationalism'.[2] The diversity of Shaw's often contradictory commentary, whether on the topic of Shakespeare or Ireland, was also largely the product of his dialecticism, his ability to see and assume both sides of a debate, in a voice characteristically punctuated with hyperbole, and to stage such debate as we find in *Shakes versus Shav*. Shaw's style in this late work, however, is not wholly dialectical, with Shaw speaking for and pulling the strings of his literary rival, and engaged in his own tense, evidently violent, negotiation of counter-identity. Even at this very late, perhaps retrospective, point in his career, Shaw's is a conscious self-fashioning within and against a literary tradition, a tradition inevitably defined, however dismissively, by an antagonism between Irish and British writing.

Irish by birth and, throughout his life, ineffably bound to the landscape of his youth, Shaw spent the vast majority of his life and the entirety of his professional writing career in England. After a brief stint as a cashier in a Dublin estate office, Shaw emigrated to London at the young age of twenty in the mid-1870s because he believed that his literary aspirations could not be accommodated in Dublin. Emigration, therefore, 'was practically compulsory'.[3] Once in England – and he would not return to Ireland for twenty-nine years – his literary career, though slow to start, flourished, and the inertia of success and establishment kept Shaw writing, first, in London, and later, from the ascetic comfort of the Rectory House, 'Shaw's Corner', in Ayot St Lawrence in Hertfordshire. Unlike his expatriate contemporaries such as Joyce, Shaw rarely returned to the imaginative landscape of Ireland in his dramatic writing; his 1904 *John Bull's Other Island*, commissioned by Yeats, though never produced for the Abbey Theatre, is the only play directly connected with Ireland. Nor was he particularly invested in the Irish Renaissance whose literary highpoints coincided with the peaks of his own career. Shaw had little sympathy for the Celtic Revival and the mythology of a rustic Irish past idealised in the works of his Irish contemporaries. He would write later in his life: 'If I had gone to the hills nearby to look back upon Dublin and to ponder upon myself, I too might have become a poet like Yeats, Synge, and the rest of them.'[4] He clearly believed, with little trace of regret, that his own writing was not distinctly Irish because he did not engage in the introspective nationalism of his Irish contemporaries, looking on Dublin and pondering upon himself. Instead, he turned his sights to London, and beyond to Europe, to the land of Ibsen and Chekhov.

At the same time, Shaw would periodically reference his Irish birth as a marker of his difference, to position his work strategically against that of his

English contemporaries and predecessors in his own dramatic and theatrical campaigns. Just before *Shakes versus Shav*, he wrote: 'I have lived for twenty years in Ireland and for seventy-two in England; but the twenty came first, and in Britain I am still a foreigner and shall die one.'[5] His status as a foreigner in England allowed him an objective view of the English, an objectivity of which no English writer was capable, while, by the same token, his Irish birth made an objective view of Ireland impossible. In a different and contradictory vein, Shaw would also suggest that his own writing was more Irish than that of any of his contemporaries because only by leaving Ireland could the writer come to a real understanding of what it meant to be Irish.[6] His Irishness was therefore rhetorically convenient, and could be called upon in his social and literary commentary to serve different purposes. In one moment, he might be disparaging the idea of an Irish literary renaissance that erroneously romanticised Ireland's past rather than negotiating its place within and against the rich tradition of British literature. In another moment, he might be renouncing, as an outsider, a British theatre that had yet to acknowledge and accommodate the New Drama of Europe that he was both advocating and writing.

Throughout his writing career, Shaw worked in this manner both within and against a canonical British literature, importantly, a literature whose own sense of what it meant to be British was being renegotiated by Britain's gradual devolution through the same period, a devolution most vocally punctuated in England by the ongoing debate about, first, Irish Home Rule, and later, independence and unity. Shaw's voice, though perhaps not prominently, was heard within this debate because, being Irish and being Shaw, he could be neither complacent nor silent. Shaw was an early advocate of Irish Home Rule, though he was cautious to note that fierce partisanship would make difficult any attempt at self-government either within a devolved Britain or, later, as an independent nation. He argued, however, that any Irish nationalism would need to be ancillary to the objectives of European socialism more broadly.[7] Shaw's tendency to speak from different sides of the debate, and to punctuate his positions with rhetorical overstatement, was combined with an unsentimental view of contemporary Ireland, a view no doubt determined by his own childhood experiences in the religious minority of an impoverished Dublin. The complications produced by his polemics were confusing, if not occasionally inflammatory for the Irish themselves, especially his unpopular disavowal of an Irish nationalism. Writing in 1913 for *The New Statesmen*, Shaw would argue that nationalism in general was 'nothing but a mode of self-consciousness, and a very aggressive one at that'.[8] But Shaw was also aware of the practical need to recognise a politically autonomous Ireland as an antidote to British Empire, empire itself the ultimate consequence of a European capitalism antithetical to his own socialist agenda, and he advocated for Ireland's place within a devolved British commonwealth. If, on the one hand, Shaw repudiated a romanticised Irish nationalism as a dangerous and potentially volatile form of political self-actualisation, on the other hand, he also recognised that he was himself invested in ethnicities determined by both shared and distinct cultural traditions bound to the geography and history of a diverse and ever-changing Great Britain.[9]

In his ninety-second year, Shaw would thus define his identity as externally British and eternally Irish, a nostalgic, perhaps unsatisfying, but ultimately pragmatic and personal negotiation of identity.[10] If Shaw's rhetorical polemics complicate his identity as an Irish expatriate living in England from the turn to the middle of the twentieth century, as a writer, Shaw himself complicates the distinction, necessarily a politically charged one, between Irish and British writing. Shaw's relationship to Shakespeare, I would argue, is similarly charged by a mixture of rivalry and censure combined with admiration and nostalgia. Even while Shaw's sense of Irishness rarely enters his commentary on Shakespeare explicitly or directly, and this is perhaps a revealing omission, what I want to explore here through a range of direct and indirect Shavian encounters with Shakespeare – including *Caesar and Cleopatra*, *The Dark Lady of the Sonnets*, *Saint Joan*, *Cymbeline Refinished*, and *Shakes versus Shav* – are the connections between Shaw's conflicted, often antagonistic, relationship to Shakespeare and his own identity, fond as he was of paradox, as both an Irish and British writer.

SHAKESPEARE REFINISHED

The combative pretext for Shaw's encounter with Shakespeare largely began when he was invited by Frank Harris in late 1894 to write as theatre critic for the *Saturday Review*. Shaw had already made his reputation in London as a music critic with a penchant for inflammatory rhetoric writing for *The World*. It was during this earlier period that Shaw was beginning to carve out his dramatic career with a series of controversial and mostly unsuccessful plays that would later be collected as his *Plays Unpleasant* in 1898.[11] When he moved to Harris's magazine, G. B. S., as he now signed himself in his columns, turned his delightfully witty venom on such histrionic actor-managers as Augustin Daly, Herbert Beerbohm Tree and, his favourite target, Henry Irving. In what is perhaps his best known Shakespeare review, of Irving's 1896 *Cymbeline* at the Lyceum Theatre, Shaw wrote of Irving: 'This curious want of connoisseurship in literature would disable Sir Henry Irving seriously if he were an interpretive actor. . . The truth is that he has never in his life conceived or interpreted the characters of any author except himself' (*Saturday Review*, 26 September 1896).[12] Shaw here took aim at what was thought to be Irving's particular talent for breaking the moulds of theatrical tradition to create his own unique character interpretations (he had even been knighted for it), and that a relatively minor theatre critic with ambitious and, as yet, unfulfilled dramatic aspirations of his own should do so was nothing short of scandalous.

The majority of the column, however, places blame for the production's deficiencies squarely upon Shakespeare: '[*Cymbeline*] is for the most part stagey trash of the lowest melodramatic order, in parts abominably written, throughout intellectually vulgar, and judged in point of thought by modern intellectual standards vulgar, foolish, offensive, indecent, and exasperating beyond all tolerance.' Fittingly, Shaw titled the review 'Blaming the Bard'. Shakespeare, according to Shaw, was a pilferer of other men's stories and ideas, whose 'rhetorical fustian' and 'unbearable platitudes' reduced the 'subtlest problems of life to commonplaces'. The inevitable self-comparison would then follow: 'With the single exception of Homer, there is no single eminent writer, not even Sir Walter Scott, whom I can despise so entirely as I despise Shakespear when I measure my mind against his.' Shaw's insistence on the unusual spelling of 'Shakespear', certainly in the spirit but without the sense of his other spelling reforms, amplified the belligerence of his irreverent treatment of Shakespeare, who was, quite remarkably for Shaw, intellectually sterile. Within the space of a few lines, though, he would continue: 'But I am bound to add that I pity the man who cannot enjoy Shakespear. He has outlasted thousands of abler thinkers, and will outlast a thousand more.' Despite an intellectual vacuity, Shakespeare had an unparalleled gift for story-telling combined with an 'enormous power over language', what Shaw would repeatedly describe throughout his career as Shakespeare's word-music.[13] Where Shakespeare failed in content, he excelled in style, particularly by way of the incomparable musical quality of his verse with its carefully measured cadences and rhythms.

But Shakespeare needed to be refined intellectually, even corrected, a task that Shaw would undertake some forty years later in his *Cymbeline Refinished*. His reworking of Shakespeare's play was first begun in 1936, occasioned by what he called an emergency in the theatre, when it was proposed that *Cymbeline* be revived for production at the Shakespeare Memorial Theatre. As a member of the SMT Committee, Shaw proposed, partly in jest, to rewrite the final act because, 'though one of the finest of Shakespeare's later plays now on the stage', *Cymbeline* 'goes to pieces' in the end: 'the act is a tedious string of unsurprising *dénouments* sugared with insincere sentimentality after a ludicrous stage battle', he wrote in his 1945 preface. To his surprise, the proposal was met with applause, and the reworked version soon followed. While it retains eighty-nine of Shakespeare's lines, *Cymbeline Refinished* dispenses with such 'stagey trash' as the descent of Jupiter on eagle's wings as *deus ex machina* and the identification of Guiderius by a mole on his neck, supplying in place of the 'melodrama' a largely naturalistic and significantly pared down single scene written competently in blank verse. 'This came very easily to me', he wrote. 'It happened when I was a child that one of the books I delighted in was an illustrated Shakespear, with a picture and two or three lines of text underneath it on every third or fourth page. Ever since, Shakespearean blank verse has been to me as natural a form of literary expression as the Augustan English to which I was brought up in Dublin.'[14] As in the later preface to *Shakes versus Shav*, Shaw's self-identification with Shakespeare's word-music is closely bound up here with a nostalgic recollection of his Irish boyhood.

His otherwise low opinion of *Cymbeline*, as he also wrote in 1945, derived from what was to his memory the last known revival of Shakespeare's play, Irving's 1896 production. During the period leading up to his caustic review in 1896, Shaw had engaged in a long correspondence with Ellen Terry who was to play Imogen to Irving's Iachimo (a 'statue of romantic melancholy' in Shaw's fifty-year-old memory).[15] Their correspondence was motivated on Shaw's part by his desire to lure her from the Lyceum under Irving's management to a new kind of drama and a new kind of theatre; to roles he was writing especially for her, such as Lady Cicely Waynflete in *Captain Brassbound's Conversion*, a role she would eventually agree to take on in Shaw's 1906 production at the Royal Court Theatre. Shaw recognised that the actor-manager system favoured star-vehicles, plays with prominent roles for leading men whose popularity (both play and actor) would sustain long and therefore commercially lucrative runs in London's West End theatres. The system perpetuated a cult of theatre personality that ran counter to his own more naturalistic drama. More to the point, the metropolitan managers were all men, and Terry would therefore always have second billing in plays chosen, and often horribly butchered, to showcase Irving's talent. But Shaw's criticism of Irving was inseparably bound to his belief that Shakespeare was also and equally 'as dead *dramatically* as a doornail'. Thus, he wrote to Terry, 'when you have finished with Imogen, finish with Shakespeare . . . Time flies; and you must act *something* before you die.'[16]

There is obvious irony not only in the fact of Shaw's later involvement in the committee to establish a permanent memorial theatre for the production of Shakespeare, despite Shakespeare being dead as a doornail, but also in the fact of Shaw's revision of Shakespeare after the fashion of eighteenth and nineteenth-century theatrical improvers of whom he was so critical. While he acknowledged the irony, there was an important difference to note. When he began to study the play for the purpose of revision in 1936, Shaw realised that his judgement of the writing had been clouded by his memory of Irving's performance: the doggerel was not doggerel, but versified masque written in the style of popular courtly entertainment. The court masque was *de rigueur* in the time of 'King Jamie', and Shakespeare was therefore obliged to indulge his audience with dramatic fashion. In the absence of music and pictorial spectacle, the last act of the play was otherwise tedious melodrama. Updating *Cymbeline* for a modern audience therefore meant rewriting 'the act as Shakespeare might have written it if he had been post-Ibsen and post-Shaw instead of post-Marlowe' (Preface, p. 183).

Shaw had experimented, somewhat less directly, with such updating of Shakespeare in the past. In 1898, he wrote his *Caesar and Cleopatra*, published in 1901 as one of the *Three Plays for Puritans* that also included *Captain Brassbound's Conversion*. Shaw's history play stages the encounter – though, importantly, not an affair – between Julius Caesar and Cleopatra that occurs prior to the narrative events of Shakespeare's own *Julius Caesar* (*c*.1599). The historical material is derived principally from Plutarch and Roman sources, though filtered through the work of the nineteenth-century German classicist Theodor Mommsen. Shaw's Caesar is evidently indebted to Mommsen's multivolume *History of Rome* (1854–6) in which Caesar is portrayed as a noble and gifted statesman, unlike the 'admitted failure' of Shakespeare's character: 'But Shakespear, who knew human weakness so well, never knew human strength of the Caesarian type', Shaw wrote in the long preface to *Three Plays for Puritans*. 'Caesar was not in Shakespear, nor in the epoch, now fast waning, which he inaugurated.'[17] Shakespeare's characters – including the eponymous characters from the later play *Anthony and Cleopatra* (*c*.1606) – lacked heroism and idealism because Shakespeare himself was limited by the inadequate philosophical outlook of renaissance England. This was the extent of Shaw's revision of Shakespeare, rewriting historical events and persons presented to him 'in light of his own time' (p. 45). In this manner, Shaw corrected the libel of Caesar's character that, he believed, had been perpetuated by Shakespeare's *Julius Caesar* over the course of three centuries to recast Caesar as a model of heroism and leadership in the present tense.[18]

Such historical revisionism was also the project of Shaw's 1923 play *Saint Joan*, written in the period following the canonisation of Joan of Arc in 1920. This later play was a much greater critical success for Shaw, and is thought to have been one of the main reasons that he was awarded the Nobel Prize for Literature in 1925, though he had established a critical reputation following such plays as *Man and Superman* (first staged in 1905), *Pygmalion* (in England, in 1914), and *Heartbreak House* (in 1921). *Saint Joan* is more obviously a case of revising received history, Shaw having sought to counter the vilification of Joan of Arc by both her French contemporaries and by the 'scurrilous' representation of her character in Shakespeare's chronicle history play, *Richard, Duke of York* or the first part of *Henry VI* (*c*.1590), where she appears as Joan La Pucelle. The English chronicles, from which Shakespeare derived the Joan La Pucelle character, demonised her for seeking to expel the English from France, and this was precisely the anti-English, anti-imperialist nationalism that Shaw sought to foreground in his characterisation of Joan of Arc in his own play.[19] Joan proved an attractive figure for Shaw precisely because he believed her to have been an unattractive figure, a strong woman of unassuming appearance 'whose genius was turned to practical account mainly in soldiering and politics' (Preface, p. 20). The task of recasting Joan of Arc as a figure of determination and strength who openly embraced typically masculine behaviour and attire at the expense of her femininity represented Shaw's attempt to de-romanticise her, to free her from the prejudices and biases of the nineteenth century, especially from those who viewed women as a separate species of animal 'with specific charms and specific imbecilities' (p. 20).

The long preface written in 1924 to accompany the play's publication is therefore an exercise in demystification (not unlike his demystification of Shakespeare), Shaw's broad objective being to address the historical misrepresentation of her character and, in particular, to debunk the lore of her Catholic martyrdom and visions (the title is deliberately ironic), even while the play pays tribute to her strength as a woman and 'visionary' in the context of medieval France. As a result, much of the preface is concerned with matters of historiography: the distance between historical epochs, in this case, the religious and political disparities that separate the medieval from the modern; the distortions produced by literary conventions of narrative, particularly the generic conventions of tragedy; and the inevitable moulding of history to reflect the present. The play's Joan, while, according to Shaw, more accurately medieval than any other previous version of her character, is also a model of the 'unwomanly woman' that he praised in the drama of Ibsen in the seminal essay of his early career, *The Quintessence of Ibsenism* (1891): 'She was the pioneer of rational dressing for women', Shaw wrote in the preface to *Saint Joan*, 'she refused to accept the specific woman's lot, and dressed and fought and lived as men did' (p. 15). While we may want to question the nature of his feminism, such praise for Joan as a woman who scorned conventional femininity was in keeping with Shaw's own practical support for the rights of women in the post-Suffrage period.

Neither *Caesar and Cleopatra* nor *Saint Joan* are revisions of Shakespeare in the sense of *Cymbeline Refinished*; indeed, in the preface to *Saint Joan*, Shaw questions Shakespeare's authorship of the early Henriad plays altogether, suggesting that they were, at best, merely improved by Shakespeare, and not by much, after minor revisions. But the fact that Shaw made the effort to link both plays in their respective prefaces to Shakespeare and his time by way of shared subject matter not only gives evidence to his desire to rewrite and correct history, but raises the point that Shaw's relationship to Shakespeare was largely determined by his understanding of history. That Shaw could extol Shakespeare's word-music even while he abhorred the lack of noble ideas or characters in his plays was not a contradiction, but rather a distinction between form and content, a distinction that was historically contingent. He could never improve upon Shakespeare's style, nor claim to write better plays: in a section of the preface to *Three Plays for Puritans* titled 'Better than Shakespear?' – a title that claims a place for Shaw as Shakespeare's successor even while it questions the presumptuous act of self-comparison—he admitted, 'do not be surprised by my modesty – I do not profess to write better plays . . . No man will ever write a better tragedy than Lear' (pp 41–2). Shaw could, however, answer to the philosophical inadequacy, the intellectual paucity, that marked the difference between Shakespeare's epoch and his own. Such claims about the limitations of Shakespeare's philosophy were shocking, and intentionally so, in an era dominated by such essayists as Walter Raleigh and, later, A. C. Bradley, both of whose works perpetuated a romanticist belief in the universality and timelessness of Shakespeare's characters and dramas.[20] For Shaw's contemporary and critic, G. K. Chesterston, such iconoclasm was motivated by Shaw's Irishness, by 'the attitude of the Irishman objecting to the Englishman turning his mere artistic taste into a religion; especially when it was a taste merely taught him by his aunts and uncles. In Shaw's opinion (one might say) the English do not really enjoy Shakespeare or even admire Shakespeare; one can only say, in the strong colloquialism, that they swear by Shakespeare. He is a mere god; a thing to be invoked.'[21] In the 1901 'Better than Shakespear?', Shaw would give the name 'bardolatry' to such unquestioned and uncritical reverence of Shakespeare, a neologism combining praise of the bard with the worship of idols.

SHAVIAN HISTORY

In another moment of characteristic bluster, Shaw would write that Shakespeare was 'for an afternoon, but not for all time', rephrasing lines from Ben Jonson's dedicatory poem to the 1623 First Folio.[22] The outrageousness of such claims made his criticism of Shakespeare hard to swallow for many of his contemporaries such as Chesterton: how could Shaw, in the face of 300 years of critical appreciation and a long heritage of performance in the theatre, deride so vehemently Shakespeare's critical faculty, denying the scope and variety of his thought, even while he praised his word melodies? On the one hand, Shaw's sense of history, as evidenced by his belief in the philosophical sophistication of his own time relative to that of Shakespeare, is demonstrative of a Shavian grand narrative that is essentially Hegelian in nature: Shakespeare stands at the threshold of an epochal modernity at the other end of which stands Shaw on the point of epochal change. This was the view of history that lay behind Shaw's correction of Joan of Arc. The Elizabethans were too close to see her clearly, where Shaw could write with a full view of the Middle Ages: 'The Renascence [*sic*] of antique literature and art in the sixteenth century, and the lusty growth of Capitalism, between them buried the Middle Ages; and their resurrection is a second Renascence' (p. 70). Shaw's understanding of such historical change is undoubtedly connected to his reading of Marx, his subsequent turn to and advocacy of English Fabianism, and the role he envisioned for the theatre in the turn to international socialism. Importantly, Shaw's long campaign against Shakespeare was always connected to practical Shavian agendas, whether he was extolling the virtues of leadership and heroism in a demoralised modern world, advocating for the role of women in society, or campaigning for a nationally subsidised repertory theatre. Moreover, his position on Shakespeare was, unlike his politics, far from doctrinal, but was rather, not unlike his Irishness, rhetorically useful and could be called upon to serve his political agendas as required. Shaw's Irishness allowed him that external perspective, that critical vantage point from which he could critique Shakespeare in ways that his English contemporaries could not, even while he remained invested in the long tradition of British literature.

On the other hand, Shaw's tendency was to read this modernity almost exclusively in terms of the nineteenth century and, by extension, the romanticist idealisation of Shakespeare. Even when he looks back to the Elizabethan period, Shaw's Shakespeare is the Romantic Shakespeare. His childhood edition, remembered fondly from his boyhood in Ireland, is one of the popular and inexpensive illustrated editions that proliferated in the mid-nineteenth century, perhaps a children's volume modelled upon Mary and Charles Lamb's 1807 *Tales from Shakespeare*.[23] His theatrical memories are those of the actor-managers who dominated the London stage from the period of his residency in London from the 1880s to the early twentieth century. His critical encounter with Shakespeare is filtered through the readings of eighteenth and nineteenth-century essayists such as Johnson, Hazlitt and Coleridge, whose own volumes were still in frequent reprint. Not unlike many of his later modernist contemporaries in England, from T. S. Eliot to L. C. Knights, when Shaw took aim at Shakespeare, he took aim at romanticist conventions of performance and criticism. His targets in the theatre were the lavish productions by those actor-managers who mangled the texts and decorated their stages with superfluous settings and costumes to attract the growing bourgeois audiences of London. By comparison, he would often praise the semi-professional and often non-commercial productions by little-known amateur and repertory groups, including antiquarian productions such as those by William Poel. While Shaw was not a Shakespeare essayist and did not write Shakespeare criticism, in his theatre reviews and play prefaces, he would often take aim at those critics who assumed they were writing about a god and therefore 'rejected every consideration of fact, tradition, or interpretation, that pointed to any imperfection in their hero'.[24] When Shaw remembers

Shakespeare warmly as a formative experience of his boyhood, his nostalgia is precisely that, an act of memory that marks a separation, a necessary disjuncture, between a romanticised, sentimentalised past and a de-romanticised present.

No other play exemplifies Shaw's anti-romantic platform better than *The Dark Lady of the Sonnets*, written and performed in 1910, and later published in a 1914 collection. This short dramatic piece not only incorporates Shakespeare as a character, but also turns upon a biographical interpretation of Shakespeare's sonnets, in particular, as the title would suggest, his relationship to the so-called 'dark lady' to whom sonnets 127 to 152 are addressed. In the play, the dark lady is Mary Fitton, historically, a young woman in Queen Elizabeth's court who was at the centre of a court disgrace involving Lord William Herbert. Fitton had conducted an affair with the young Herbert, Earl of Pembroke, whose initials were thought, in the accompanying sonnet theory, to evidence his identity as the dedicatee of the 1609 Quarto edition, the 'onlie begetter of these insuing sonnets Mr W. H.', and ostensibly the mysterious youth to whom sonnets 1 to 126 are addressed. The play stages an imaginary encounter between Shakespeare and Fitton, a midnight tryst in the gardens of the Palace at Whitehall, that occurs prior to her affair with Pembroke (in the theory, after being introduced to one another by Shakespeare, who is later betrayed by them). In the 1914 preface to the play, Shaw actually denied the viability of the Pembroke/Fitton theory altogether. The play's plot had been given to him by Edith Lyttleton after Shaw had been invited by the National Shakespeare Memorial Committee to produce a short dramatic piece in aid of its cause. The 1914 preface is largely devoted to discussing Shaw's confrontation with Frank Harris over the Fitton theory. Harris had published his own play in 1910, *Shakespeare and His Love*, an altogether more serious, and decidedly inferior, attempt to stage the triangular relationship between Shakespeare, Pembroke and Fitton. When he read the announcement in late 1910 that Shaw's play was to be produced in the theatre, while his own play had yet to inspire the interest of a theatrical manager, Harris was incensed and accused Shaw of plagiarising, of wholly annexing, his Pembroke–Fitton theory. Shaw's defence against Harris was to deflate the sonnet theory that lay behind the play, and to emphasise the irony of his own comic 'pièce d'occasion'.[25]

Despite the humour, however, the play's portrait of Shakespeare is recognisably Shavian. Before he encounters Fitton, 'Shakespear' first comes across the cloaked figure of Queen Elizabeth, sleepwalking like Lady Macbeth and cursing the spots of blood that will not out. When Shakespear mistakes her for Mary Fitton, the audience learns that Elizabeth is suffering a furtive guilt for the execution of Mary, Queen of Scots, as she mutters in her sleep a line that echoes *Macbeth*: 'Mary! Mary! Who would have thought that woman to have had so much blood in her!' (p. 313). Shakespear is immediately enamoured by the music of her words and their perfect melody, and when he is warned by the powerful Queen, now awoken from her somnambulant state, to 'season his admiration for a while', he reaches for his tablets to write down what his extremely poor memory will not retain: 'What was it? "Suspend your admiration for a space –"' (p. 314). Shakespear and the cloaked lady continue their conversation, during which she accuses him of being 'saucy' and 'overbold'. Even after the entrance of the dark lady Fitton, and the revelation of Queen Elizabeth's identity, Shakespear remains impudent, confident in his own immortal talent: '"not marble nor the gilded monuments of princes shall outlive" the words with which I make the world glorious or foolish at my will' (p. 321). The portrait of Shakespeare drawn in the play is so evidently characteristic of Shaw. His Shakespear has an ear for word music, though he lacks the imagination to write his own melodies, and he is more than happy to pilfer ideas and phrases from other sources, even while suffering from an overconfidence in his own greatness and immortality.

Through the second half of the play, Shakespear takes up the cause of the National Theatre, pleading to the Queen the necessity to establish a permanent home for a national drama, a theatre that would be both repertory and non-commercial. Shaw had been involved in the National Theatre campaign in England from its earliest days, a campaign that began in the 1880s with such prominent advocates as William Archer, a campaign that would continue until the National Theatre Act of 1949. The Royal Court Theatre, run by the joint management of Shaw, Harley Granville-Barker and John Vedrenne between 1904 and 1907, had witnessed the production of many of Shaw's early plays, his first important successes, under this repertory subscription system. Granville-Barker, whose own plays were also frequently produced at the Court Theatre, had authored with William Archer the most important volume in the campaign, *A National Theatre: Schemes and Estimates*, a scheme modelled upon the successful Court experiment. *The Dark Lady of the Sonnets*, written in 1910, thus appeared at the height of the National Theatre fervour. For Shaw, however, such a theatre would not only house a national drama, but would serve as a venue for the New Drama of the continent, combining the work of the Court Theatre with that of such groups as the Stage Society, widely acclaimed in the early twentieth century for their English productions of Ibsen and Chekhov.

This is the model of theatre that Shaw envisions through the medium of Shakespear, an antidote to the commercial theatres of London: 'Madam,' he explains to the Queen, 'these [commercial theatres] are the adventures of needy and desperate men that must, to save themselves from perishing of want, give the sillier sort of people what they best like; and what they best like, God knows, is not their own betterment and instruction' (p. 322). The notion of a didactic drama used to educate a 'sillier sort of people' in want of betterment and instruction is wholly in keeping with Shaw's Fabianism. The Fabian

Society, of which Shaw was a prominent member from 1884, advocated a model of gradual or evolutionary socialist reform, achieved by patient debate and discussion, the kind which we find staged in *The Dark Lady of the Sonnets*. Moreover, such debate would characterise the governing style of the new intellectual class, who would use such platforms as the theatre to build a society that cultivated an ethos of individual, social and moral improvement. As Shaw's Shakespear argues, this theatre would have to be endowed out of public revenue for the playing of a drama that no merchant would touch, a new drama of intellectual and moral ideas.

In an earlier letter to Ellen Terry, Shaw, trying to impress upon her the importance of the 'New Drama' and the role that the theatre would play in his social reform, wrote: 'My capers are part of a bigger design than you think: Shakespear, for instance, is to me one of the towers of the Bastille, and down he must come.'[26] If this metaphor of theatrical revolution ran counter to the evolutionist agenda of his socialism, such rhetorical hyperbole was entirely in keeping with his iconoclastic treatment of Shakespeare throughout his career. Moreover, this iconoclasm was informed and enabled by his dual identity as both Irish and British. Shaw, not unlike his contemporaries of the Irish literary renaissance such as Yeats and Synge, recognised the role that theatre would play in the political transformation of society, and while they differed vastly in their styles and ideas, they all cultivated a sense of the drama as theatre of opposition and agent of transformation.[27] Shaw's Britishness meant that he would remain thoroughly invested in the political and artistic future of England, an investment that both resonated with his nostalgic admiration of Shakespeare, even while it required the dislocation of Shakespeare's cultural centrality. At the same time, he saw the necessity to situate this investment within the broader scope of an evolving Europe and its changing political landscape. This is what he imagined for Ireland as well – most apparently, in his *John Bull's Other Island* – a new form of political and social organisation that would transcend the economies of an outmoded empire, and one that would accommodate and sustain the intellectual and moral integrity of a new Europe. Importantly, for both Ireland and the English theatre, this required a substantive break with the romanticism of the nineteenth century, whether the cultural nationalism that looked back to Ireland's mythic past at the expense of a pragmatic, integrated future, or the bardolatry that held up Shakespeare erroneously as a model of the universal human condition.

Of course, at the end of his career in 1949, when he was writing *Shakes versus Shav*, Shaw's rhetorical antagonism was beginning to seem not a little outdated. The nineteenth century had long since passed. Ireland, though partitioned, had very recently severed its ties to the British Commonwealth to become a Republic. Though he would still write on the topic of Ireland to the end of his life, Shaw's claim to authority on that matter was diminished by the fact that he was more than seventy years removed from Ireland. Shakespeare commentary had also been replaced by professional criticism. For that matter, Shaw's own works had entered professional criticism, now firmly ensconced within the canon of British literature. By this point in his career, he had become a genuine rival to Shakespeare, the next great British dramatist, and he no longer needed to play the role of his own apologist. The antagonism intended by the title of *Shakes versus Shav*, an antagonism entirely consistent with his life's worth of writing, seems therefore ironic, a comic exaggeration of a rivalry, complete with boxing match in the play itself, that surrenders to a muted reconciliation between Shaw and his rival Shakespeare in the final moments before their brief candles are extinguished. Perhaps it was a similar turn from antagonism to nostalgia that led Shaw to imagine himself late in his career as externally British and eternally Irish. When he made this distinction, Shakespeare could not have been very far from his mind – he never was. In the same manner, Shaw would return, as he wrote to conclude his own dramatic legacy with *Shakes versus Shav*, to the warmly remembered Shakespeare of his boyhood in Ireland.

Notes

1   George Bernard Shaw, *Shakes versus Shav*, in *The Bodley Head Bernard Shaw Collected Plays and their Prefaces*, 7 vols (London: Max Reinhardt, The Bodley Head, 1974), VII, 469–77 (p. 469). All subsequent references will be made to this edition and given within the text.

2   George Bernard Shaw, 'A Note on Aggressive Nationalism', *The New Statesman*, 12 July 1913, in *The Matter with Ireland*, 2nd edn, ed. by Dan H. Laurence and David H. Greene (Gainesville: University of Florida Press, 2001), pp 91–4 (p. 93).

3   Quoted in Michael Holroyd, *Bernard Shaw, The One-Volume Definitive Edition* (London: Chatto & Windus, 1997), p. 36.

4   Quoted in the Introduction to *The Matter with Ireland*, p. xvi.

5   George Bernard Shaw, 'Ireland Eternal and External', *The New Statesman*, 30 Oct. 1948, in *The Matter with Ireland*, pp 339–41 (p. 339).

6   George Bernard Shaw, 'Literature in Ireland', a lecture delivered in Dublin, 26 Oct. 1918, in *The Matter with Ireland*, pp 176–9 (pp 178–9).

7   Gearóid O'Flaherty, 'George Bernard Shaw and Ireland', in *The Cambridge Companion to Twentieth-Century Irish Drama*, ed. by Shaun Richards (Cambridge: Cambridge University Press, 2004), p. 130. O'Flaherty provides the argument that Shaw only supported Irish nationalism as a corrective to English imperialism: 'Shaw accepted nationalism as beneficial only if its ultimate consequence was the formation of a "federation of nations, each subject only to the whole empire, and not to the nucleus or strongest member of it".' (p. 129).

8   Shaw, 'A Note on Aggressive Nationalism', p. 91.

9   I use the term 'ethnicity' to mean a mode of self-identification in communities organised heterogeneously and discontinuously by geography, language and culture, and whose heterogeneity

naturally counters the homogeneity of such concepts as 'race' and 'nationality'. While Shaw predates critical race theory, I think such distinctions usefully qualify Shaw's own sense of 'Irishness' in contrast to his refutation of 'Irish nationalism'.

10 Shaw, 'Ireland Eternal and External', pp 339–40.

11 These include *Widowers' Houses* (1892), *The Philanderer* (1893) and *Mrs Warren's Profession* (1893).

12 Later collected in Shaw's *Our Theatres in the Nineties*; quoted here from George Bernard Shaw, *Shaw on Shakespeare: An Anthology of Bernard Shaw's Writings on the Plays and Production of Shakespeare*, ed. by Edwin Wilson (New York: E. P. Dutton & Co., Inc., 1961), pp 54–61.

13 Wilson provides an excellent overview of Shaw's interest in Shakespeare's word-music in the Introduction to *Shaw on Shakespeare*, esp. pp xix–xxi.

14 George Bernard Shaw, *Cymbeline Refinished: A Variation on Shakespeare's Ending*, in *The Bodley Head Bernard Shaw*, VII, 179–99 (p. 183). All subsequent references will be made to this edition. Shaw's earlier play, *The Admirable Bashville* (1901), was his not wholly successful attempt to write an entire play in Elizabethan blank verse.

15 Collected in *Ellen Terry and Bernard Shaw: A Correspondence*, ed. by Christopher St. John (New York: G. P. Putnam's Sons, 1931).

16 Quoted in *Shaw on Shakespeare*, p. 43.

17 In the Preface to George Bernard Shaw, *Three Plays for Puritans*, in *The Bodley Head Bernard Shaw*, II, 11–430 (p. 39). All subsequent references will be made to this edition.

18 In *Shaw's Sense of History* (Oxford: Clarendon Press, 1988), J. L. Wisenthal writes: 'One might say that Shaw, like Mommsen, wanted to write history in the present tense. He wanted to make his audiences see that historical figures are real people, and that historical issues are real issues' (p. 105).

19 In *The Marriage of Contraries: Bernard Shaw's Middle Plays* (Cambridge, Mass.: Harvard University Press, 1974), J. L. Wisenthal argues that Shaw must have been drawn to the anti-English element in the story precisely because of his Irishness: 'The parallel between early twentieth-century Ireland and early fifteenth-century France would have been in Shaw's mind: both France and Ireland were struggling for freedom from English domination, and the Irish case was based on the nationalism that Shaw ascribes to Joan in the play' (p. 173).

20 Sir Walter Raleigh first published his volume on *Shakespeare* in the English Men of Letters series in 1907; A. C. Bradley's *Shakespearean Tragedy* appeared in 1904 in the first of many editions.

21 Gilbert K. Chesterton, *George Bernard Shaw* (New York: John Lane Company, 1909), p. 110.

22 Quoted in the Introduction to *Shaw on Shakespeare*, p. ix.

23 On the proliferation of inexpensive illustrated editions in the nineteenth century, see Andrew Murphy, *Shakespeare in Print: A History and Chronology of Shakespeare Publishing* (Cambridge: Cambridge University Press, 2003), esp. p. 174.

24 In the Preface to George Bernard Shaw, *The Dark Lady of the Sonnets*, in *The Bodley Head Bernard Shaw*, IV, 269–339 (p. 292). All subsequent references will be made to this edition.

25 For a longer discussion of the running debate between Harris and Shaw, see my own *Shakespeare and Modernism* (Cambridge: Cambridge University Press, 2006), esp. ch. 2.

26 Letter dated 27 Jan. 1897, in *Ellen Terry and Bernard Shaw*, p. 136.

27 In *The Irish Art of Controversy* (Ithaca: Cornell University Press, 2005), Lucy McDiarmid makes the argument that Ireland's high cultural nationalism, prominently between the years of 1908 and 1913, was played out by cultural controversies of the period, one of which she identifies as the Abbey Theatre's 1909 production of Shaw's *The Shewing-up of Blanco Posnet* which had been banned by the Lord Chamberlain in England.

CHAPTER 8

William Shakespeare, Oscar Wilde and the Art of Appeal

Noreen Doody

In his novel, *The Picture of Dorian Gray*, Wilde's eponymous hero remarks that one is influenced by one's biological and racial ancestors and by the great thinkers and artists who have gone before: 'one had ancestors in literature, as well as in one's own race'.[1] Wilde propounds a similar theory in his essay on literary criticism, 'The Critic as Artist', where he contends that one is subject to the influential effect of a powerful ancestry of the imagination.[2] It is within this ancestry that Wilde numbers William Shakespeare, foremost creator of imaginative life, whose artistic authority Wilde calls on at crucial moments during his lifetime to both explain and endorse his style of living, his art and his style of loving. Shakespeare was pivotal to Wilde's sense of his own identity: national, artistic and sexual. This essay explores the relationship between Wilde and Shakespeare and will focus on these three areas in which Wilde makes appeal to the authority of William Shakespeare. It will also consider how Shakespeare's aesthetics appeal to Wilde and are to some extent appropriated by him in his creative work.

Wilde, born in Dublin in 1854, was the heir to a bi-cultural inheritance: the great, canonical writers of the English language had been available to him from an early age and his parents' interest in Irish culture and folklore had ensured him an equal education in the cultural legacy of his own country. Wilde's mother, Lady Wilde, was a poet and translator while his father, the aural surgeon Sir William Wilde, was an amateur archaeologist, collector of folktales and author of several books including *Lough Corrib: Its Shore and Islands*. Wilde moved easily in the imaginative world of ideas and images. Had he chosen, he might have made a name for himself in the active world of politics – he was offered a safe seat in government but declined it, making a decision to remain in the imaginative realm of literature. In this realm, racial imposition and colonisation did not figure as the difficult issues they represented in actual life; in the imaginative world of art, Wilde felt free either to bypass the problematic political conditions of the time or to engage in a subversive, tactical form of combat. Wilde embraced a bi-cultural literary identity and indulged his English and Irish cultural inclinations. In his poem on John Keats, 'Heu Miserande Puer' (1877), Wilde includes the phrase: ' O sweetest singer of our English land!' In reply to the Rev. Matthew Russell, SJ, editor of *The Irish Monthly*, to whom Wilde had sent the poem for publication, Wilde writes: 'I am sorry you object to the words "our English land". It is a noble privilege to count oneself of the same race as Keats or Shakespeare.' Wilde's appeal to Shakespeare indicates his accepted version of colonisation as culturally and not politically based. Ultimately, however, Wilde concedes to the editor's wishes and drops the offending possessive pronoun for a more neutral definite article changing the line to 'O sweetest singer of the English land!' Wilde's accompanying remark to the editor is heavily ironic: 'I would not shock the feelings of your readers for anything', he tells him.[3] The magazine would have had a predominantly nationalist readership and while Wilde would politically have had nationalist sympathies, poetically his espousal of Shakespeare as literary forefather allowed him the freedom to make use of the epithet of Englishness. When Wilde published this poem in *Poems* in 1881 he changed the title to 'The Grave of Keats' and reverted to the original phrase, 'our English land'. Writing in a letter to Edmond de Goncourt in 1891, Wilde gives this succinct rendition of his identity: 'Français de sympathie, je suis Irlandais de race, et les Anglais m'ont condamné à parler la langage de Shakespeare.'[4] While Wilde's description may be delivered tongue-in-cheek, his phrase 'condemned to speak the language of Shakespeare' resonates with anterior meaning. Wilde's reference to the imposition of language forefronts the unequal political relationship that then existed between Ireland and England and the real circumstance of colonial enforcement. Ideologically opposed to English domination of Ireland, Wilde, in his journalistic writing, had castigated the obtuseness of British Rule in Ireland and its attendant injustices.[5] At the same time, he suggests its cultural compensations.

This ambivalent attitude towards Ireland's relationship with England was very much in evidence among Irish literary people at the time. Shakespeare was still being held in high regard by 'influential revolutionary Irish Republicans' in the early twentieth century, among them writers Ernest O'Malley, Seán O'Faoláin and Peadar O'Donnell.[6] One of the chief protagonists in O'Faoláin's novel, *Bird Alone* (1936), is an eccentric old Fenian who continuously quotes Shakespeare at his grandchildren. O'Donnell encountered Shakespeare while a prisoner of the Free State troops during the Civil War in Ireland (1922) and read him enthusiastically.[7] Ernest O'Malley, while also a republican prisoner in 1923, writes at the time of his incarceration: 'I have a decent library now and have ample time to browse deep in Chaucer, Shakesp[eare], Dante and Milton.' While O'Malley eagerly embraced Shakespeare and the literary culture of England he adamantly rejected imperial rule; in the same year that he writes of his delight in Shakespeare he also proclaims 'the inborn hate of things English, which I expect all Irishmen inherit'.[8]

The poet W. B. Yeats used almost this exact division between the literary culture of England as exemplified by Shakespeare and the political rule of England to delineate the frustrated position he held as an Irishman:

> No people, Lecky said [. . .] have undergone greater persecution, nor did that persecution altogether cease up to our own day. No people hate as we do in whom that past is always alive, there are moments when hatred poisons my life [. . .] [but] I owe my soul to Shakespeare, to Spenser and to Blake, perhaps to William Morris, and to the English language in which I think, speak and write, that everything I love has come to me through English; my hatred tortures me with love, my love with hate.[9]

Yeats clearly describes the ambiguous nature of colonised identity and the emotional struggle for a sense of unbiased belonging to which it gave rise. He expresses the dilemma of the Irish lover of English literature who embraces the language and ideas of the great English writers while at the same time being conscious that these writers belong within the fold of the political oppressor. Yeats professes an almost intolerable strain in the simultaneous adoption of both positions.

Yeats's assertion that Shakespeare contributed fundamentally to his artistic sensibility could be echoed by many of his Irish contemporaries, including Wilde. Shakespeare was widely read and revered in nineteenth-century Ireland. Edward Dowden, Professor of English Literature at Trinity College Dublin, an entrenched Unionist, was a family friend of the Yeatses, and wrote his seminal and widely acclaimed work, *Shakspere: A Critical Study of his Mind and Art*, in 1875. In the summer of that year a twenty-year-old Wilde saw *Hamlet* performed at Verona in the old Roman amphitheatre and wrote home to his mother of the indifferent nature of the production but of the romance of seeing Shakespeare by moonlight in such a place.[10] Evidently, the reality of the poor performance in no way detracted from Wilde's creative perception of Shakespeare nor his appreciation of the imaginative experience. Wilde's deep knowledge of Shakespeare's drama is evidenced in the many references he makes to it within his own literary work, while his short story, 'The Portrait of Mr W. H.', illustrates his subtle, close critical reading of Shakespeare's *Sonnets*. In May 1885 Wilde reviewed *Hamlet*, produced by Henry Irving at the Lyceum Theatre[11] and published an article in *The Nineteenth Century* entitled 'Shakespeare and Stage Costume', an article which he later included in his book of literary criticism, *Intentions* (1891), under the title 'The Truth of Masks'. In this essay, which demonstrates his familiarity with Shakespeare's dramatic oeuvre, Wilde argues that Shakespeare's architectural accuracy in the staging of his plays promotes the illusory nature of his drama. It is this illusory world of Shakespeare's that gives Wilde a place of belonging that is separate and distinct from the ignominious state of colonisation into which he was born. Wilde's remarks to Edmond de Goncourt are a declaration of identity and, in electing to assert Shakespeare as a hierarchical figure of authority, within that declaration Wilde is selecting a colonial narrative that is more acceptable to him and which places Shakespeare in a cultural rather than a political setting. Shakespeare permits Wilde to elide the affront of actual colonisation and provides him with a site of imaginative belonging.

However imaginatively secure Wilde might have felt within the language and landscape of Shakespeare's creation, the disjunction between his origins of birth and his acquired culture become visible in his approach to the language of his mentor. W. B. Yeats discerns that Wilde's style of writing in the English language is born out of his fascination with it as an outsider: 'It was precisely because he was not of it by birth and by early association that he caught up phrases and adjectives for their own sake, and not because they were a natural part of his design.'[12] Wilde himself spoke to Conan Doyle about his preoccupation with fine language and beautiful words for their own sake, describing his inclination to 'throw probability out of the window for the sake of a phrase'.[13] Wilde's propensity to adopt words for no reason other than for their glamour and intrinsic beauty may well be accounted for by his cultural bifurcation and, similarly, his powerful play with language often arises from this circumstance. Many times in his writing Wilde makes use of his celebrated wit to enter virtual combat on behalf of the colonised and, indeed, claims a decisive cultural victory on their behalf in relation to language. Wilde contends that the Irish who were 'condemned' to speak the language of Shakespeare succeed in reversing the hierarchical order in colonising the English language. In a lecture he gave in San Francisco (1882) Wilde talks of how Irish lands were confiscated and devastated by English forces while the English language was adopted and enhanced by the colonised Irish: 'We took their language,' he writes, 'and added new beauty to it.'[14] Wilde's choice of habitat, the imaginative world of art wherein Shakespeare is figurehead, allows him an autonomy denied in the actual political sphere. Wilde's contention that the Irish improved the language of Shakespeare indicates his perception that in the imaginative world of art, vanquished and victor are interchangeable terms; he undermines the notion that force and violence are necessary to world order and allows for the real possibility of cultural exchange and mutual gain.

Wilde attributes great power to the imaginative faculty, even going so far as to espouse the idea that Art creates life. He contends that what is realised in fact is first imagined in fiction[15] and credits Shakespeare with having accurately depicted both human nature and human personality. Harold Bloom's contention in recent times that Shakespeare invented the human owes much to his precursor, Oscar Wilde.[16] As Bloom writes: 'Shakespeare [. . .] produced Falstaff and Hamlet as art's tribute to nature. More even than all the other Shakespearean prodigies [. . .] Falstaff and Hamlet are the invention of the human, the inauguration of personality as we have come to recognise it.'[17] Wilde holds that there is a fundamental sameness about human nature and that it is the individual formulation of this base material into the expression of personality, the details of self expression, which differentiates one from the mob. 'The brotherhood of man,' he writes, '[. . .] is a most depressing and humiliating reality.' What is interesting, according to Wilde, is the mask and not that which lies behind it. Wilde recognises the sublime achievement of Shakespeare in imbuing his characters, Hamlet and Falstaff, with personality and so he singles them out to illustrate his theory that each of us, no matter how distinctive, is alike in our humanity. Wilde observes Falstaff and Hamlet, undeniably rich in personality, one playful, the other sombrely dramatic, and finds in each of them reflections of the other: 'The fat knight has his moods of melancholy and the young prince his moments of coarse humour.'[18] Behind the contrasting masks of these vibrant personalities lies a similarly drab human nature. Shakespeare has created both. Wilde applauds the accuracy of Shakespeare's observation of the real, but he also expresses his reservation that in his use of the realistic Shakespeare may have sown the seeds of decay for the imaginative drama of future generations. Yeats recalls hearing Wilde say, 'Give me *The Winter's Tale*, "Daffodils that come before the swallow dares", but not *King Lear*. What is *King Lear* but poor life staggering in the fog?'[19]

However, Wilde sees Shakespeare primarily as the defender of the imaginative and many times invokes him in support of his own aesthetic principles. Wilde takes real exception to art being used as a social document and accuses the nineteenth-century English public of continually confusing art with reality. Following the first publication of *Dorian Gray* in novella form in *Lippincott's Magazine* in 1890 Wilde was vilified both personally and as an artist for what was generally considered an indecent book; the behaviour of Wilde's fictive characters was seen as immoral and, by extension, so was that of their author. Wilde immediately appeals to Shakespeare in his defence against what he saw as gross philistinism, stating in a letter to *The Scots Observer*, 'An artist, sir, has no ethical sympathies at all. Virtue and wickedness are to him simply what the colours on his palette are to the painter [. . .] Iago may be morally horrible and Imogen stainlessly pure. Shakespeare, as Keats said, had as much delight in creating the one as he had in creating the other.'[20] Wilde continues to call on the authoritative figure of Shakespeare, in an essay of the following year, to indict the erroneous conception of art as a factual testimony to its author's moral character: 'To call an artist morbid because he deals with morbidity as his subject matter is as silly as if one called Shakespeare mad because he wrote *King Lear*.'[21]

Wilde's abhorrence of the notion of a concrete connection between the real life doings of authors and their created subjects was balanced by the belief that the imagined world of art offered insights into life beyond the laboured plagiarism of the actual. He admired Shakespeare's ability to do this and singles out, as an example, the lesser characters of Rosencrantz and Guildenstern in *Hamlet*. Wilde admires in these two characters Shakespeare's incomparable subtlety of observation and finds in his reading of their personalities and situation a profound insight and an understanding of a circumstance of his own real life drama. As Wilde awaited his first trial in Holloway Prison, his only reading matter was the works of Shakespeare, lent to him by a friend. Almost two years later, when most of his prison sentence had been served, Wilde contemplates the details of his incarceration and the part played in it by his friend and lover, Lord Alfred Douglas. Wilde by this time was much disenchanted by Douglas and his behaviour and finds in Shakespeare's creation of Rosencrantz and Guildenstern a powerful analogy and insight into Douglas's place within his story.[22] Wilde suggests that Shakespeare's two characters, being mean and shallow, were unequal to the momentous events that were unfolding about them. They were out of their depth and, Wilde observes, interpreting Shakespeare, that it is not a necessary correlation of tragedy that those taking part in it have the stature capable of appreciating the awesome gravity of what is going on around them. Wilde comes to a clearer understanding of Douglas's place within his own personal tragedy through his reading of Shakespeare's imaginative creations, seeing his former lover as a minor, inept character unequal to and unaware of the appalling tragedy in which he took part. As Wilde had once remarked, playing on Shakespeare's lines: 'The world is a stage, but the play is badly cast.'[23]

Wilde's engagement with Shakespeare is nowhere more in evidence than in his detailed knowledge of the *Sonnets*. It is to Shakespeare of the *Sonnets* that he appeals when in 1895 he stood before a jury in a courtroom of the Old Bailey, accused of committing 'acts of gross indecencies with other male persons'. In answer to a question from the prosecuting lawyer, Wilde calls on the great names of the Renaissance in explication and justification of his position. It is a powerful aesthetic defence that Wilde puts forward. Wilde is claiming that the 'crime' with which he is being charged is as essential to his art as it once was to the art of the great artists, Shakespeare and Michelangelo, and before that, to the wisdom of the Greek world. Wilde is claiming that his association with younger men is that of the poet to his muse and furthermore that the male muse is of crucial importance to great literature.

'The Love that dare not speak its name' in this century is such a great affection of an elder for a younger man as there was between David and Jonathan, such as Plato made the very basis of his philosophy, and such as you find in the sonnets of

Michelangelo and Shakespeare. It is that deep, spiritual affection that is as pure as it is perfect. It dictates and pervades great works of art like those of Shakespeare and Michelangelo, and those two letters of mine, such as they are. It is in this century misunderstood, so much misunderstood that it may be described as 'the Love that dare not speak its name', and on account of it I am placed where I am now. It is beautiful, it is fine, it is the noblest form of affection. There is nothing unnatural about it. It is intellectual, and it repeatedly exists between an elder and a younger man, when the elder man has intellect, and the younger man has all the joy, hope and glamour of life before him. That it should be so, the world does not understand. The world mocks at it and sometimes puts one in the pillory for it.[24]

Wilde's speech from the dock was so powerful that the spectators in the courtroom stood to their feet and burst into spontaneous applause. The power of the speech may be accounted for by Wilde's delivery, his eloquence, the content of his words or his identification with Shakespeare, as though he too stood accused.

Some years earlier in his short story, 'The Portrait of Mr W. H.', Wilde proposed the theory that Shakespeare dedicated his *Sonnets* to a young and beautiful male actor, Willie Hughes. Wilde was not the first to do this, but in his short story he supports the theory with convincing internal evidence from the sonnets and also by means of a painting of the young boy that turns out to be a forgery. Wilde identifies Willie Hughes as Shakespeare's male muse. In his short story Wilde depicts this muse of Shakespeare as dangerous and desirable. Wilde writes that for several years the personality of Willie Hughes 'filled the soul of Shakespeare with terrible joy and no less terrible despair'. Wilde quotes Shakespeare, inferring that he is naming Willie Hughes as the 'tenth' muse: 'Ten times more in worth | Than those old nine which rhymers invocate.'[25]

Already in classical literature, as Wilde would know having graduated with a double First in Classics from Oxford, there had been a Pretender to the position of tenth muse. In classical literature the earlier depiction of the muses was that of the three female muses representative of memory, practice and song – guardians of an oral tradition. The muses continued in the nine female goddesses who lived on Mount Helicon, daughters of Zeus and Mnemosyne, followers of Apollo, god of Song. Poets venerated these nine goddesses and desired their favour. The muses often favoured the artists but could also be cruel and vindictive. The female image of the muse emerges from the ancient tales as an image of desire and destruction. A certain erotic presence evolves in the interdependent relationship between muse and artist; a tension exists, as though either artist or muse might devour the other. The Thracian Bard, Thamyris, declared that his song was more wonderful than that of the Nine sister muses. The muses were greatly affronted at his challenge to their position and quickly retaliated: they blinded him and robbed him of his song.

The poet Thamyris was, according to Apollodorus, the first male lover of another male and so his bid for usurpation has implications in gender terms – his song which he believes more beautiful than that of the nine goddesses is inspired by his beloved, the beautiful boy, Hyacinthus. Hyacinthus is later loved by Apollo, and it is Apollo who, in a fit of jealousy, informs the nine muses of Thamyris's proud boast that his song is more powerful than theirs. This ancient story of the triumph of the male muse and the jealousy, rivalry and desire that ensues has resonances for Wilde, whose presence in the dock, pleading the nobility of same-sex love, is by no small means attributable to the conduct of his beautiful and poisonous muse, Lord Alfred Douglas, and, indeed, Wilde refers to Douglas as Hyacinthus in a letter produced in court as evidence against him. The letter reads:

> My own boy, your sonnet is quite lovely. It is a marvel that those red rose-leaf lips [. . .] of yours should be made no less for music of song than for madness of kissing. Your slim gilt soul walks between passion and poetry. I know Hyacinthus, whom Apollo loved so madly, was you in Greek days.[26]

In his short story, 'The Portrait of Mr W. H.', Wilde proclaims Shakespeare's muse, Willie Hughes, the 'very cornerstone of Shakespeare's art; the very source of Shakespeare's inspiration; the very incarnation of Shakespeare's dreams'.[27] These are powerful claims for Shakespeare's purported beloved. It seems, according to Wilde, that Shakespeare's entire creative impulse, its execution and success springs from his relationship with Willie Hughes; it is as though the boy were Shakespeare's creativity incarnate. Indeed, Wilde relies on this interpretation of the inextricability of Shakespeare and his muse in his speech from the dock when he urges the vitality of the male muse to the creative process. Writing from Reading Gaol some years later, Wilde expands on this idea, describing his own relation to the male muse in somewhat similar terms to those which he used to express Shakespeare's creative reliance on Willie Hughes. Wilde explains his own relationship with his muses in the phrase 'feasting with panthers'[28]: the young men are represented as sleek, dangerous, dark and forbidden. The phrase suggests sensual and artistic appetite and communicates the richness and rawness of the experience which gives sustenance to the creative appetite of the artist. Wilde places himself among the exotic creatures that both attend and compose the feast and at any moment may become the feasters – a delicate, dangerous situation which holds the artist always at a point of creative tension with his muse.

Wilde claims that Shakespeare, like many others in the sixteenth century, was fascinated by Plato's *Symposium* and the notion of spiritual conception, or the meeting of true minds resulting in the incarnation of the idea in a living form. Wilde himself subscribed to liberalised Platonist thinking current at

Oxford in the nineteenth century, which proposed the spiritual nature of love and the view that eros converts to the aesthetic. It is because of this idealised neo-Platonic concept of same-sex love that Wilde was free to appeal publicly to the canonical figure of Shakespeare as his precursor in acclaiming a male muse. The passionate language suggesting sexual involvement is explained by Wilde in Platonic terms in 'The Portrait of Mr W. H.' where he writes that while the erotic is spiritualised, the language of passion remains in place, leaving the vulgar and uninitiated believing that the sensual language is proof of sexual appetite. The Hyacinthus letter referred to during the court proceedings had been the subject of a failed blackmail attempt prior to the trial and was produced during the trial in an attempt to show the sexual nature of Wilde's same-sex relationships. Anticipating the threat this letter might pose, Wilde had arranged for a friend to convert the incriminating love letter into a sonnet in an attempt to depersonalise it and neutralise its passionate language by using it in the socially acceptable format of a sonnet.

Forgery and authenticity are central themes in Wilde's short story, 'The Portrait of Mr W. H.'. The young protagonist, Cyril Graham, acquires a forged painting of Willie Hughes to prove the young man's existence and ultimately to prove his own interpretation of the *Sonnets*. The unnamed narrator of the story spends many hours in laborious and painstaking study of the sonnets looking for supporting evidence for the existence of Shakespeare's male muse. While Wilde's narrator is busy scrupulously assembling facts, Wilde, at practically the same time, is stating in another essay, 'The Decay of Lying' (published six months prior to the short story on Mr W. H.), the merits of deception and extolling the virtues of the lie: 'A fine lie,' he writes, '[is] that which is its own evidence.' Again, he declares: 'It's style that makes us believe in a thing [. . .] nothing but style.'[29] Indeed, Wilde had once professed that 'Where there is no illusion there is no Illyria, where there is no style there is no Shakespeare'.[30] Wilde here makes the claim that his great precursor William Shakespeare owes his art to his consciousness of the crucial importance of style to art. Implicated in Wilde's assertion of Shakespeare's acknowledgment of style is his own admission of aesthetic indebtedness to Shakespeare. 'The Decay of Lying' is an exposé of Wilde's aesthetic principles; in it Wilde expresses total opposition to the fastidious type of search for explanations and proofs his protagonists have undertaken in 'The Portrait of Mr W. H.'. Wilde mischievously inserts in 'The Portrait of Mr W. H.' the mention of a 'fascinating critic' who is currently writing on the matters of art that he discusses in 'The Decay of Lying'. The 'fascinating critic' is, of course, Wilde himself and this reference provides a strong creative link between both essays, indicating Wilde's ultimate critical intentions.

Wilde extends the idea of forgery to encompass Shakespeare's creative capacity to produce female characters that surpass any realist depiction of women. Wilde sees the muse of Shakespeare's *Sonnets* as possessing both male and female attributes; he describes Willie Hughes as having 'a beauty that seemed to combine the charm of both sexes'.[31] Wilde extends the notion of male muse, suggesting that not only has Shakespeare's muse usurped the female role in the area of poetic inspiration but that Shakespeare in writing female roles for young boy actors has given something of the life and joyful essence of these actors to his great female characters. It seems that the actors are in themselves muses and in the collaboration of artist and muse a new type of girl or woman has come into being. Wilde seems to be suggesting that Juliet, Viola, and Portia owe their vivacity and integrity as women to not being fully modelled on actual women. For Wilde, Shakespeare has rendered them perfect works of art precisely because they are not wholly intended to be copies of the real thing but because they are counterfeit images of women.

Wilde speaks of Shakespeare in terms of precursor to his thought that Life follows Art and that art deals with the imaginative and creative.[32] He celebrates him as 'he who made Prospero the magician, and gave him Caliban and Ariel as his servants, who heard the Tritons blowing their horns round the coral reefs of the Enchanted Isle'.[33] Wilde describes how Shakespeare concurs with himself in his belief that art is a matter of 'imaginative reality' rather than 'unimaginative realism' and condemns those tedious critics who are always in search of facts and proofs dismissing completely their claim that Shakespeare endorses their theories about Art being the reflection of reality. Wilde writes: '[they] will quote that hackneyed passage [. . .] This unfortunate aphorism about Art holding the mirror up to Nature, is deliberately said by Hamlet in order to convince the bystanders of his absolute insanity in all art-matters.' Wilde's own reaction to Hamlet's 'lunacy' was to state that, 'Life holds the mirror up to Art, and either reproduces some strange type imagined by painter or sculptor, or realises in fact what has been imagined in fiction.'[34]

Wilde's aesthetic stance that art neither imitates life nor depends on facts seems far removed from some of his protagonists' views in 'The Portrait of Mr W. H.'. Critics have noted the indeterminacy of this short story and expressed frustration that Wilde does not clearly indicate whether or not he believes in his own erudite theory of Shakespeare's *Sonnets*. However, looking at this short story in the light of 'The Decay of Lying' it is apparent that 'The Portrait of Mr W. H.' is made up of many types of imaginings, lies and forgeries: the young narrator who strives so hard to prove the theory writes up his information and then finds that it is unconvincing; the character, Erskine, begins by believing Cyril Graham's theory but because of the forged portrait, comes to doubt it, then finally believes once more in the theory. He feigns suicide in order to persuade the narrator of the authenticity of the theory. Wilde even undermines the credibility of martyrdom: 'To die for one's theological opinions is the worst use a man can make of his life; but to die for a literary theory! It seemed impossible.'[35]

In the short story, 'The Portrait of Mr W. H.', Wilde deliberately makes fun of scholarly research, the difficult and arduous pursuit of facts that they might uphold a theory, and indeed literary theory itself. He inclusively dismisses his own literary theory of Shakespeare's *Sonnets* which because of its insincerity is a type of imaginative creation, a forgery. There are all types of artifice and all sorts of imaginings in the short story: the suicide is pretence; the women played by boys are not what they seem; the muse is a mythical evolution. 'The Portrait of Mr W. H.' is a send-up of scholarly research, detailed factual enquiry and labour; Wilde throws his research out the window for the sake of his aesthetic stance.

'The Portrait of Mr W. H.' is, then, Wilde's homage to Shakespeare: at the end of the short story the theory has been exploded or at least has disappeared from the story and all that remains is the art – the beautiful portrait of Shakespeare's inspiration, the Male Muse, Willie Hughes, and Shakespeare's beautiful *Sonnets* themselves. Beauty and Art, according to Wilde, require no explanation. 'Better to take pleasure in a rose,' Wilde writes, 'than to put its roots under a microscope.'[36]

Wilde's aesthetics privilege the power and acuity of the imaginative faculty and it is from Wilde's perception of Shakespeare as the inimitable Creator of a wondrous, fantastical cosmology that his deep admiration of him derives. Wilde lived at a time (1854–1900) during which his country was colonised by England so that deferring to the artistic authority of Shakespeare allowed him to exchange a literal set of unequal circumstances for an alternative, imaginative community wherein parity of esteem might be possible. Shakespeare's world not only provides Wilde with a place of belonging but reinforces his aesthetic of the imaginative nature of being; it is the artist, according to Wilde, who shapes our perception of life or in Shakespeare's words: 'gives to airy nothing | A local habitation and a name.'[37] Wilde not only applauds the world of Shakespeare's imagination but also finds in his creative process an elucidation of his own creativity in his perception of the male muse as intrinsic to the creative work of the artist. It is a measure of Wilde's faith in the iconic power of Shakespeare that he appeals to his name in a nineteenth-century courtroom to make clear the nobility and rightness of same-sex love. A similar trust is apparent in Wilde's demands on Shakespeare at crucial moments in his lifetime for the ratification of his art and his style of living. Shakespeare was always for Wilde an authoritative presence, a source of imaginative wisdom and foremost arbiter of life and art.

Notes

1   Oscar Wilde, *The Picture of Dorian Gray*, in *Collins Complete Works of Oscar Wilde* (Glasgow: HarperCollins, 2003), p. 108.

2   Ibid., 'The Critic as Artist' in *Collins Complete Works of Oscar Wilde*, p. 1138.

3   Ibid., *The Complete Letters of Oscar Wilde*, ed. by Merlin Holland and Rupert Hart-Davis (London: Fourth Estate, 2000), p. 53.

4   Ibid., *The Complete Letters of Oscar Wilde*, p. 505.

5   Ibid., 'Mr. Froude's Blue Book [on Ireland]', review of J. A. Froude, *The Two Chiefs of Dunboy. The Pall Mall Gazette* (13 Apr. 1889), p. 3. Collected in *The Artist as Critic: Critical Writings of Oscar Wilde*, ed. by Richard Ellmann (London: W. H. Allen, 1970).

6   Richard English, 'Shakespeare and the Definition of the Irish Nation' in *Shakespeare and Ireland: History, Politics, Culture*, ed. by Mark Thornton Burnett and Ramona Wray (Basingstoke: Macmillan, 1997), p. 136.

7   Grattan Freyer, *Peadar O'Donnell*, Irish Writers Series (PA: Bucknell University Press, 1973), p. 58.

8   Richard English, '"The Inborn Hate of Things English": Ernie O'Malley and the Irish Revolution 1916–1923', *Past and Present*, 151: 1 (1996), 174–99 (p. 177).

9   W. B. Yeats, 'A General Introduction for my Work,' in *Essays and Introductions* (Dublin: Gill & Macmillan, 1961), p. 519.

10   *The Complete Letters of Oscar Wilde*, p. 12.

11   Oscar Wilde, *Selected Journalism*, ed. by Anya Clayworth (Oxford: Oxford University Press, 2004), p. 47.

12   W. B. Yeats, *W. B Yeats: Uncollected Prefaces and Introductions by Yeats to Words by Other Authors and to Anthologies edited by Yeats*, ed. by William H. O'Donnell (London: Macmillan, 1988), p. 150.

13   *The Complete Letters of Oscar Wilde*, p. 478.

14   Oscar Wilde, 'Irish Poets of the Nineteenth Century: Unpublished Lecture Notes of Oscar Wilde', in *University Review*, 1: 4 (Spring 1955), ed. by Michael J. O'Neill, p. 29.

15   Ibid., 'The Decay of Lying', p. 1,085.

16   See Noreen Doody, 'Precursor and Ephebe: Oscar Wilde, Harold Bloom and the Theory of Poetry as Influence', in *Barcelona English Language and Literature Studies*, ed. by Mireia Aragay and Jacqueline A. Hurtley (Barcelona: Universitat de Barcelona, 2000).

17   Harold Bloom, *Shakespeare: The Invention of the Human* (London: Fourth Estate, 1999), p. 4.

18   Oscar Wilde, 'The Decay of Lying', p. 1,076; p. 1,075.

19   W. B. Yeats, *Autobiographies* (London: Macmillan, 1991), p. 130.

20   Oscar Wilde, *The Picture of Dorian Gray*, ed. by Michael Patrick Gillespie (New York: W. W. Norton, 2007), p. 367.

21   Ibid., 'The Soul of Man Under Socialism', in *Collins Complete Works of Oscar Wilde*, p. 1188.

22   Ibid., *De Profundis*, in *Complete Letters*, p. 772.

23   Ibid., 'Lord Arthur Savile's Crime', in *Collins Complete Works of Oscar Wilde*, p. 165.

24   Richard Ellmann, *Oscar Wilde* (London: Hamish Hamilton, 1987), p. 435.

25   Oscar Wilde, 'The Portrait of Mr W. H.', in *Collins Complete Works of Oscar Wilde*, p. 307.

26 Merlin Holland, *Irish Peacock and Scarlet Marquess: The Real Trial of Oscar Wilde* (London: Fourth Estate, 2003), p. 267; p. 268.

27 Oscar Wilde, 'The Portrait of Mr W. H.', p. 307.

28 Ibid., *De Profundis*, p. 1042.

29 Ibid., 'The Decay of Lying', p. 1072.

30 Ibid., 'Twelfth Night at Oxford', in *Selected Journalism*, p. 59.

31 Ibid., 'The Portrait of Mr W. H.', p. 328.

32 Ibid., 'The Decay of Lying', p. 1091.

33 Ibid., p. 1082.

34 Ibid., p. 1082; p. 1085.

35 Ibid., 'The Portrait of Mr W. H.', p. 348.

36 Ibid., 'The Truth of Masks', p. 1169.

37 Shakespeare, *A Midsummer Night's Dream*, v. 1. 16–17.

CHAPTER 9

'Lips that Shakespeare taught to speak'

Wilde, Shakespeare, and the Question of Influence

Richard Meek

In a letter to Edmond de Goncourt written in December 1891, Oscar Wilde comments that 'One can adore a language without speaking it well, as one can love a woman without understanding her. French by sympathy, I am Irish by race, and the English have condemned me to speak the language of Shakespeare.'[1] Goncourt had previously published a journal entry in which he described Wilde as 'this individual of doubtful sex, with a ham-actor's language, and tall stories'.[2] Wilde's response (which was itself written in French) thus served as an act of self-defence and self-justification, attributing Goncourt's misreading of his character to Wilde's own inadequate grasp of the French language. Yet Wilde's comment also opens up larger questions about his relationship with Shakespeare. On the surface, Wilde is asserting his political and linguistic independence: an Irishman, he has been forced to forsake his mother tongue and speak English. By referring to the English language as 'the language of Shakespeare', Wilde implies that Shakespeare somehow equates to, or stands for, the English language, or even Englishness more generally. For some critics, this comment is an eloquent expression of the ways in which Irish writers have found themselves 'troubled by Shakespeare's symbolization of English cultural hegemony'.[3] In other words, this apparent ambivalence towards Shakespeare is bound up with Wilde's ambivalence towards Englishness. Yet it seems ironic that, at the very moment when Wilde is asserting his Irishness, he simultaneously asserts his affinity with Shakespeare – a writer that, as we shall see, he clearly admired.[4] What this passage seems to suggest is that Wilde's Irishness, while an important aspect of his identity, may also have served as a convenient way for him to emphasise his status as an iconoclast and an outsider, and to reflect upon his own artistic abilities.

Wilde's tendency to identify matters of national identity with aesthetic issues is also apparent in a comment he made in 1892 when it seemed that his play *Salome*, which was written in French, might be banned: 'If the Censor refuses *Salome*, I shall leave England to settle in France where I shall take out letters of naturalization. I will not consent to call myself a citizen of a country that shows such narrowness in artistic judgement. I am not English. I am Irish which is quite another thing.'[5] Here Wilde rejects England because of its 'narrowness' in artistic judgement, and threatens to relocate to France – rather than return to Ireland – the implication being that in France he will find artistic judgements more open and agreeable to him. This comment suggests that Wilde's relationship to these different nations was, to a large extent, governed by artistic concerns. It thus raises the possibility that Wilde conceived of the world in terms of literary and aesthetic communities as well as national identities. Indeed when we turn to Wilde's comments about Shakespeare, we find that Wilde is more concerned to emphasise Shakespeare's artistry, and his place amongst the world's other great writers, than his Englishness. He describes Shakespeare as 'the greatest figure in the world's literature since Greek days', and as 'the most purely human of all the great artists'.[6] Both of these comments suggest that Wilde considered Shakespeare to be an artist whose greatness transcends questions of race or nationality. Thus while the declaration with which we began is ostensibly concerned with issues of politics and nationhood it also relates to a recurrent Wildean preoccupation with the question of influence. By reminding us that English is 'the language of Shakespeare', Wilde underlines his own status as one of Shakespeare's heirs, and perhaps even appropriates something of Shakespeare's literary and cultural legacy. At the same time, however, the phrase 'the language of Shakespeare' implies that the English language *belongs to* Shakespeare. Is it ever possible for a writer – whatever their nationality – to appropriate the words of Shakespeare for themselves? Are the many Shakespearean quotations that appear throughout Wilde's writings a way for Wilde to assert his own creative genius? Or do they rather allow Shakespeare to speak for him, or even through him?

Wilde seems to acknowledge that – to borrow from Mikhail Bakhtin – 'The word in language is half someone else's'.[7] As we shall see, this is a concern that is repeatedly played out and explored in Wilde's writings. In *De Profundis*, for example, Wilde suggests that influence is unavoidable, an inevitable fact of existence: 'Most people are other people. Their thoughts are someone else's opinions, their lives a mimicry, their passions a quotation.'[8] Yet this Wildean aphorism immediately follows a quotation from Ralph Waldo Emerson that addresses the impossibility of originality: 'Nothing is more rare in any man . . . than an act of his own.'[9] When Wilde writes about influence, then, he often enacts the very process that he describes; and this seems to be especially the case when he writes about Shakespeare. In this essay, I explore Wilde's preoccupation with what happens when we try to 'speak' Shakespeare, and the question of whether quoting Shakespeare can be a creative act in itself, or if it turns one into a kind of passive mouthpiece for Shakespeare's art. After exploring several references to Shakespeare in Wilde's critical writings and poems, I discuss Wilde's engagement with Shakespeare in *The Picture of Dorian Gray*. I want to suggest that this novel represents Wilde's most provocative and complex engagement with Shakespeare. As we shall see, this intertextual relationship leads Wilde to explore a series of related questions about the possibility of originality and the ethics and aesthetics of influence.

I

Wilde clearly liked to associate his own life – as well as his art – with Shakespeare. Margot Asquith recalls how she first came across Wilde at a garden party given by Lady Archibald Campbell, explaining why he thought he resembled Shakespeare. According to Asquith, he 'ended a brilliant mono-logue by saying he intended to have a bronze medallion struck of his own profile and Shakespeare's'.[10] It is tempting to see Wilde's fantasy of being immortalised alongside Shakespeare in bronze – the counterfeit presentment of two great artists – as an expression of his desire that they would be placed alongside each other by posterity.[11] And when Wilde moved to London in 1879 he reportedly compared his situation to that of Shakespeare: 'Shakespeare wrote nothing but doggerel lampoon before he came to London and never penned a line after he left.'[12] For Wilde, then, Shakespeare's career seems to have served as a kind of pattern for his own life, and even as a way of expressing his artistic ambitions. Interestingly, Wilde seems to conceive of London in terms of its literary meanings and associations: not simply as the political capital of the nation, but rather the place that inspired Shakespeare to write his best work, and which might inspire Wilde to do the same.

This fascination with Shakespeare has been noted by several of Wilde's critics and biographers. Kate Chedgzoy, for example, comments that 'in both his writings and the social self-presentation which formed almost as sub-stantial a part of his *œuvre* Wilde liked to weave a net of allusions which implied special kinship between himself and Shakespeare'.[13] Yet critics – including Chedgzoy – who have written about this special relationship have tended to focus their attention on 'The Portrait of Mr W. H.', an explicitly Shakespearean tale that recounts the attempts of three men to unlock the riddle of Shakespeare's *Sonnets*. Such critics often discuss the tale as an allegory of homosexual desire, or even a kind of intertextual liaison with Shakespeare.[14] And yet, as I have suggested above, Wilde's engagement with Shakespeare extends far beyond 'The Portrait of Mr W. H.', and indeed beyond questions of national identity or sexuality. Throughout his writings – from his early dramatic work *The Duchess of Padua* to his remarkable letter to Lord Alfred Douglas *De Profundis* – we find Wilde quoting Shakespeare's words, or reading his own life via the works of Shakespeare.[15] Yet it is when he writes about art, acting, and the theatre that Wilde's engagement with Shakespeare becomes particularly vexed and complex.

In 'The Decay of Lying' (1889), Wilde's flamboyant and playful dialogue on artistic creativity and truth telling, Cyril and Vivian repeatedly refer to Shakespeare to back up their arguments. Vivian counters the commonsensical notion that art imitates life by arguing that a famous passage from *Hamlet* should not be taken at face value, or as evidence of Shakespeare's own views upon the subject: 'this unfortunate aphorism about Art holding the mirror up to Nature, is deliberately said by Hamlet in order to convince the bystanders of his absolute insanity in all art-matters.'[16] Here Hamlet's idealistic claims about dramatic art – that 'the purpose of playing' is 'to hold as 'twere the mirror up to nature' (III.2.20–2) – are turned on their head. But perhaps we might also see this as Wilde turning one of the greatest works of English literature on its head, reinventing this immensely canonical text as a play about insincerity and lying. This moment thus represents a potentially subversive act on Wilde's part, in the sense that Hamlet's words are severed from their dramatic context – and their author – and successfully appropriated as evidence for Wilde's thesis that life imitates art.[17] Later in the essay, Vivian again cites *Hamlet* as another example of the ways in which life imitates art: 'Schopenhauer has analysed the pessimism that characterises modern thought, but Hamlet invented it. The world has become sad because a puppet was once melancholy' (p. 180). Here Wilde anticipates some of the bolder claims made by Harold Bloom in recent years, by audaciously suggesting that Hamlet has somehow 'invented' the pessimism of modern life.[18] Wilde thus argues that Shakespeare's influence goes beyond the merely literary, and that a text such as *Hamlet* affects the emotional life of the whole world. On the one hand, then, 'The Decay of Lying' demonstrates that it is possible to populate Shakespeare's words with one's own intention and one's own accent.[19] On the other hand, however, Wilde reminds us of the extent to which we cannot escape Shakespeare or his influence; he even seems to concur with Bloom that Shakespeare 'largely invented us'.[20]

Wilde also explores such concerns when he writes about theatrical performances of Shakespeare's works. As Adrian Poole has recently commented, 'Shakespeare was a prominent contributor to Wilde's developing conception of life as art, as theatre, show, play.'[21] Wilde seems to have been especially preoccupied with the question of how much creative input an actor has when they perform Shakespeare's plays. Is an actor, he asks, simply a mouthpiece for Shakespeare's creative genius? Or are Shakespearean performances a kind of artistic collaboration between actor and playwright? At times Wilde argues for a relatively positive view of actors and their part in artistic creation. Here, for example, is Wilde's extravagant praise of the actress Sarah Bernhardt, and her performances as Lady Macbeth in Paris:

> There is nothing like it on our stage, and it is her finest creation. I say her creation deliberately, because to my mind it is utterly impertinent to talk of Shakespeare's *Macbeth* or Shakespeare's *Othello*. Shakespeare is only one of the parties. The second is the artiste through whose mind it passes. When the two together combine to give me an acceptable hero, that is all I ask. Shakespeare's intentions were his own secret: all we can form an opinion about is what is actually before us.[22]

In this celebration of the art of the actor, Wilde states that Bernhardt is as much the creator as Shakespeare himself. Shakespeare, Wilde suggests, should not be regarded as the single source of the play: he is only 'one of the parties'. The fact that *Macbeth* passes through Bernhardt's mind makes her the joint owner – perhaps even co-author – of Shakespeare's play. Similar views are expressed in Wilde's effervescent dialogue 'The Critic as Artist' (1890). As Gilbert puts it,

> When Rubinstein plays to us the *Sonata Appassionata* of Beethoven, he gives us not merely Beethoven, but also himself, and so gives us Beethoven absolutely – Beethoven re-interpreted through a rich artistic nature, and made vivid and wonderful to us by a new and intense personality. When a great actor plays Shakespeare we have the same experience. His own individuality becomes a vital part of the interpretation.[23]

By performing an artwork – whether it is one of Beethoven's sonatas or a play by Shakespeare – the performer adds something of his or her own personality to the original. For Gilbert the two cannot be separated. These reflections upon Shakespearean performances also comment implicitly upon Wilde's own relationship with Shakespeare. Of course, Wilde was not an actor, and yet it is clear that Shakespeare's words frequently passed through Wilde's mind as he wrote. We might even suggest that Wilde wanted his allusions to Shakespeare to be thought of as a kind of artistic collaboration in the manner of his description of Bernhardt's Shakespearean performances. It is as if Wilde wanted to become 'one of the parties' alongside Shakespeare – perhaps even in the manner of the bronze medallion that he wanted to have struck.

At the same time, however, Wilde displays an awareness that any actor who performs Shakespeare's plays risks becoming a mere spokesperson, passively reciting Shakespeare's powerful words. In his sonnet 'Fabien Dei Franchi' (1881), dedicated to the actor Henry Irving, Wilde encourages Irving to leave aside lesser plays, and to act instead in works better suited to his great talents:

'These things are well enough, – but thou wert made | For more august creation!'[24] It is no surprise, perhaps, that Wilde has Shakespeare in mind. Wilde suggests that 'frenzied Lear | Should at thy bidding wander on the heath' (9–10), and that Romeo 'For thee should lure his love' (11–12). As Wilde expresses it, these Shakespearean characters will be at Irving's command. And yet, in the last line of the sonnet, Wilde reminds us that Shakespeare will be the authority lying behind Irving's performances: 'Pluck Richard's recreant dagger from its sheath – | Thou trumpet set for Shakespeare's lips to blow!' (13–14). In this intriguing formulation, Wilde suggests that Irving acts as Shakespeare's trumpet, a kind of mouthpiece for Shakespeare's own creative powers. It is unclear, then, who is in control of these imagined Shakespearean performances. The sonnet thus prompts us to ask just how much agency or artistic freedom an actor or artist who speaks Shakespeare's words really has. Such matters of agency, influence and appropriation are further complicated in *The Picture of Dorian Gray* (1891), and here these issues take on an additional ethical dimension.

II

Various critics have noted that *Dorian Gray* is one of Wilde's most allusive texts, and certainly at times the novel resembles a tissue of quotations. Jerusha McCormack has even claimed that 'It is hard to say anything original about *The Picture of Dorian Gray*, largely because there is so little that is original in it'.[25] McCormack goes on to note the various sources and influences that scholars have identified in the novel, including Poe, Balzac, Goethe, Radcliffe, Tennyson, Arnold, and Pater. Yet it seems to me that the novel's engagement with Shakespeare is far more central than other critics have previously noted.[26] We might suggest that the irony of *Dorian Gray* is that while it is deeply indebted to various external influences, the novel dramatises the ethical and moral problems that emerge when one allows influence – literary or otherwise – to take over one's life. And, as we shall see, Shakespeare offers a way for both Wilde and his characters to articulate and explore these ideas.

From the outset, the novel self-consciously reflects upon the idea of influence. As the charismatic Lord Henry Wotton puts it to the impressionable Dorian,

> There is no such thing as a good influence, Mr. Gray. All influence is immoral – immoral from the scientific point of view . . . to influence a person is to give him one's own soul . . . His virtues are not real to him. His sins, if there are such things as sins, are borrowed. He becomes an echo of some one else's music, an actor of a part that has not been written for him.[27]

Lord Henry suggests that, by allowing oneself to be influenced by someone else, one effectively stops being responsible for one's actions, or what Henry ominously calls one's 'sins'. He suggests, then, that the notion of influence is bound up with ethical as well as aesthetic questions. Yet this warning about the dangers of influence seems especially ironic in a text that is as wilfully and persistently allusive as *Dorian Gray*. Is there a danger that Wilde's novel at times becomes an echo of someone else's music? Indeed we might note that this passage is quoted in the opening pages of Harold Bloom's *The Anxiety of Influence*, in the context of a discussion about Wilde's failure as a poet.[28] We have already seen how Wilde's reflections upon Henry Irving and Sarah Bernhardt – two Shakespearean actors – implicitly comment upon Wilde's own appropriations of Shakespeare. Here Lord Henry *explicitly* uses the idea of acting as a metaphor for influence. And yet, unlike Wilde's model of collaboration between actor and playwright, Lord Henry's formulation suggests that by allowing oneself to be influenced by another, one becomes like an actor who is both passive and miscast, speaking lines that have already been written by – and indeed for – someone else.

Yet we find that Dorian has not entirely heeded Lord Henry's advice: 'He [Dorian] was dimly conscious that entirely fresh influences were at work within him. Yet they seemed to him to have come really from himself' (p. 18). This description again seems to reflect upon the dynamics of literary influence. It is unclear whether Lord Henry's words have influenced Dorian, or whether they have stimulated something that was there already. Is Lord Henry merely 'one of the parties' in this model of influence? Is it ever possible for influence to be 'entirely fresh'? The language of the novel becomes curiously overwrought as the narrator muses upon the influence of Lord Henry's words upon Dorian: 'Words! Mere words! How terrible they were! How clear, and vivid, and cruel! One could not escape from them. And yet what a subtle magic there was in them!' (p. 19). It seems all the more ironic that while Dorian is dimly aware of having been influenced by someone else, these two paragraphs of the novel are *themselves* deeply indebted to Walter Pater's *Gaston de Latour*.[29] We might note, then, that there is a peculiar similarity here between the novel's author and its main character. Should Pater be regarded as a 'fresh influence' upon Wilde, or does Wilde – like Dorian – imagine that these florid passages have really come from himself?

As the novel continues we find that Dorian is not only influenced by the words of Lord Henry, but also overly influenced by Shakespeare, in the sense that Shakespeare's plays become one of Dorian's principal models for reading and interpreting the world. This is perhaps another way in which Dorian might remind us of Wilde himself. Dorian reveals that he has fallen in love with an actress named Sybil Vane. He informs Lord Henry of how he came across 'an absurd little theatre, with great flaring gas-jets and gaudy play-bills' (p. 48), and found himself watching a shabby production of *Romeo and Juliet*. Dorian admits that he was 'rather annoyed at the idea of seeing Shakespeare done in such a wretched hole of a place', but acknowledges that he was 'interested, in a sort of way' (p. 50).[30] Romeo and Mercutio, we are told, were 'as grotesque as the scenery' (p. 50), yet Dorian is captivated by the young lady playing Juliet. Dorian goes to see her Shakespearean performances night after night:

> One evening she is Rosalind, and the next evening she is Imogen . . . I have watched her wandering through the forest of Arden, disguised as a pretty boy in hose and doublet and dainty cap. She has been mad, and has come into the presence of a guilty king, and given him rue to wear, and bitter herbs to taste of. She has been innocent, and the black hands of jealousy have crushed her reed-like throat. (pp 50–1)

In this rapturous description of Sybil Vane's performances as Rosalind, Imogen, Ophelia, and Desdemona, Dorian seems to have forgotten the difference between life and art. He describes the events of *Hamlet* and *Othello* as if they have actually taken place. Dorian stresses Sybil's innocence, contrasting it with the guilt of Claudius or the jealousy of Othello. Dorian even seems to take a peculiar pleasure in describing Sybil's demise at the 'black hands of jealousy'. When the proprietor of the theatre – described by Dorian as a 'horrid old Jew' (p. 52) – offers to introduce Sybil to him, Dorian is still enraptured by the fictional world of the play: 'I was furious with him, and told him that Juliet had been dead for hundreds of years, and that her body was lying in a marble tomb in Verona' (p. 52). For Dorian, Sybil Vane does not exist separately from the Shakespearean characters that she plays. Wilde seems to be hinting at the problems of using Shakespeare – and perhaps art more generally – as a way of making sense of the world.

Certainly there is a hint of homoerotic desire when Dorian suggests that he actually prefers Sybil Vane in masculine attire: 'When she came on in her boy's clothes she was perfectly wonderful' (p. 75). But perhaps the important point here is not the question of Dorian's sexuality, but the fact that he only finds Sybil Vane attractive when she is someone else. He appears to have fallen in love with an idea, or even a collection of quotations. When Dorian declares his love for Sybil Vane to Basil Hallward he does so in terms that are particularly suggestive and revealing:

> I have been right, Basil, haven't I, to take my love out of poetry, and to find my wife in Shakespeare's plays? Lips that Shakespeare taught to speak have whispered their secret in my ear. I have had the arms of Rosalind around me, and kissed Juliet on the mouth. (p. 76)

Here Dorian admits that his love for Sybil Vane is bound up with the language of Shakespeare. His perception of Sybil is deeply influenced by his perception of the Shakespearean roles she plays, and perhaps Dorian finds himself trying to imitate her male counterparts, such as Orlando and Romeo. Indeed *Dorian Gray* draws attention to these questions of mimicry and emulation: when Basil suggests that 'Love is a more wonderful thing than Art', Lord Henry counters with the proposition that they are 'both simply forms of imitation' (p. 84). We might note, however, that Sybil Vane is strangely absent from the passage quoted above. Only her lips are present in the description, and, what is more, it is Shakespeare who has 'taught' them to speak. The problem with Dorian's love for Sybil Vane, then, is not that he uses Shakespeare as a way of expressing himself – as many lovers do – but that he actually *substitutes* Shakespeare for the 'real' world. It would appear that Dorian has actually fallen in love with Shakespeare; or – perhaps more accurately – with Shakespeare's language. Dorian does register a degree of uncertainty about the fact that he has fallen in love with an idea: 'I have been right, Basil, haven't I . . . ?' (p. 76). Nonetheless, Dorian's description of his love for Sybil Vane suggests that she functions, at least for Dorian, as a kind of conduit, allowing him to experience communion – perhaps even a kind of textual intercourse – with Shakespeare.

Dorian takes Basil and Lord Henry to see Sybil Vane's performance as Juliet. And several fragments of verse from *Romeo and Juliet* itself appear in the text of the novel, with the narrator introducing one extract from the balcony scene as a 'beautiful passage', and another as 'those wonderful lines' (p. 83). Yet Sybil Vane's acting has become less than convincing, and the narrator informs us that these wonderful lines were spoken badly: 'the staginess of her acting was unbearable . . . Her gestures became absurdly artificial . . . It was simply bad art. She was a complete failure' (p. 83). Far from defending his fiancée, however, Dorian apologises to his companions, noting the extent to which Sybil Vane's star has fallen: 'Last night she was a great artist. This evening she is merely a commonplace, mediocre actress' (p. 84). We discover that Sybil Vane had thought that art – in this case Shakespearean art – was the only reality; now that she has discovered Dorian, however, and has fallen in love, she finds herself unable to act. As Sybil herself puts it,

> To-night, for the first time, I became conscious that the Romeo was hideous, and old, and painted, that the moonlight in the orchard was false, that the scenery was vulgar, and that the words I had to speak were unreal, were not my words, were not what I wanted to say. You had all brought me something higher, something of which art is but a reflection . . . I have grown sick of shadows. (p. 86)

Yet this passage once again highlights the novel's complex exploration of the very notion of influence. Sybil Vane suggests that there are times when life cannot be summed up by using a Shakespearean quotation. She emphasises the fact that the words of *Romeo and Juliet* are not her own; to adapt Lord Henry's formulation, she feels like an actor of a part that has been written for someone else.

In 'Discourse in the Novel', Bakhtin suggests that the appropriation of other people's words is not always an easy process:

> not all words for just anyone submit easily to this appropriation, to this seizure and transformation into private property: many words stubbornly resist, others remain alien, sound foreign in the mouth of the one who appropriated them and who now speaks them; they cannot be assimilated into his context and fall out of it; it is as if they put themselves in quotation marks against the will of the speaker.[31]

This phenomenon that Bakhtin describes seems to correspond with the attempts of Wilde – and his characters – to appropriate the language of Shakespeare. Now that Sybil Vane is actually in love with Dorian Gray, she finds that Shakespeare's words do *not* speak for her. They remain, as Bakhtin puts it, alien to her, and sound foreign in her mouth. Yet we might suggest that Wilde is playing a somewhat risky game here. Sybil Vane's anxiety about the unreality and otherness of Shakespeare's language threatens to expose Wilde's novel as a patchwork of quotations. The further irony is that Sybil's optimistic rejection of art and literature is itself reliant upon other people's words. The phrase 'I have grown sick of shadows' is an echo of Tennyson's 'The Lady of Shallot'.[32] Once again, at the very moment when one of Wilde's characters reflects upon the idea of influence, or originality, they end up quoting the words of another. For both Wilde and his characters, then, influence is problematic, perhaps even dangerous, and yet at the same time unavoidable. Sybil Vane's experiences with Shakespeare even raise the possibility that Shakespeare's words will prove too powerfully canonical for Wilde to appropriate them. For Harold Bloom, it is precisely Wilde's inability to escape from the shadow of other writers that makes a work like *The Ballad of Reading Gaol* an artistic failure.[33] And yet the fact that *The Picture of Dorian Gray* offers such a self-conscious and ambivalent exploration of the idea of influence suggests that to accuse the novel of lacking originality is to miss the point. When we turn to the latter part of the novel, which charts Dorian's moral decline, we find that Wilde makes some intriguing links between Dorian's portrait and the characters' appropriations of Shakespeare.

We have seen how *Dorian Gray* explores the perils of influence, and the problems and limitations of reading the world via the works of Shakespeare. As the novel continues, and becomes a kind of 'strange tragedy' (p. 93), it also explores its characters' attempts to use art – both pictorial and literary – to try to disguise or even conceal unsavoury truths about themselves. In particular, Dorian's portrait prompts us to reflect further upon the relationship between aesthetics and ethics. On the one hand, the painting suggests that art can aestheticise and thus hide the unpleasant elements of life from us. On the other hand, however, the portrait also reminds us of the extent to which art can serve a moral function, and can, as Hamlet puts it, 'show virtue her feature, scorn her own image' (III.2.22–3). Dorian finds that the painting does indeed 'bear the burden of his passions and his sins', and is 'seared with the lines of suffering and thought' (p. 90). Dorian's moral decline actually alters and disfigures the portrait: it reflects his own sins back to him. This ambivalence regarding the role and function of art is also, we might note, explored by Dorian and Lord Henry when they come to discuss Sybil Vane's tragic suicide. And, once again, Shakespeare plays an important role in their discussion.

Dorian admits to Lord Henry that he has effectively murdered Sybil, recalling his earlier description of her death at the hands of Othello: 'as surely as if I had cut her little throat with a knife' (p. 98). At the same time, however, he fails to take any responsibility for his actions, preferring to think about his life as if it were a scene in a book or a play: 'How extraordinarily dramatic life is! If I had read all this in a book, Harry, I think I would have wept over it' (p. 98). Dorian suggests that Sybil Vane's death would only have moved him had it been part of a fictional narrative. Yet despite Dorian's lack of feeling, he nonetheless suggests that art can be a way of eliciting empathy. For Lord Henry, however, art is a way of denying moral responsibility. Earlier in the novel he expresses his *inability* to empathise with others, seemingly regarding art as a kind of convenient anaesthetic: 'I can sympathize with everything, except suffering', he tells us. 'One should sympathize with the colour, the beauty, the joy of life. The less said about life's sores the better' (pp 39–40). And when discussing the demise of Sybil Vane, Lord Henry attempts to lessen the gravity of the situation by offering a barrage of epigrams and quotations, even appropriating and distorting the language of *Hamlet* in order to back up his arguments: 'Conscience makes egotists of us all' (p. 102), he says, recalling Hamlet's 'conscience does make cowards of us all' (III.1.85). Lord Henry reminds Dorian of the various Shakespearean heroines that Sybil Vane played: 'if she died as Juliet, she came to life as Imogen' (p. 103). And yet as Dorian himself points out these comparisons with Shakespeare's characters simply reveal the gulf between life and art: 'She will never come to life again now' (p. 103). Shakespeare thus provides a lens through which Dorian and Lord Henry debate the question of whether art encourages empathy or aestheticises suffering.

In one of the most striking and disturbing passages in the novel, Lord Henry encourages Dorian to think of Sybil Vane's death as a fiction – a scene from the plays of Shakespeare or one of his contemporaries:

> you must think of that lonely death in the tawdry dressing-room simply as a strange lurid fragment from some Jacobean tragedy, as a wonderful scene from Webster, or Ford, or Cyril Tourneur. The girl never really lived, and so she has never really died. To you at least she was always a dream, a phantom that flitted through Shakespeare's plays and left them lovelier for its presence, a reed through which Shakespeare's music sounded richer and more full of joy. (p. 103)

Lord Henry proposes a dangerous and scandalous forgetting of the difference between life and art. Sybil Vane is effectively depersonalised as a 'reed' through which Shakespeare's verbal music sounded. Far more appropriate and worthwhile, Lord Henry suggests, to grieve for Shakespeare's tragic heroines: 'Mourn for Ophelia' if you like. Put ashes on your head because Cordelia was strangled. Cry out against Heaven because the daughter of Brabantio died. But don't waste your tears over Sybil Vane. She was less real than they are' (p. 103). While Dorian had previously mistaken Sybil Vane for Rosalind, Imogen, and Juliet, now Lord Henry compares her unfavourably to these characters. The two men thus deny Sybil Vane any kind of independent existence outside the world of Shakespeare's plays. According to Lord Henry, Shakespeare's heroines are just as 'real' as – perhaps *more* real than – Sybil Vane herself.

At the same time, however, Lord Henry's description of Sybil Vane under-lines Dorian's part in her death. Lord Henry attempts to depersonalise her, describing Sybil as 'a reed through which Shakespeare's music sounded' (p. 103). Sybil, he suggests, is nothing more than a trumpet set for Shakespeare's lips to blow. And yet the novel has already shown us that Sybil is far more than a mere mouthpiece, not least when she suggests that Shakespeare's words do not speak for her. What is even more suggestive is that this phrase recalls Dorian's earlier description of Sybil's 'reed-like throat', which is crushed by Othello's 'black hands of jealousy' (p. 51). Lord Henry's use of the word *reed* thus inadvertently associates Dorian with Othello. At the end of Shakespeare's tragedy, we might remember, Othello attempts to redescribe himself as an 'honourable murderer' (v.2.300), and one who 'loved not wisely but too well' (v.2.353); yet he is nonetheless largely responsible for Desdemona's tragic death. These connections with *Othello* are further reinforced when the narrator – whose voice seems to merge with that of Dorian – describes the portrait in strikingly Shakespearean terms:

Was it to become a monstrous and loathsome thing, to be hidden away in a locked room, to be shut out from the sunlight that had so often touched to brighter gold the waving wonder of its hair? The pity of it! the pity of it! (pp 105–6)

This last exclamation echoes Othello's comments to Iago when he thinks that Desdemona's infidelity has been confirmed: 'Nay, that's certain. But yet the pity of it, Iago. O, Iago, the pity of it, Iago!' (IV.I.191–2). This allusion to *Othello* further complicates *Dorian Gray*'s engagement with Shakespeare, as well as its exploration of the question of influence. After all, *Othello* – a play that explores Iago's attempts to manipulate and poison Othello's mind – can itself be read as a warning about the dangers of being too easily influenced by another. Lord Henry's attempts to use Shakespeare to hide Dorian's part in Sybil Vane's suicide – and his own influence upon Dorian – are thus only partially successful.[34] For these interconnected Shakespearean allusions not only emphasise Dorian's responsibility for Sybil's death by aligning him with Othello, but also, we might suggest, implicitly align Lord Henry with Iago. What this suggests is that Shakespeare's art functions in the novel in an analogous way to the portrait: it does not simply conceal but rather exaggerates Dorian's moral failings.

We have seen, then, that *The Picture of Dorian Gray* both explores and enacts the complex and ambiguous processes of literary (and non-literary) influence. The novel alerts the reader to the ethical dimensions of art, and encourages him or her to engage empathetically with others. It exposes the dangers of allowing art to distract us from or aestheticise immoral actions. At the same time, the novel suggests that art – whether it is the portrait, one of Shakespeare's plays, or even *The Picture of Dorian Gray* itself – is a kind of Rorschach test, reflecting and revealing the values of the reader or viewer. As Wilde puts it in 'The Portrait of Mr W. H.',

We become lovers when we see Romeo and Juliet, and Hamlet makes us students . . . Art, even of the fullest scope and widest vision, can never really show us the external world. All that it shows us is our own soul, the one world of which we have any real cognizance . . . It is Art, and Art only, that reveals us to ourselves.[35]

This passage emphasises the difficulty, even impossibility, of concealing one's moral failings through art. Clearly Dorian Gray's portrait serves this function; as Basil Hallward puts it to Dorian, 'Sin is a thing that writes itself across a man's face. It cannot be concealed' (p. 149). Yet we have also seen that something similar happens when the novel's characters try to appropriate Shakespeare for their own ends. Both forms of art expose or even exaggerate the characters' moral failings rather than disguise them. These links are further emphasised in the novel's penultimate chapter, when Dorian himself uses the language of *Hamlet* to describe his feelings about the painting.[36] Indeed this comparability between Shakespeare's art and the art of the portrait suggests that Wilde was not aligning himself with his characters – as some anxious contemporary reviews of *Dorian Gray* suggested – but rather using Shakespeare as a way of critiquing them, or even allowing them to critique themselves.

It seems both apt and striking, then, that when Wilde wrote to the editor of the *Scots Observer* to defend his novel, he compared his own art to that of Shakespeare: 'Your critic then, sir, commits the absolutely unpardonable crime of trying to confuse the artist with his subject-matter. For this, sir, there is no excuse at all. Of one who is the greatest figure in the world's literature since Greek days Keats remarked that he had as much pleasure in conceiving the evil as he has in conceiving the good.'[37] Even after the novel was published we find that Wilde was still using Shakespeare to articulate and conceptualise the questions of art and morality that it raises. Wilde suggests that he shares with Shakespeare a kind of moral relativism or detachment; he proposes that neither artist should be mistaken for their characters. At the same time, Wilde effectively aligns himself with Shakespeare, and applies Keats's comments on Shakespeare's genius to himself, using them to defend and justify his own art.[38] Thus while *Dorian Gray* highlights the problems of using Shakespeare's language as a means of expressing oneself, and using his art as a way of making sense of the world, it would appear that Wilde did not always heed these warnings. If Wilde did indeed consider himself 'condemned' to speak the language of Shakespeare, this may not have been due to the suppression of his Irish language or identity, but rather to the sheer power and pervasiveness of Shakespeare's literary afterlife. For a writer such as Wilde, whose ambivalent fascination with Shakespeare seems to have persisted throughout his career, this may have been a condemnation devoutly to be wished.

Notes

1   *The Complete Letters of Oscar Wilde*, ed. by Merlin Holland and Rupert Hart-Davies (London: Fourth Estate, 2000), p. 505: 'On peut adorer une langue sans bien la parler, comme on peut aimer une femme sans la connaître. Français de sympathie, je suis Irlandais de race, et les Anglais m'ont condamné à parler le langage de Shakespeare.'

2   Quoted in Richard Ellmann, *Oscar Wilde* (London: Hamish Hamilton, 1987), p. 331.

3   Mark Thornton Burnett, 'Introduction' to *Shakespeare and Ireland: History, Politics, Culture*, ed. by Mark Thornton Burnett and Ramona Wray (Basingstoke: Macmillan, 1997), pp 1–5 (p. 1).

4   See Declan Kiberd, 'Oscar Wilde: The Artist as Irishman', in *Wilde the Irishman*, ed. by Jerusha McCormack (New Haven and London: Yale University Press, 1998), pp 9–23, in which he notes that, for Wilde, being condemned to speak the language of Shakespeare 'was not the most onerous of sentences' (p. 11).

5   Interview with Robert Ross, *Pall Mall Budget*, 30 June 1892, quoted in Ellmann, *Oscar Wilde*, pp 351–2.

6   Letter to the Editor of the *Scots Observer*, 9 July 1890, repr. in *The Soul of Man Under Socialism and Selected Critical Prose*, ed. by Linda Dowling (Harmondsworth: Penguin, 2001), p. 115; *De Profundis*, in *De Profundis and Other Writings* (Harmondsworth: Penguin, 1976), p. 167.

7   Mikhail Bakhtin, 'Discourse in the Novel' (1934–5), in *The Dialogic Imagination: Four Essays*, ed. by Michael Holquist (Austin: University of Texas Press, 1981), pp 259–422 (p. 293).

8   *De Profundis*, p. 169.

9   Ibid., p. 169. The Emerson quotation is taken from his lecture 'The Preacher', published in Ralph Waldo Emerson, *Lectures and Biographical Sketches* (Boston: Houghton, Mifflin, 1893). See *Complete Letters*, ed. by Holland and Hart-Davies (p. 744, n. 3).

10   Margot Oxford [Asquith], *More Memories* (London: Cassell, 1933), p. 116.

11   Lady Campbell's wry response ('And I suppose your profile will protrude *beyond* Shakespeare's!') suggests that she perceived a degree of competitiveness or emulation on Wilde's part (quoted in Asquith, *More Memories*, p. 116).

12   Quoted in Elizabeth Robins, *Both Sides of the Curtain* (London: William Heinemann, 1940), p. 9. See also Ellmann, *Oscar Wilde*, p. 105.

13   Kate Chedgzoy, '"Strange worship": Oscar Wilde and the Key to Shakespeare's *Sonnets*', in *Shakespeare's Queer Children: Sexual Politics and Contemporary Culture* (Manchester: Manchester University Press, 1995), pp 135–76 (p. 148).

14   Richard Ellman offers a biographical reading of 'The Portrait of Mr W. H.', commenting that Wilde 'imagined Shakespeare, a married man with two children like himself, captivated by a boy as he had been captivated by Ross' (*Oscar Wilde*, p. 281). For other considerations of the relationship between Wilde and Shakespeare that focus on 'Mr W. H.' see William A. Cohen, 'Willie and Wilde: Reading *The Portrait of Mr W. H.*', *South Atlantic Quarterly*, 88 (1989), 219–45; Chedgzoy, 'Strange worship'; Joseph Bristow, '"A complex multiform creature": Wilde's Sexual Identities', in *The Cambridge Companion to Oscar Wilde*, ed. by Peter Raby (Cambridge: Cambridge University Press, 1997), pp 196–218 (see esp. pp 204–9); Lawrence Danson, *Wilde's Intentions: The Artist in his Criticism* (Oxford: Clarendon Press, 1997), pp 102–26; Rebecca Laroche, 'The Sonnets on Trial: Reconsidering *The Portrait of Mr W. H.*' in *Shakespeare's Sonnets: Critical Essays*, ed. by James Schiffer (New York: Garland, 1999), pp 391–409; and Russell Jackson, 'Oscar Wilde and Shakespeare's Secrets', in *In the Footsteps of Queen Victoria*, ed. by Christa Jansohn (Münster: Lit Verlag, 2003).

15   Towards the end of *De Profundis*, for example, Wilde offers a brief meditation on *Hamlet*, and seems to present Hamlet's tragedy as a precedent for his own downfall: 'Instead of trying to be the hero of his own history, he seeks to be the spectator of his own tragedy' (p. 201).

16   'The Decay of Lying', in *Selected Critical Prose*, ed. by Dowling, pp 163–92 (p. 178).

17   Wilde certainly seems to have been aware of the subversive potential of reinventing Shakespeare. Before 'The Portrait of Mr W. H.' appeared, he is reported to have said that 'Our English homes will totter to their base when my book appears', quoted in Hesketh Pearson, *The Life of Oscar Wilde: A Biography* (1954; repr. London: Macdonald and Jane's, 1975), p. 127.

18 See Harold Bloom, 'Shakespeare, Center of the Canon', in *The Western Canon: The Books and School of the Ages* (London: Macmillan, 1995), ch. 2; and *Shakespeare: The Invention of the Human* (London: Fourth Estate, 1999).

19 Cf. Bakhtin, who suggests that the word in language 'becomes "one's own" only when the speaker populates it with his own intention, his own accent, when he appropriates the word, adapting it to his own semantic and expressive intention' (Bakhtin, 'Discourse in the Novel', p. 293)

20 Bloom, *The Western Canon*, p. 40.

21 Adrian Poole, *Shakespeare and the Victorians* (London: Thomson Learning, 2004), p. 235. The whole of Poole's 'Dublin Epilogue' (pp 231–9) is relevant here. Poole suggests that Wilde's relationship with Shakespeare was far less anxious – or hostile – than it was for certain other Irish writers: 'Wilde would have been happy to drink champagne with Shakespeare: Shaw would have thrown it in his face' (pp 235–6).

22 *Morning News*, article headed 'Paris, Tuesday June 10, 1884', quoted in Ellmann, *Oscar Wilde*, p. 236.

23 'The Critic as Artist', in *Selected Critical Prose*, ed. by Dowling, pp 213–79 (p. 246). Gilbert is referring to Anton Rubinstein (1829–94), an acclaimed Russian pianist and composer.

24 'Fabien Dei Franchi', first published in Wilde's *Poems* (London, 1881), quoted from *De Profundis and Other Writings*, p. 221 (lines 8–9).

25 Jerusha McCormack, 'Wilde's Fiction(s)', in *The Cambridge Companion to Oscar Wilde*, pp 96–117 (p. 110).

26 Hortst Breuer is one of the few critics to consider the relationship between *Dorian Gray* and Shakespeare, but even he focuses on Shakespeare's *Sonnets* rather than the many references to Shakespeare's plays that permeate the novel. See his 'Oscar Wilde's *Dorian Gray* and Shakespeare's Sonnets', *English Language Notes*, 42 (2004), 59–68.

27 Oscar Wilde, *The Picture of Dorian Gray*, ed. by Isobel Murray (Oxford: Oxford University Press, 1981), p. 17. Further references to the novel will be from this edition.

28 See Harold Bloom, *The Anxiety of Influence: A Theory of Poetry* (New York: Oxford University Press, 1973), p. 6. Bloom suggests that Wilde 'knew he had failed as a poet because he lacked strength to overcome his anxiety of influence, knew also the darker truths concerning influence' (pp 5–6). Bloom comments that Wilde's lyrics 'anthologize the whole of English High Romanticism' (p. 6), but does not mention his relationship with Shakespeare.

29 See Murray, n. 18 (p. 226). On Wilde's fascination with Pater, see Ellmann, *Oscar Wilde*, p. 46. In *De Profundis* Wilde describes Pater's *The Renaissance* as 'that book which has had such strange influence over my life' (p. 158).

30 Harold Bloom may also have found something of interest in this performance. Bloom writes that 'A bad production of Shakespeare, dreadfully directed and performed by actors who cannot speak verse . . . differs in kind as well as degree from good or bad productions of Ibsen and Molière. There is the shock of a verbal art larger and more definitive than any other, so persuasive that it seems to be not art at all but something that was always there' (*The Western Canon*, p. 49).

31 Bakhtin, 'Discourse in the Novel', p. 294.

32 See Tennyson, 'The Lady of Shallot': 'I am half sick of shadows' (line 71), in *The Poems of Tennyson*, 2nd edn, ed. by Christopher Ricks, 3 vols (London: Longman, 1987), I, 387–95.

33   Bloom writes that '*The Ballad of Reading Gaol* becomes an embarrassment to read, directly one recognizes that every lustre it exhibits is reflected from *The Rime of the Ancient Mariner*' (*The Anxiety of Influence*, p. 6).

34   Interestingly, Bakhtin refers briefly to *The Picture of Dorian Gray* in the context of a discussion about how the 'speaking person' in a novel is always an '*ideologue*'. He writes: 'The novel, being a dialogized representation of an ideologically freighted discourse . . . is of all verbal genres the one least susceptible to aestheticism as such, to a purely formalistic playing about with words. Thus when an aesthete undertakes to write a novel, his aestheticism is not revealed in the novel's formal construction, but exclusively in the fact that in the novel there is represented a speaking person who happens to be an ideologue for aestheticism, who exposes convictions that then are subjected in the novel to contest' ('Discourse in the Novel', p. 333).

35   'The Portrait of Mr W. H.' in *Selected Critical Prose*, p. 91.

36   As Dorian puts it to Lord Henry, 'The memory of the thing is hateful to me. Why do you talk of it? It used to remind me of those curious lines in some play – "Hamlet," I think – how do they run? – "*Like the painting of a sorrow, / A face without a heart.*" Yes: that is what it was like' (p. 214).

37   Letter to the Editor of the *Scots Observer*, 9 July 1890, repr. in *Selected Critical Prose*, p. 115.

38   Keats commented that Shakespeare 'has as much delight in conceiving an Iago as an Imogen', rpt in *The Romantics on Shakespeare*, ed. by Jonathan Bate (Harmondsworth: Penguin, 1992), p. 199.

CHAPTER 10

'Like Shakespeare,' she added . . . 'or isn't it?'

Shakespearean Echoes in Elizabeth Bowen's
Portrait of Ireland

Heather Ingman

Theories of intertextuality remind us that, since all texts are potentially poly-phonic, no reading of a text can be final. Every conclusion will be, as Terence Harpold terms it, a 'contingent conclusion', a product of a reader's selection of some intertextual echoes and avoidance or ignorance of others.[1] In recent years, discussions of early twentieth-century Irish writers' appropriations of Shakespeare have focused on the theme of writing back to the empire in the period prior to and during decolonisation.[2] What such discussions have neglected, however, is the role of gender in Irish re-readings of Shakespeare. This essay attempts to supply that omission by looking at Elizabeth Bowen's use of Shakespeare. Bowen's appropriations of Shakespeare throughout her work are many and various, as I will indicate below; but in keeping with this volume's emphasis on Shakespeare in Ireland, I have chosen to concentrate on Bowen's re-reading of Shakespeare in an Irish context, specifically her use of *Twelfth Night* in *The Last September* and of *The Tempest* in her short story, 'Sunday Afternoon'. Such an approach not only highlights issues of inter-textuality and intentionality, but also points to Bowen's interrogation of gender and identity in the context of Irish politics. A consideration of Shakespearean echoes in Bowen's work underlines, moreover, her status as a precursor of a series of twentieth-century women writers – Angela Carter, Kate Atkinson, Marina Warner, to name only three – who have reclaimed Shakespeare for female-centred experience.[3]

Although Bowen did not write an essay specifically on Shakespeare, his influence permeates so much of her writing that it is remarkable that, to date, little has been made generally of the echoes of Shakespeare in her work. Hermione Lee notes the resemblance between Hamlet and the spy, Robert Kelway, in Bowen's Second World War novel, *The Heat of the Day* where

Hamlet-like echoes are particularly evident in Robert's relationship with his dead father and his over-controlling mother.[4] In Bowen's post-war novel, *The Little Girls*, references to the three witches from *Macbeth* provide a subtext to the reunion of the three school friends, while her last novel, *Eva Trout*, is studded with references to *Hamlet*. In keeping with Bowen's use of pastiche and parody in that novel, the *Hamlet* references are intentionally misleading, their playfulness serving to underline Bowen's critique of the vacuity of modern culture.

Some of Bowen's novels demonstrate a more sustained engagement with Shakespearean themes. As Ann Ashworth has pointed out, the question 'Why was she called Portia?' reverberates through *The Death of the Heart*, a novel where the heroine's future is constrained by her dead father's wishes and she has to learn, as Shakespeare's heroine advises, to temper justice with mercy.[5] Like Shakespeare's Portia, Bowen's heroine has to negotiate her father's arrangement for her that does not necessarily have her best interests at heart. Thomas Quayne has bequeathed his daughter to his son and daughter-in-law in the mistaken impression that with them she will experience English family life. But, like *The Merchant of Venice*, *The Death of the Heart* depicts a worldly, shallow society whose values are centred on commerce.[6] In a society such as this, both Portias have to learn to rely on their own judgement. At the same time, their fathers' wills must be satisfied – the right casket must be chosen, Portia must be welcomed properly into the Quaynes' home. In her quest for a home and a sense of identity, Bowen's Portia has to choose between three mother figures: the worldly, glittering Anna, the less glamorous Mrs Heccomb, and the stolid, leaden servant Matchett who, despite her unpromising appearance, is the one who finally brings Portia home.

In all these works, the Shakespearean echoes merit further analysis. However, I would like to focus here on Bowen's rereading of Shakespeare in the Irish context of her second novel, *The Last September*. The novel was published in 1929 but it is set during the War of Independence and depicts the final loss of power for Bowen's class, the Anglo-Irish. It has been noted that the names of Lois's two girlfriends in *The Last September* recall the leading female characters in *Twelfth Night*: Viola being the name of the English school friend with whom Lois corresponds, and Olivia her Irish friend whose name has become abbreviated to Livvy.[7] Neil Corcoran, who makes this point, also discusses the explicit reference to Shakespeare in the course of Marda's conversation with Hugo about the political situation in Ireland – 'Like Shakespeare,' Marda says, 'or isn't it?' (p. 82). Corcoran relates this to Shakespeare's history plays, taking Marda to be drawing a parallel between the insecurity of the Anglo-Irish and that of the baronial and monarchical classes in Shakespeare's history plays. However it could be argued that Marda's words continue the references to *Twelfth Night* for it is my contention that *Twelfth Night* illuminates some of the central themes of *The Last September*. I am not arguing that Elizabeth Bowen deliberately placed direct references to *Twelfth Night* in her novel but rather that bearing Shakespeare's play in mind helped her imagination focus on certain themes. This chapter explores three areas of the play in connection with Bowen's novel: the fragility of Illyria; the sexual ambiguity of the characters; and the fluidity of desire.

To take the first: the fragility of Illyria. In *Twelfth Night* an elegiac mood is established at the outset as Orsino calls for more music to stir up his feelings of doomed love for Olivia. A sense of stasis is conveyed, of idle, self-indulgent gentry as Orsino opts for music over action, against his adviser's wish that he get out and do a spot of hunting. The elegiac quality of Bowen's novel is established in the opening paragraphs by such phrases as 'in those days, girls wore crisp white skirts'.[8] Words like 'transitory' and 'out-moded' echo through the text. A picture is painted of an irresponsible, leisured class which continues to visit, entertain, and organise tennis parties and dances, despite the dangers lurking outside. Danielstown is presented as a world of its own, sealed off by armed patrols from the nationalist rebels. Similarly, in Shakespeare's play, Illyria is depicted as an unreal place where its leisured inhabitants eat, flirt and analyse their feelings despite talk of naval engagements and pirates. As Michael Dobson comments, 'The choice of Illyria as a setting places love and escapism alongside danger and death.'[9]

It is this insularity of the Anglo-Irish recurring in the conversation between Hugo and Marda, two Anglo-Irish visitors to Danielstown, which prompts the latter's reference to Shakespeare. Marda has asked: 'How far do you think this war is going to go? Will there ever be anything we can all do except not notice?' (p. 82). To which Hugo responds that the Anglo-Irish will simply carry on with 'their tenacity to something that isn't there – that never was there' (p. 82). Their position in the country is no more than an illusion, he suggests, a point which is echoed in several other passages in the novel: for example, Lois and Hugo, after speaking with Michael O'Connor whose son is fighting with the nationalists, feel their presence in the country is an 'illusion' (p. 65). Marda then takes this up in Bowen's characteristically fragmented sentences: 'But the hold of the country *was* that, she considered. "Like Shakespeare," she added, more vaguely, "or isn't it?"' (p. 82). Contrary to Corcoran's argument that this refers to the history plays, Marda's comment may be read as a continuation of Bowen's reference to *Twelfth Night*, specifically her use of Shakespeare's play to critique aspects of Anglo-Irish life. Danielstown, like Illyria, is a fragile, unreal place and its very fragility exerts a hold on its inhabitants. This is a feature noted many times by Bowen in her descriptions of life in the Irish Big House. In an essay on that topic published in 1940, she describes: 'the spell that falls on the visitor from the moment he passes in at the gates.'[10] In *Bowen's Court*, published two years later, she speaks of life there as 'a continuous semi-physical dream' where her ancestors, cut off from the life of the country-side around them, became prone to fantasy.[11] Bowen's only other novel set in Ireland, *A World of Love* published in 1955, likewise portrays inhabitants of a decaying Big House trapped in a fantasy dream world where life seems to have stopped still after the First World War. The teasing ambiguity of Marda's remark simultaneously discloses and disguises Bowen's reliance on the Shakespearean text for her critical portrayal of the Anglo-Irish.

Like Illyria, the Big House is a fantastical place where the inhabitants carry on their revels despite the dangers ('armed patrols', the Black and Tans and so on) lurking outside. In her preface to the second US edition of *The Last September*, Bowen remarks: 'In such an atmosphere, the carrying on of orthodox conventional social life might seem either foolhardy or inhuman. One can only say, it seemed the best thing to do.'[12] The Anglo-Irish may be in the wrong, and even at times acknowledge themselves to be in the wrong, but they are determined to go on enjoying their cakes and ale while they still can. The autumnal quality of both novel and play and their time-specific titles reinforce the notion that these will be the last of the revels. The Twelfth Night, or Feast of Epiphany, will give way to the working world. The dance in the British Army barracks will be the last occasion for revelry before violence shatters the old political order. Despite Bowen's class loyalties, she fully recognised that the Anglo-Irish way of life could not continue, acknowledging in her afterword to *Bowen's Court* that: 'my family got their position and drew their power from a situation that shows an inherent wrong . . . With the Treaty . . . a new hopeful phase started: I believe in its promise' (p. 453). In the novel, Laurence and Lois, representatives of the younger generation of Anglo-Irish, rebel against their elders' willed ignorance, angry at being obliged to take part in a way of life that has no future: 'they both sat eating tea with dissatisfaction, resentful at giving so much of themselves to what was to be forgotten' (p. 118). *Twelfth Night* provided Bowen with the perfect example of a society on the brink of danger but determined to ignore that danger for as long as possible.

Shakespeare's play and Bowen's novel share more than tone and atmosphere. The themes of gender ambiguity and the fluidity of desire are common to both. *Twelfth Night* is, as commentators have pointed out, a play about young people. Viola's youth is central to the plot, allowing her to masquerade successfully as a male: 'Not yet old enough for a man, nor young enough for a boy,' says Malvolio (1.5.139–40). Barbara Hodgdon has commented that Viola's gender 'remains tenuously constituted, adaptable to circumstance'.[13] Similarly, Penny Gay suggests that 'Viola always exists in the margins between genders', playing out a fantasy of not being obliged to choose – she can be both Viola *and* Sebastian.[14] The fantasy aspect of this is underlined by the statement in the play that Viola and Sebastian are identical twins, a biological impossibility for female/male twins, and one which Shakespeare added to his source in Barnabe Rich's *Farewell to Military Profession* (1581), where it is simply a brother and a sister who become separated.

The play's gender trouble is echoed in Bowen's novel where Lois's unstable sense of self is highlighted. A central theme of *The Last September* is that eighteen-year-old Lois has reached adulthood but cannot bring herself to assume the role of a woman: 'I hate women' she tells Marda, 'But I can't think how to begin to be anything else' (p. 99). Like Viola she seems to be between genders. In contrast, both Lois's friends, Viola and Livvy (Olivia), are adept at assuming the feminine role. Viola's letters reveal a young woman already accomplished at assessing the suitability of men, provoking in Lois the realisation that Viola must have only played at being a schoolgirl as she, Lois, now has to play at being grown-up. Livvy is similarly effective in stage managing her engagement to the bewildered David. Both Viola and Livvy are more skilled in the world of sexual politics than Lois so that, although Lois cannot imagine them together, her two friends have more in common than she believes; unlike Lois, they have no difficulty in performing their appropriate gender role. In comparison with Shakespeare's lively Viola, Lois seems passive, even lethargic. Is Bowen suggesting that Lois's difficulty in assuming the life of a woman is somehow due to the uncertain political position in which she finds herself? Accidentally encountering a nationalist, Lois knows that she cannot share whatever impulse is inspiring him to hurry through the Irish countryside at night. She lacks confidence in her class in the same way as she lacks confidence in herself as a woman.

But there is more to Lois's difficulty in performing the feminine role than simple loss of confidence. The theme of sexual ambiguity in *The Last September* has been noted by several critics, in particular by Patricia Coughlan who cites Marda as an example of someone who exudes sexual attractiveness for both genders.[15] After getting to know Marda, Lois has moments of wanting to be 'a woman's woman' (p. 99) and wishing Gerald 'were a woman' (p. 172). In relation to *Twelfth Night* Stephen Greenblatt has argued, on the basis of Sebastian's comment to Olivia in Act V, Scene 1 (lines 252–3) that the play suggests to be legally, socially and theologically acceptable, love must swerve from the straight course of love of one's own sex to heterosexual love.[16] Bowen's novel echoes this movement. After the revelation in the mill scene of Hugo's passion for Marda, Lois feels that she has no alternative but to marry Gerald, despite his disappointing kisses. 'She felt quite ruled out, there was nothing at all for her here . . . She thought: "I must marry Gerald"' (p. 125). As in the play, any latent homosexual attraction is quickly eroded by a heterosexual society. However, ambiguities remain in both novel and play. Lois insists that Gerald take account of her feelings about Marda: 'Don't you wonder at all if I miss her?' (p. 153). With Gerald's death, Lois's future once again becomes uncertain. In *Twelfth Night*, despite her betrothal to Orsino, Viola remains in male clothes to the end, referred to by Orsino as 'boy', 'man' and 'Cesario'. Sebastian's assurance to Olivia that she is betrothed to both 'a maid [ie a male virgin] and a man' (v.1.256), only reinforces the ambiguity of the play's ending, an ambiguity which Shakespeare seems to have been at pains to insist upon, downplaying his source's emphasis on the celebration of heterosexual marriage.

In Bowen's novel, Lois's difficulty with her assigned gender role is echoed by some of the male characters. Hugo is well aware that, at a time when masculinity was bound up with a willingness to die in defence of one's country and its women, the political situation in Ireland robbed Anglo-Irish males of a heroic role. He complains of being 'deprived of heroism by this wet kind of smother of commiseration' (p. 82), which is indeed expressed in the novel by English Army wives like Mrs Vermont whose statement 'We came to take care of all of you' is not well received by the Anglo-Irish (p. 47). Hugo pushes his emasculation to its logical conclusion by adopting the female role of care giver in relation to his wife. Laurence shares Hugo's feelings of vacancy produced by the political situation: 'I know nothing,' he complains, 'this might all just as well be going on in the Balkans' (p. 92). His desire to take on the rebels is constantly thwarted. When he does finally encounter them, the episode, like much in this novel, is anticlimactic (they simply rob him of his shoes and watch). Bowen's critique of masculinity interweaves gender with the political situation in Ireland by connecting Anglo-Irish males' passivity in responding to the rebels with emasculation. Her interrogation of masculinity curiously echoes Shakespeare's play. The equation of masculinity with valour in war is scrutinised in *Twelfth Night* where Sir Andrew Aguecheek reveals himself a coward, in contrast with Viola who cannot fight properly because of her sex. 'Viola's manhood queries Sir Andrew's' comments Juliet Dusinberre.[17] If masculinity is related to the ability to fight, neither Sir Andrew in the play nor Hugo nor Laurence in the novel perform it satisfactorily. In *The Last September* it is Marda and Lois, not Hugo, who face the IRA gunman in the mill.

As well as interrogating gender roles, both play and novel emphasise the fluidity of desire. For Stephen Greenblatt, 'the delicious confusions of *Twelfth Night* depend upon the mobility of desire.'[18] Indeed, he characterises 'the unmooring of desire, the generalising of the libidinal' as 'the special pleasure of Shakespearean fiction' (p. 89). In *Twelfth Night*, unusually for Shakespeare, there is no older generation of fathers to arrange or block marriages and this makes desire extraordinarily fluid. Indeed, part of the pleasure for the audience of *Twelfth Night*, as Valerie Traub suggests, is 'derived from a transgressive glimpse of multiple erotic possibilities'.[19] Viola disguised as the young page, Cesario, is in love with Orsino; Orsino, despite his proclaimed love for Olivia, is drawn to Cesario; Olivia falls in love with Cesario and Viola/Cesario is not immune to the erotic excitement of finding herself the object of a woman's desire. The subtitle, 'What You Will', seems entirely appropriate.

Desire is equally unstable in Bowen's novel; indeed Patricia Coughlan speaks of desire generally in Bowen's work as possessing 'a strikingly labile quality'.[20] *The Last September* opens with Lois's misconceived crush on Hugo. Similarly, Hugo, Laurence and Lois all have crushes on Marda. Lois would love to be able to solve the problem of her future by loving Gerald but by the end of the novel, she is disconcerted to find herself intrigued by one of his fellow soldiers, Daventry. The strange relationship between Daventry and Gerald, noted by Corcoran, appears to involve a homoerotic element. 'Gerald and Daventry passed in the dark with, it seemed, a queer silent interchange' (p. 153). As in this episode, there is always a shadowy third in the relationships in *The Last September*: Lois's mother comes between Hugo and Lois; between Lois and Gerald there is first Marda, then Daventry; between Lois and Marda there is Hugo and also Marda's fiancé, Leslie Lawe. In *Twelfth Night* in the conversations between Viola and Orsino, there is always Olivia; between Viola and Olivia there is always Orsino. Once again, consciously or unconsciously, Shakespeare's play underpins Bowen's novel, specifically here in its treatment of the complications of desire.[21]

As well as the instability of desire, the novel, like the play, dwells on the illusions of love. Olivia thinks she wants Cesario but gets what she really wants in Sebastian, a male version of Viola. Lois thinks she wants Gerald but gets her freedom instead, arguably what she really wants. Orsino believes himself to be in love with Olivia but his love is domineering and controlling and he has no clear image of Olivia herself. He is inclined to dogmatise about women's love, denying women a will of their own and an independent perspective. In Bowen's novel, such conventionality about women is shared by Gerald whose sense of chivalry impels him into a protective attitude towards both Lois and Ireland. As Viola resists Orsino's ideas about women, so Lois resists Gerald's colonising efforts and draws a parallel between England's misplaced sense of chivalry in regards to Ireland – their refusal to declare outright war on the country – and male chivalry towards women: 'Can you wonder this country gets irritated?' she remarks. 'It's as bad for it as being a woman. I never can see why women shouldn't be hit' (p. 49). However Lois is unable to change Gerald's feelings: 'Some idea he had formed of herself remained inaccessible to her; she could not affect it' (p. 48). Her moment of outrage only strengthens Gerald's feelings of protectiveness. Like Orsino, his idealisations about women prevent him from understanding the real woman in front of him, a feminist point, perhaps, but one which is already explicit in Shakespeare's play.

None of the lovers take responsibility for their love. Viola looks to time to untangle the knot with Olivia (11.2. 38–9); Olivia blames fate for her love for Viola (1.5. 280–1). Hugo does nothing to suppress his feelings for Marda, which are perfectly plain to his wife; Marda simply flees the havoc she has caused. There are other hints of irresponsibility: Laurence shares Malvolio's self-interested approach to love. As Malvolio desires social advancement in his fantasies of marriage to Olivia, so Laurence envies Marda for settling her future advantageously by her engagement to Leslie Lawe. Orsino's narcissistic use of music to work on his emotions (1.1.1–8) finds its echo in the novel in the scene at Mrs Fogarty's where the British soldiers and the young women indulge their emotions by singing love songs. Inspired by the music they evince a sentimentality about love which Lois eventually resists: 'All that fuss, if you know what I mean, about just somebody' (p. 74).

Danielstown, like Illyria, is a place where a youthful cast can play at love, where Laurence, the incipient novelist, can rewrite the scenario of their lives, marrying Hugo to Lois's mother, Sir Richard to Hugo's wife, turning himself into a tortured literary genius and writing Lois out of the script altogether. In *Twelfth Night*, it is Viola who recounts stories about herself: what she would do if she were Olivia's lover, 'Make me a willow cabin at your gate' (1.5.237), or her tale to Orsino of her imaginary sister pining for love (11.4.105–17). This theme of the infinite possibilities of role playing underlines the fragility of the worlds depicted in the novel and the play. As the period of revelry comes to an end, so Laurence recognises that there is a limit to the number of roles one can play: 'there is a narrow and fixed compulsion, Laurence recognised, inside the widest ranges of our instability' (p. 107). This is underlined by Marda's marriage to the conventional Leslie Lawe: 'So much of herself that was fluid must, too, be moulded by his idea of her' (p. 129). Both novel and play thus allow us to glimpse the erotic possibilities of a world where gender binaries are undermined. They both mourn the fact that identity has in the end to be fixed.

Nevertheless *The Last September* ends with Lois and Laurence continuing to challenge their respective gender roles. He refuses to take responsibility for her luggage, she refuses his protection. In the play, everything is rounded off by marriages, yet instabilities and discords remain. The audience is left wondering how Sebastian's feelings for Antonio will be reconciled with his sudden marriage to Olivia, and just how comfortable the relationship between Viola and Olivia as sisters-in-law is going to be after Olivia's revelations of love to Viola/Cesario and the latter's momentary response. As Malvolio's threat of revenge hangs over the ending of *Twelfth Night*, so in *The Last September*, Daventry's judging glance at Danielstown in the wake of Gerald's death foreshadows its later burning.

'Like Shakespeare', Marda says in *the Last September*, before adding, in keeping with the novel's ambivalence, 'or isn't it?' I would argue that it is like Shakespeare but that Bowen's intertextual reading of *Twelfth Night* not only adds layers to her own novel, but also draws out what is only briefly referred to in Shakespeare's play, namely that a place like Illyria must always be under threat from the world outside. The threat may come from pirates, or from

Irish rebels, or merely from the workaday world which does not permit dalliance in Utopia for long. It is easy to see why the precariousness of Illyria had a particular resonance for an Anglo-Irish writer looking back to the brief period in her adulthood before her class finally lost power.

In keeping with the teasing playfulness of Marda's allusion to Shakespeare, it has not been my intention to insist on deliberate parallels between play and novel. In none of her works is Bowen's use of Shakespeare heavy-handed or obtrusive. Rather an examination of the echoes, conscious and unconscious, of *Twelfth Night* suggests that Bowen used the play as an aid for her imagination in working out the themes of her novel. The explicit reference to *Twelfth Night* in the naming of Lois's friends provides a clue to the underlying Shakespearean subtext in Bowen's novel and that subtext in turn alerts us to central themes in her novel, namely the fragility of the Anglo-Irish world, the unsettling of fixed categories of gender and unfocused desire.

Bowen's appropriation of Shakespeare's play for her own imaginative purposes remarkably anticipates contemporary women novelists' deliberate claiming of Shakespeare for women's writing. In her exploration of the fluidity of gender and her interest in carnival time when the usual societal structures are disrupted, she anticipates contemporary women writers' more explicitly feminist appropriations of Shakespeare, such as Barbara Trapido in *Juggling* (1994) or Angela Carter in *Wise Children* (1992).[22] What distinguishes Bowen from these writers, however, is her appropriation of Shakespeare into a specifically Irish political context.

Intriguingly, this use of Shakespeare to comment on Irish politics is repeated later in Bowen's career in her short story, 'Sunday Afternoon', published in 1941. In this story, there is a clear reference to *The Tempest* in Bowen's portrayal of the young girl, Maria, whom Henry insists on calling Miranda, wishing to leave her enchanted home (neutral Ireland) in order to participate in the war effort in London. Henry Russel, who has lost all his possessions during the bombing of his London flat, is on a brief visit back to friends in Ireland. All now elderly, his friends' way of living has not been altered by the war. Their lives have for Henry 'an air of being secluded behind glass'.[23] They are horrified, in a Jamesian way, to hear of the loss of 'his beautiful things' but really would prefer him not to enter into details about life in the Blitz.

The Shakespeare reference allows Bowen to depict the static, unreal quality of life in Ireland during the 'Emergency', in contrast with the grim realities of life in London during the Blitz. The story has several autobiographical resonances. Like Henry Russel, Bowen stayed in London throughout the war, working as an ARP warden and offering her services to the Ministry of Information. The reference to the bombing of Henry's flat and the loss of all his possessions recalls the fear with which Bowen lived daily and, in fact, in July 1944 her house in Clarence Terrace was partially destroyed by a bomb.

'Sunday Afternoon' may be based on one of several trips Bowen made back to Ireland during the course of the war.[24]

In 'Sunday Afternoon', only Maria is energised by Henry's description of life in London. She ruthlessly dismisses the Ivy Compton-Burnett type dialogue of her elders, who wish to keep her in Ireland, and is determined to escape the paralysis of life in neutral Ireland, 'this eternalized Sunday afternoon' (p. 617). While recognising this paralysis, Henry refuses to aid Maria's getaway, telling her that the brave new world she envisages is one where the brutality of war has caused language, and even personal identity, to all but disappear. In contrast with the stylised civilities of the Anglo-Irish in neutral Ireland, life in London has been reduced to the mere will to survive. Depersonalisation and the brute struggle for survival are all that await Maria this world-weary Prospero warns: 'with nothing left but our brute courage, we shall be nothing but brutes' (p. 621).

The middle-aged Henry is positioned between the older generation represented by his friends and the younger represented by Maria. Though he recognises the necessity of another way of life that the war has called into being, in contrast with Maria's eagerness to embrace the new, Henry feels all the charm of the older generation's aesthetic of living. Again, the word 'spell' is used to describe the enchantment of the Anglo-Irish way of life. Henry warns Maria that, in losing all this, she will lose her identity. Like Prospero at the end of *The Tempest*, Henry, only too aware of what awaits him in the grim world of London bombings, looks back with nostalgia to his time spent on this enchanted isle. In contrast, Maria, like Miranda facing her brave new world, thinks only of the adventures that await her in her new life.

Bowen's appropriation of Shakespeare in her short story again foregrounds what is only briefly suggested in his play, namely the change in Miranda's personality that will be a consequence of her departure from the enchanted island and entrance into the world of Italian *Realpolitik*. As Stephen Orgel points out, during the chess game with Ferdinand, the formerly unworldly Miranda eagerly enters into his stratagems and even suggests that were he to cheat she would forgive him: 'Yes, for a score of kingdoms you should wrangle, | And I would call it fair play' (v.1.176–7).[25] Bowen's short story picks up this hint and, through Henry's speeches, elaborates on the threat to self involved in Maria/Miranda leaving her island.

What is missing in Bowen's appropriation of *The Tempest* are the kind of post-colonial readings of Shakespeare's play in which Caliban is interpreted sympathetically as the native whose island has been cruelly usurped by Prospero the coloniser. Such readings are discussed by Declan Kiberd in *Inventing Ireland* in the specific context of early twentieth-century Irish politics, when writers like Yeats, Wilde and Joyce were attempting to rescue Shakespeare from the trappings of English imperialism. Post-colonial interpretations have become common in Irish stagings of *The Tempest*, for example, during the 1993 Dublin Theatre Festival, the Island Theatre Company presented a Caliban who represented the native Irish colonised by the English.[26] Writing from an Anglo-Irish standpoint and having a Burkean distrust of revolutions, Bowen would have felt no need to subvert readings of Prospero as the wise ruler of an enchanted island threatened by primitive forces which he has to tame and civilise. If Caliban's influence is present at all in her story, it is in the suggestion that at work in wartime London are primitive forces which threaten the continuation of civilised life and the dissolution of language. Maria's eagerness to embrace this life attracts to her the label of 'savage' even before she has stepped off her island (p. 620; p. 622).

If equating Caliban with English, rather than Irish, barbarism is suggestive of an Irish writer turning the tables on imperialist interpretations of the play, a momentary glance back to *The Last September* is sufficient to refute any such radical intentions on Bowen's part. For Caliban's presence lurks too in *The Last September*, where rebels are out to destroy Danielstown's enchanted way of life. When Lois and Marda come across one of the rebels in the mill, he points a gun at them while 'looking at them with calculating intentness, like a monkey' (pp 124–5). This description not only recalls representations of an ape-like Caliban but also awakens unpleasant echoes of nineteenth-century racist cartoons in which the native Irish were depicted with simian features.[27] With her dread of the dispossessed and of the loss of civilised values in the wake of modern life, Bowen, unlike Joyce, was never likely to rehabilitate Caliban at the expense of Prospero.

Like all re-readings, Bowen's appropriations of *Twelfth Night* and *The Tempest* compel us to approach Shakespeare's plays with fresh eyes but they also remind us that no reading can be final. If Bowen anticipates contemporary feminist reworkings of Shakespeare in the area of gender politics, in the area of Irish politics her reading of *The Tempest*, at least, reveals a more conservative tendency. At the same time, her exploration of gender instability in *The Last September* raises the question whether, consciously or unconsciously, the novel demonstrates that Irish political identity is also more fluid than it might at first seem. Certainly the younger generation, represented by Laurence and Lois, are fascinated by the rebels and long to make contact with them. The portrayal of Lois as a rebel against the feminine role she is expected to play, wittingly or unwittingly, creates several parallels between the Irish nationalists and herself.[28] As Lois awakens to her place in society, she finds herself unable straightforwardly to accept the identity prepared for her by her sex but also by her class. Like those fighting for the Irish nation, she begins to construct her identity in opposition to the role she is expected to play in the Anglo-Irish scheme of things. At the end of the novel Lois's future is left uncertain, just as the nation that the rebels are fighting for has not yet come into being. As often with re-readings of Shakespeare, Bowen's exploration of gender trouble in the light of *Twelfth Night* may have led her further than she intended to go in opening up, also, the question of the instability of political identity and adding a further layer of complication to her novel.

Notes

1 Terence Harpold, 'Conclusions', in *Hyper/Text/Theory*, ed. by George Landow (Baltimore MD and London: Johns Hopkins University Press, 1994), pp 189–222 (pp 192–3).

2 See, for example, Declan Kiberd's chapter, 'Writing Ireland, Reading England', in *Inventing Ireland: The Literature of the Modern Nation* (London: Jonathan Cape, 1995), pp 268–85.

3 See Julie Sanders, *Novel Shakespeares: Twentieth-Century Women Novelists and Appropriation* (Manchester: Manchester University Press, 2001).

4 Hermione Lee, *Elizabeth Bowen* 2nd edn (London: Vintage, 1999), p. 175.

5 Ann Ashworth, '"But Why Was She Called Portia?": Judgement and Feeling in Elizabeth Bowen's *Death of the Heart*', *Critique*, 28: 3 (1987), 159–66.

6 In this context, an interesting point of comparison with Bowen's novel is Marina Carr's play, *Portia Coughlan*, where the heroine also takes her name from *The Merchant of Venice*. As Paula Murphy has argued, Carr uses Shakespeare and other historical literary references to point out unease at social changes in Celtic Tiger Ireland ('Staging Histories in Marina Carr's Midlands Plays', *Irish University Review*, 36: 2 [2006], 389–402).

7 Neil Corcoran, *Elizabeth Bowen: The Enforced Return* (Oxford: Clarendon Press, 2004), pp 43–4.

8 Elizabeth Bowen, *The Last September* [1929] (Harmondsworth, Penguin, 1987), p. 7.

9 Shakespeare, *Twelfth Night*, ed. by M. Mahood, intro. by Michael Dobson (Harmondsworth: Penguin, 2005), p. xxvi.

10 Elizabeth Bowen, *The Mulberry Tree: Writings of Elizabeth Bowen*, ed. by Hermione Lee (London: Vintage, 1999), p. 25.

11 Elizabeth Bowen, *Bowen's Court and Seven Winters* (London: Virago, 1984), p. 451.

12 Cited in Bowen, *The Mulberry Tree*, p. 125.

13 Barbara Hodgdon, 'Sexual disguise and the theatre of gender', in *The Cambridge Companion to Shakespearean Comedy*, ed. by Alexander Leggatt (Cambridge: Cambridge University Press, 2002), pp 179–97 (p. 187).

14 Penny Gay, *As She Likes It: Shakespeare's Unruly Women* (London: Routledge, 1994), p. 17.

15 Patricia Coughlan, 'Women and Desire in the Work of Elizabeth Bowen', in *Sex, Nation and Dissent in Irish Writing*, ed. by Éibhear Walshe (Cork: Cork University Press, 1997), pp 103–34.

16 Stephen Greenblatt, *Shakespearean Negotiations: The Circulation of Social Energy in Renaissance England* (Oxford: Clarendon Press, 1988), p. 68.

17 Juliet Dusinberre, *Shakespeare and the Nature of Women*, 3rd edn (Basingstoke: Palgrave, 2003), p. 255.

18 Greenblatt, *Shakespearean Negotiations*, p. 93.

19 Valerie Traub, 'The Homoerotics of Shakespearean Comedy', in *Shakespeare's Comedies* ed. by Emma Smith (Oxford: Blackwell, 2004), p. 176.

20 Coughlan, 'Women and Desire', p. 105.

21 For a recent discussion of triangular relationships in one of Bowen's 1920s short stories, see Patricia Coughlan, 'Bowen, the 1920s and "The Dancing Mistress"', in *Elizabeth Bowen*, ed. by Éibhear Walshe (Dublin: Irish Academic Press, 2009), pp 40–64. See also Maud Ellmann's discussion of the 'shadowy third' that haunts relationships between men and women in *Elizabeth Bowen: The Shadow Across the Page* (Edinburgh: Edinburgh University Press, 2004), pp 22–5.

22 See Sanders, *Novel Shakespeares*, pp 14–37.

23 Elizabeth Bowen, *Collected Stories* (Harmondsworth: Penguin, 1985), p. 616.

24 For more on Bowen's life at this time and the general context of the period, see Clair Wills, *That Neutral Island: A Cultural History of Ireland during the Second World War* (London: Faber & Faber, 2007).

25 Shakespeare, *The Tempest*, ed. by Stephen Orgel (Oxford: Oxford University Press, 1987), pp 29–30.

26 For an account of this performance, see Claudia W. Harris, '*The Tempest* as Political Allegory', in *The Tempest: Critical Essays*, ed. by Patrick Murphy (London: Routledge, 2001), pp 57–77.

27 For a reproduction of one of these cartoons, see Dymphna Callaghan, *Shakespeare without Women: Representing Gender and Race on the Renaissance Stage* (London: Routledge, 2000), p. 136.

28 For precise details of these parallels, see Heather Ingman, *Twentieth-Century Fiction by Irish Women: Nation and Gender* (Burlington: Ashgate, 2007), pp 31–7.

CHAPTER II

'Nothing will come of nothing'

Zero-Sum Games in Shakespeare's

King Lear and Beckett's *Endgame*

David Wheatley

Shakespeare does not loom as large in accounts of Samuel Beckett's influences as Dante, Racine, Proust or Joyce, but is an ever-present sounding board in his early poetry and fiction. The young Beckett's love of French drama is well documented, and as a lecturer at Trinity College he starred, for two nights only, in the student revue *Le Kid*, staged at the Peacock Theatre, but even though here already his reference points were French (Corneille) rather than Anglophone, his time at Trinity was not without a Shakespearean backdrop. Trinity College had been the university of Edward Dowden, eminent Irish Victorian and author of *Shakespeare: A Critical Study of His Mind and Art*. In 1931 Beckett describes (in a letter to Thomas MacGreevy) writing to James Joyce on another Trinity Victorian, Thomas Ebenezer Webb (1821–1903), a diligent promoter in his day of Francis Bacon's claims to authorship of Shakespeare's plays;[1] but a more vivid influence on the undergraduate Beckett would have been W. F. Trench, whose lectures on Shakespeare are credited by James Knowlson with having 'laid the groundwork for [Beckett's] close knowledge of Shakespeare's major plays'.[2] The publication in 2009 of the first volume of Beckett's letters offered further reminders of Shakespeare's role in shaping the young Beckett. He attends a performance of *Romeo and Juliet* at the Gate (possibly the production at which Murphy remembers having seen Ticklepenny);[3] praises George Eliot's *Mill on the Floss* as 'at least superior to Shakespeare's Histories'; puts the words 'A cow, a cow, my Free State for a cow' in the mouth of a publican in Bray; and muses in Hamburg on the correct delivery of Ophelia's flower speech in *Hamlet*.[4]

Allusions to Shakespeare in Beckett's work, the *Faber Companion to Samuel Beckett* informs us, 'range from clarion calls to distant echoes.'[5] As its exhaustive checklist reminds us, bardic echoes are everywhere in Beckett, from schoolboy tags in *Dream of Fair to Middling Women* and *More Pricks Than Kicks*, to *A Winter's Tale* in *Ohio Impromptu* ('The sad tale a last time told'),[6] nods to *Hamlet* and *Love's Labour's Lost* in *Company* ('bourneless dark', 'labour lost'),[7] and an appearance by the little-read poem 'The Passionate Pilgrim' in the equally unfavoured *Rough for Radio II* (Shakespeare's 'Crabbed age' inverted to Beckett's 'Crabbed youth').[8] An early reference to *King Lear* occurs in the poem 'Casket of Pralinen for a Daughter of a Dissipated Mandarin',[9] while Belacqua is in love 'from the girdle up' with the Smeraldina Rima.[10] Another early poem, 'Sanies II' travesties Sonnet 116 as 'suck is not suck that alters', and a later poem echoes Petruchio's question from Act IV Scene 1 of *The Taming of the Shrew*, 'Where is the life that late I led?' ('there /the life late led /down there /all done unsaid').[11] Perhaps the most prolific of Beckett's magpie quoters is Winnie in *Happy Days*, who mixes inconsequential wittering and learned allusion, displaying a fondness for *Romeo and Juliet*, *Twelfth Night* and *Cymbeline* ('ensign crimson', 'pale flag', 'no damask', 'fear no more the heat o' the sun').[12]

James Knowlson's biography describes Beckett using Shakespeare's plays to teach English to his fellow wartime refugee in Roussillon, Miss Beamish (the original of Miss McGlone in *Krapp's Last Tape*), and making notes on *King Lear* in a notebook he kept during the composition of the 'second trilogy' of *Company*, *Ill Seen Ill Said* and *Worstward Ho*. A dramatic fragment from the mid-1980s, *Bare Room*, involves a dialogue between two figures set on a snowy New Year's Eve on the theme of Sonnet 71, 'No longer mourn for me when I am dead.' *King Lear*'s tragic 'Undo this button' is colloquialised by Arsene as 'bugger these buttons!' in *Watt*,[13] and in his late prose Beckett repeatedly found himself drawn back to the play. Gloucester's 'vile jelly' appears in *Ill Seen Ill Said*,[14] and *Worstward Ho* is ghosted by 'The worst is not; so long as we can say, "This is the worst"' (IV.1.27).[15] Further evidence of Beckett's return to Shakespeare late in life can be found in Anne Atik's 2001 memoir *How It Was*. Atik describes Beckett reciting *Macbeth* and *Lear*, and dwelling, again, on Edgar's lines 'The worst is not . . .'. She comments:

> *King Lear* was the play he could say least about, its power being indescribable as well as unstageable, perhaps because anything one could say was foredoomed to fall short. I noticed only that his face darkened, his lips tightened whenever it was mentioned. He expressed his feelings about it mostly by conveying that one couldn't.[16]

The desire to test the worst against the limits of both experience and language frequently brings Beckett up against another piece of wisdom he would have found in *Lear*: 'Nothing will come of nothing' (I.1.90).[17] *Lear* and *Endgame* can both be described as playing zero-sum games, but to trace a line of descent from Shakespeare's nothings to Beckett's gives a pleasingly fecund spin to that sterile-seeming line. For such an ostensibly empty subject, the Beckett file on nothing could hardly be fuller. 'Nothing' is, after all, the first word of *Waiting for Godot*: 'Nothing to be done.' 'Nothing is more real than nothing', Malone announces (Beckett's Malone rather than the eighteenth-century Irish Shakespearean), as Murphy had earlier done, tracing the insight back to a 'guffaw of the Abderite', otherwise Democritus. 'To bore one hole after another in [language], until what lurks behind it – be it something or nothing – begins to seep through; I cannot imagine a higher goal for a writer today', Beckett wrote (in German) to Axel Kaun in 1937.[18] 'He must have had the vision of *positive* annihilation', Beckett wrote of Dr Johnson to Joseph Hone in the same year.[19] His first post-trilogy efforts in prose were the *Texts for Nothing* or *Textes pour rien*, borrowing a trick from the musical designation of silence in French (an empty bar is a *mesure pour rien*).

At the heart of Beckettian nothingness is a rhetorical paradox, profound and playful at once. In a moment of ill-judged rabble-rousing, politician Robert Kilroy-Silk once proclaimed that the Arabs had given European civilisation nothing. As the history of Western numeral systems shows, this is all too true: the Arab word *sifr* gives us the English 'cipher', a number or a nothing, or both. Pondering the problems of arithmetical representation, the Greeks wondered how 'nothing' could be 'something' in paradoxes such as those of Zeno of Elea and Eubulides of Miletus (the same paradoxes that reappear in the problem of the 'impossible heap' in *Endgame*). 'Nothing is better than the kingdom of heaven', begins a syllogism that proceeds 'A crust of bread is better than nothing' before pouncing to sophistic victory: 'A crust of bread is better than the kingdom of heaven.' Lear's fool and not a few Beckettian ne'er-do-wells might be inclined to agree. John Donne explored the productive womb of absence in 'A Nocturnall Upon S. Lucies Day', in which love expresses 'A quintessence even from nothingnesse':

> He ruin'd me, and I am re-begot
> Of absence, darknesse, death: things which are not.[20]

'There is nothing between us', Sylvia Plath writes in 'Medusa', in a pun that brilliantly conflates intimacy, distance and denial.[21] Wallace Stevens provides one of the most celebrated modern inflections of 'nothing' in its positive and negative senses in 'The Snow Man', whose listener, 'nothing himself, beholds | Nothing that is not there and the nothing that is.'[22] As a perform-ative contradiction, this recalls the characterisation of Joyce's *Ulysses* as an attempt to turn the light on quickly enough to see the dark, but example after example from Beckett reminds us how something (or nothing) can simul-taneously be and not be, be present and absent at once.

A similar, punning Shakespearean use predating *Lear* occurs in Sonnet 20, where nature debars the young man as a love object for the poet by 'adding one thing to my purpose nothing.'[23] Shakespeare is trading on the common Elizabethan equation of 'nothing' with the female genitalia, a tradition that reaches its apogee in Rochester's 'On Nothing'. The renunciation of procreation, it might be noted, is a shared feature of *Lear* and *Endgame*. 'The sex goes on at the end', Clov says of Hamm's toy dog in *Endgame*, the question of sex arising as an irrelevant afterthought in a world long since accounted for and finished: 'Finished, it's finished, nearly finished, it must be nearly finished.'[24] 'Let copulation thrive', a disgusted Lear proclaims on the heath, 'But to the girdle do the gods inherit; | Beneath is all the fiends' (IV.5.112; 123–4). This is to start at the end of *Lear*, but under both plays' fatalistic logic the end is in the beginning (and yet we go on). A sage in Jorge Luis Borges abominates mirrors and copulation more than anything else in the world, as both increase the numbers of men, and Hamm and Clov's indignation at finding a flea too expresses itself in anti-reproductive fury, though it does breed separate puns on the subject in English and French: in English they fear the flea may be, not lying, but 'laying' 'doggo' (in which case 'we'd be bitched' (19), while in French Clov's '*A moins qu'elle ne se tienne coïte*' is quickly corrected by Hamm to '*coïte*' ('*Si elle se tenait coïte nous serions baisés*').[25]

Where then to start, in these two plays that place all beginning under a fatal taboo? If only to ensure that a juxtaposition of *Lear* and *Endgame* involves comparing like with like, it might be pertinent to ask whether *Endgame* is in fact, unequivocally, a tragedy. *Godot* was billed by Beckett as a tragicomedy, and in his ingenious reading of the play Wolfgang Iser has shown how its effect depends on a pendulum-like oscillation in the audience between contradictory responses. Vladimir and Estragon wait for Godot, who never comes: this is tragic, but their clowning suggests they do not take their situation seriously, whatever pity we feel for them; the play is obviously a comedy. Yet no sooner do we relax into hearty laughter at their antics than the ever-present pathos corrects our reaction: no, what we find so funny is not amusing at all; we are laughing at, not with Vladimir and Estragon, and our laughter catches in our throat.[26] As a reading of Beckett's tragicomedy, this would have the backing of Nell in *Endgame* when she insists that 'Nothing is funnier than unhappiness, I grant you that' (11). Opportunities for clowning are thinner on the ground in *Endgame*, and the jokes all seem to have fallen flat, but as Nell goes on:

[I]t's always the same thing. Yes, it's like the funny story we have heard too often, we still find it funny, but we don't laugh any more (11–12).

The obverse of which is that we need no longer weep, either, at pains grown long familiar, even if weaker souls may occasionally succumb: 'He's crying',

Clov says of the 'bottled' Nagg; 'Then he's living', answers Hamm (32). *Lear*'s status as a tragedy is not in doubt: here the problem, rather, has been the overwhelming piling up of grief upon grief, to the point where even Dr Johnson approved of Nahum Tate's rewriting of the play with a happy ending, a version that held the stage until the nineteenth century (not that Shakespeare's version is without humour, as we shall see). Like Beckett, Tate was a graduate of Trinity College Dublin, but no modern-day Tate has (yet) arisen to provide a happy ending to *Endgame*, though the tendency to soften the play's harshness, or to introduce a *grand guignol* element, is all too familiar from contemporary productions (consider Conor McPherson's self-proclaimed 'Tarantinoesque' *Endgame* for the *Beckett on Film* series of 2002).[27]

Another starting point for comparisons is the extent to which, like *Lear*, *Endgame* is a family drama. Hamm's treats his parents as human detritus – 'The old folks at home! No decency left!' (7), but grudgingly endures them as the necessary audience to his storytelling. The storyteller tells a never-ending tale to a captive family audience, forever skirting its end but hinting that, once reached, it can only mean death (here Tom Murphy's debt to *Endgame* in *Bailegangaire* is unmistakable). Hamm's relationship with Clov, meanwhile, is more ambivalent. Is Clov the child from Hamm's tale? Is he Hamm's (adoptive?) son or not? *Lear* by contrast begins with a father overweaningly sure of his role at the head of his family. Where Hamm and Clov's relationship is ambivalent, Goneril and Regan begin with the advantage of blood kinship; but if their later treatment of Lear destroys their father–daughter bond, Lear's initial treatment of Cordelia is crueller still. His image of her as a loving daughter is what destroys her, when she cannot enact her role with the show of daughterly tribute he demands:

LEAR	[W]hat can you say to draw
	A third more opulent than your sisters? Speak.
CORDELIA	Nothing, my lord.
LEAR	Nothing?
CORDELIA	Nothing.
LEAR	Nothing will come of nothing. Speak again.
CORDELIA	Unhappy that I am, I cannot heave
	My heart into my mouth. I love your majesty
	According to my bond, no more nor less. (1.1.85–93)

As Alexander Leggatt observes, 'she is not real to Lear; he has constructed a version of her in his mind, as Othello does Desdemona.'[28] What is particularly galling to Lear is that, in another nothing-themed paradox, Cordelia should say 'Nothing' rather than simply remaining mute. Her 'Nothing' is over-eloquent in its failure, over-insistent on what she does not say besides. In his rage Lear annuls her identity not just in the present but retrospectively: 'Better thou | Hadst not been born than not t'have pleased me better' (1.1.233–4). As Leggatt further argues, the logic of Lear's enslavement of Cordelia to his fantasy of devotion is that she is indeed, already, nothing: 'When she asserts her own reality, and he counter-attacks by reducing her to nothing, this simply brings to the surface what he was doing to her all along.'[29] The remainder of the play flows from the consequences of that 'nothing'. When in the next scene Gloucester surprises Edmund reading a letter he hastily conceals – 'What paper were you reading?' 'Nothing, my lord' – his blithe insistence that 'The quality of nothing hath not such need to hide itself' (1.2.31–5) underlines the opposition between positive and negative 'nothings': seeing no evil, Gloucester grasps nothing of what is afoot, whereas Edmund is already putting his malign 'nothings' to work, in a moral darkness that eclipses Gloucester's transparent virtue. In the same way, the wronged Edgar becomes a mere rather than a malign 'nothing' when Edmund's machinations force him into disguise: '"Poor Turlygod! Poor Tom!" | That's something yet. Edgar I nothing am' (II.2.183–4).

Lear's vain dreams of overflowing love from all three of his daughters are pricked by Cordelia's employment of the language of measurement and division – 'Why have my sisters husbands if they say | They love you all?' (1.1.99–100) – foreshadowing the divisions that will flow from Lear's division of his kingdom while imagining he can remain its one symbolic overlord. Hamm forswears the language of filial piety in his angry exchange with his 'accursed progenitor':

HAMM   Scoundrel! Why did you engender me?
NAGG   I didn't know.
HAMM   What? What didn't you know?
NAGG   That it'd be you. (26)

Where the failure of Goneril and Regan's daughterly instincts is presented in *Lear* as a breach in nature and a sinful failure of femininity, in *Endgame* family antagonism is perfectly natural now that sterility has become the natural order of things, as hammered home by Clov:

HAMM   Did your seeds come up?
CLOV   No.
HAMM   Did you scratch round them to see if they had sprouted?
CLOV   They haven't sprouted.
HAMM   Perhaps it's still too early.
CLOV   If they were going to sprout they would have sprouted. [*Violently.*] They'll never sprout! (9)

A comparison might be drawn here with the poisoned no-man's-land territories that dot the films of Tarkovsky, such as *Solaris* and *Stalker* or the post-apocalyptic world of *The Sacrifice*. While on one level these sites stand for the pollution wrought on nature under Soviet Communism or nuclear warfare, on another they suggest the emergence of a post-natural space that begins to form an ecosystem in its own right, as in the mysterious Chernobyl-like 'zone' to which the Stalker ventures. For, as with Vladimir and Estragon's apparent nihilism in *Godot*, the wonder in *Endgame* is not that things are grim and unbearable, but that no matter how bad they are Beckett's characters go on regardless.

Hamm's essence is that of the dethroned patriarch, the familiar Beckettian sadist (Pozzo, Moran) crashing to earth but clinging to the tatters of privilege and self-image, and recycling them as bad drama. Significantly, he is also blind. Lear is morally blind, and certainly blinder than the sightless Gloucester (we shall return to the theme of blindness and insight). Ham-actor that Hamm is, he freely spouts Shakespearean tags ('Our revels now are ended', 'My kingdom for a nightman').[30] Although Beckett's stagecraft would seem to favour a ruthless minimalism, this is not to say that he could not accommodate a more fustian style on occasion; in Walter Asmus's productions of *Waiting for Godot*, Alan Stanford as Pozzo squints through his fingers as he holds forth for Vladimir and Estragon. The performance is revolting and enjoyable at once, allowing us to take a guilty pleasure in Pozzo's routine while leaving us in no doubt as to what bad acting it is. An added consequence of Hamm's ham-acting is its intensification of *Endgame*'s already deathly levels of claustrophobia. Beckett's plays divide into those that take place in open and those that take place in closed spaces, with *Godot* and *Endgame* occupying opposite poles, the off-stage lavatory to which Vladimir dashes contrasting sharply with Hamm's plangent cry of 'Outside of here it's death!' Even a blasted heath would be a luxury of sorts, now that 'there's no more nature' (8). Nevertheless, the play contrives to create an interior within an interior through Hamm's handkerchief, with which the play begins and ends. The act of lifting its stage curtain on his daily performances makes Hamm both actor and audience, and licenses his treatment of the other characters as adjuncts to his private psychodrama. The fact that Hamm is blind (and is also wearing dark glasses, his eyes having gone 'all white') only compounds the sense of protected interiority. Hamm's handkerchief is also a sudarium, allowing him to play St Veronica to his own Christ (compare the poem 'Enueg II', 'veronica mundi | veronica munda | give us a wipe for the love of Jesus').[31]

When he declines to throw his 'Old stancher!' away at the end of the play ('You . . . remain'), Hamm is clinging to its protective membrane around his blind eyes, and the option it allows him to turn his performances on and off, but also reserving the right to experience his predicament through play alone rather than in the Yeatsian 'desolation of reality'. (Compare the frantic insistence throughout *How It Is* that the novel is being quoted rather than spoken or experienced.) The play fights back against Hamm with its constant threats to exhaust his dramatic material, forcing him to up the ante to ever greater heights of melodrama ('Can there be misery – loftier than mine?' (4)), in what Gabriel Schwab has termed the 'Dialectic of Closing and Opening in *Endgame*',[32] with Hamm constantly trying to prise back open what the play relentlessly shuts down. It is as if the play is at war with its central character or the idea of theatricality itself, a side of *Endgame* that Declan Kiberd has compared to the Puritan shutting of the theatres.[33]

Blindness is highlighted in *Lear* too, where Gloucester's deeper insight than those around him is thrown into relief by his blinding at Cornwall's hands. If suffering and loss do not quite translate into higher moral virtues in *Endgame* (except to the self-pitying Hamm), it proceeds by a logic of inevitability whereby the will that was present a moment ago, once lost, was never really there in the first place:

> One day you'll say to yourself, I'm tired, I'll sit down, and you'll go and sit down. Then you'll say, I'm hungry, I'll get up and get something to eat. But you won't get up. You'll say, I shouldn't have sat down, but since I have I'll sit on a little longer, then I'll get up and get something to eat. But you won't get up and you won't get anything to eat. (20)

After the buffoonery of Hamm's soliloquies, this is the play's more straightforwardly philosophical side. On a deeper level, however, one shades into the other. Jan Kott finds 'philosophical buffoonery' in the blind Gloucester's predicament and his subsequent leap from a non-existent height.[34] His reading, in *Shakespeare Our Contemporary* (1965), is all the more compelling for its pioneering comparison of *Lear* and *Endgame*, not least when we consider the tone that Georg Lukács had set for critics in the Soviet bloc with his fierce denunciations of Beckett as an apolitical degenerate (even today, his reception in Communist Eastern Europe could hardly be improved on as a starting point for a reading of Beckett as a political dramatist.) Kott stresses the Job-like falling away of our human props and comforts in Beckett, and into this void inserts a 'parable of universal human fate.' So far so Theatre of the Absurd, but Kott scents a prototype of Beckett's tragicomic reversals in the particular brand of clowning on show in *Lear*: 'In Shakespeare clowns often ape the gestures of kings and heroes, but only in *King Lear* are great tragic scenes shown through clowning.'[35] Of Gloucester's suicide speech ('O you mighty gods! | This world I do renounce'), Kott comments: '[His] suicide has a meaning only if the gods exist [. . .] Even if the gods are cruel, they must take this suicide into consideration.'[36] This is in elegant counterpart to Hamm's prayer in *Endgame*, which so worried the Lord Chamberlain before the play's first London production: 'The bastard! He doesn't exist!' (29)

The subject of Beckett and religion has occupied many critics, from William Empson and Vivian Mercier to Mary Bryden and Declan Kiberd, but what the comparison to *Lear* adds to the mix is the strange complementarity of the theist and atheist viewpoints sketched above. If the gods kill us for their sport, Gloucester imagines he can shame them into feelings of guilt by giving up his life, which only then will acquire any meaning (compare the sinister nihilist Kirilov's idea of a messianic suicide in Dostoevsky's *The Possessed*). If Hamm's sadist God expects his creatures to worship him, it will be at the cost of stripping their lives of all meaning, to the point where God as principle-of-value shrinks to an empty name, devoid of any concrete existence and fit only for ritual execration, the still point at the centre of the endless reversals from comedy to tragedy and back again in a universe from which all moral absolutes have fled. If God does not exist everything is permitted, Dostoevsky worried in *The Brothers Karamazov*, to which Beckett's modern response might be that if God does not exist nothing is permitted, since without him the framework that explains actions as sinful (rather than simply meaningless) is absent; and Hamm makes a very poor example of Richard Dawkins's ebullient atheism. This is not to read *Endgame* as a piece of religious nostalgia, laying flowers on God's tomb, as Nietzsche would put it, but to insert Hamm's spitting atheism into the same context of reversal and ambivalence as that which governs the relations between tragedy and comedy in the Beckettian (and Shakespearean) universe.

Endgame and *King Lear* are both zero-sum games, in which victory or defeat threaten to end up looking much the same. A key difference between *Lear* and other Shakespeare tragedies, Kott argues, is the absence of any better future in prospect, or any Fortinbras figure promising renewal as the curtain falls (though Edgar's survival surely makes this a debatable point). Evil has been snuffed out, without any great show of penitence or justice being done, and those that survive have only a Job-like ordeal of degradation to their name and no voice of God from on high to explain their suffering away. Kott cites Lear's exchange with the disguised Kent – 'How now, what are thou?' 'A man, sir' (1.4.9–10) – as an example of the contact with identity in the raw which all the central characters in *Lear* must undergo, but where his reading parts company with more orthodox existential humanism is his insistence that the concept of 'man' too emerges from the play buckled and bruised, quoting Polish critic Andrzej Falkiewicz's comparison of maimed and mutilated humanity to a peeling onion.[37] As Beckett's 'ideal core of the onion' in *Proust* would suggest,[38] no amount of tears along the way can guarantee that anything is waiting for us at the end.

Lear and Hamm both witness their kingdoms fall away to nothing, and cling all the more jealously to their self-image as symbolic kings. But while Goneril and Regan can strip their father of his actual power, only the fool can pierce Lear's ultimate armour of self-deception with impunity:

LEAR   Dost thou call me fool, boy?
FOOL   All thy other titles thou hast given away. That thou wast born with.

$$(1.4.144-5)^{39}$$

Clov too is his master's most faithful audience and the only person who can speak the truth of his empty posturing back to him: 'I see . . . a multitude . . . in transports . . . of joy', he says of the view through his telescope: 'That's what I call a magnifier.'[40] While Lear must endure his ordeal before seeing through himself, Hamm is aware from the outset that, bar a painkiller or two and the biscuits he feeds his parents, an empty, self-dramatising power is all he has got: to Clov's challenge, 'What is there to keep me here?', he retorts 'The dialogue' (30). Unhappiness raised to the level of self-expression may seem to offer nothing much in *Endgame*'s apocalyptic scheme of things, but as in Cordelia's speech, the nothing that speaks its name, without fear or favour, unleashes all manner of action beyond the power of the nothing that merely keeps its silent counsel. 'To think perhaps it won't all have been for nothing!' Hamm hopes, or perhaps fears (18). Even if so, in the diastole-systole reflux from one nothing to the next, something will have altered, altering characters and audience in turn. Lear's final speech runs the asymptote of existence closer than ever to enclosing nothingness in words (to paraphrase the 'Tailpiece' from *Watt*). There is a fine Beckettian ambiguity on 'no life', half statement of fact and half outraged rejection, and the irony *in extremis* of requiring his button to be undone, recalling Molloy's aside on 'one dying of cancer obliged to consult his dentist':[41]

> And my poor fool is hanged. No, no, no life?
> Why should a dog, a horse, a rat have life,
> And thou no breath at all? Thou'lt come no more.
> Never, never, never, never, never.
> Pray you undo this button. Thank you, sir.
> Do you see this? Look on her. Look, her lips.
> Look there, Look there. (V.3.281-7)

'Afaint afar away over there', as Beckett also gestured at the end of his last work, 'what is the word', before adding the saving, or possibly losing word 'what'.[42] Or as he put it on the theme of nothingness in one of his late French poems, the *mirlitonnades*:

> *rien nul*
> *n'aura été*
> *pour rien*
> *tant été*
> *rien*
> *nul*[43]

Which I render, amid much margin for error, as:

> nothing no one
> will have been
> in vain
> so long as
> nothing no one
> been

Pushed close to a state of nothingness, Lear and Hamm manage almost but not quite, in their self-lacerating rage at God, man and themselves, not to have 'been'. They fail to fail outright, in other words, which as double negatives go adds up to an entirely abject form of success. As for what they do amount to, or what positive good their being there does, as Beckett wrote to Alan Schneider of *Endgame*: 'Hamm as stated, and Clov as stated, together as stated, nec tecum nec sine te, in such a place, and in such a world, that's all I can manage, more than I could.'[44]

Notes

1   Beckett to Thomas MacGreevy, 20 Dec. 1931, in *The Letters of Samuel Beckett, 1929–1940*, ed. by Martha Dow Fehsenfeld and Lois More Overbeck, 4 vols (Cambridge: Cambridge University Press, 2009), I, p. 101.

2   James Knowlson, *Damned to Fame: The Life of Samuel Beckett* (London: Bloomsbury, 1996), p. 54.

3   Beckett, *Murphy* (London: John Calder, 1963), p. 61.

4   *The Letters of Samuel Beckett* (ed. cit.), to MacGreevy 18 Oct. 1932, 1 Jan. 1935; 19 Jan. 1936; 14 Nov. 1936 (p. 136; p. 240; p. 299; p. 384).

5   C. J. Ackerley and S. E. Gontarski (eds), *The Faber Companion to Samuel Beckett* (London: Faber & Faber, 2006), p. 521.

6   Beckett, *Complete Dramatic Works* (London: Faber & Faber, 1986), p. 448.

7   Beckett, *Nohow On: Company, Ill Seen Ill Said, Worstward Ho* (London: John Calder, 1992), p. 41; p. 52.

8   Beckett, *Complete Dramatic Works*, p. 277.

9   'Gloucester's no bimbo /and he's in Limbo /so all's well with the gorgonzola cheese of human kindness', *Poems 1930–1989* (London: John Calder, 2002), p. 197.

10   Beckett, *Dream of Fair to Middling Women* (Monkstown: Black Cat Press, 1992), p. 3.

11   *Poems 1930–1989*, p. 21. 'there /the life late led' can be found in *Obra Poética Completa*, ed. by Jenaro Talens (Madrid: Hiperión, 2000), p. 126, where it is mistakenly printed as part of a poem titled 'pss'; it is in fact a separate poem.

12   *Romeo and Juliet* v.3.94–6; *Twelfth Night* ii.4.113; *Cymbeline* iv.2.258.

13   Beckett, *Watt* (London: John Calder, 1963), p. 41.

14   Beckett, *Nohow On*, p. 91.

15   The Hopkins Sonnet 'No Worst, There is None' is somewhere in the mix too, one hopes, though there is no evidence that Beckett read Hopkins.

16   Anne Atik, *How It Was: A Memoir of Samuel Beckett* (London: Faber & Faber, 2001), p. 54. Stephen Watt also notes *Lear*'s importance to Beckett: 'By the time Beckett had reached his seventies, *King Lear* was something he simply could not get round', *Beckett and Contemporary Irish Writing* (Cambridge: Cambridge University Press, 2009), p. 126.

17   References are from the Folio text. The Quarto has 'Nothing can come of nothing'.

18   Beckett, *Disjecta: Miscellaneous Writings and a Dramatic Fragment* (London: John Calder, 1983), p. 172.

19   Letter to Joseph Hone, 3 July 1937, quoted in Christopher Ricks, *Beckett's Dying Words* (Oxford: Clarendon Press, 1993), p. 15.

20   *The Complete English Poems of John Donne*, ed. by C. A. Patrides (London: J. M. Dent, 1985), pp 90–1.

21   Sylvia Plath, *Collected Poems* (London: Faber & Faber, 1981), p. 226.

22   Wallace Stevens, *Collected Poems* (London: Faber & Faber, 1954), p. 9.

23   Shakespeare, *The Sonnets and a Lover's Complaint*, ed. by John Kerrigan (Harmondsworth: Penguin, 1995), p. 86.

24   *The Theatrical Notebooks of Samuel Beckett: Volume II, Endgame*, ed. by S. E. Gontarski (London: Faber & Faber, 1992), p. 3. This text has been preferred as the closest to Beckett's final intentions currently in print; all references hereafter in text to this edition.

25   Beckett, *Fin de Partie* (Paris: Editions de Minuit, 1957), p. 51.

26   Cf. Wolfgang Iser, 'Counter-Sensical Comedy and Audience Response in Beckett's *Waiting for Godot*', in *New Casebooks: Waiting for Godot and Endgame*, ed. by Steven Connor (Houndmills: Macmillan, 1992), pp 55–70.

27   Available on *Beckett on Film* (Ambrose Video, 2002).

28   Alexander Leggatt, *Shakespeare's Tragedies: Violation and Identity* (Cambridge: Cambridge University Press, 2005), p. 145.

29   Ibid., p. 149.

30   As noticed by Katherine Worth in *Samuel Beckett's Theatre: Life Journeys* (Oxford: Clarendon Press, 2001), p. 127.

31   Beckett, *Collected Poems* (London: John Calder, 1984), p. 13.

32 Gabriel Schwab, 'On the Dialectic of Closing and Opening' in *New Casebooks: Waiting for Godot and Endgame*, pp 87–99.

33 Declan Kiberd, *Inventing Ireland* (London: Jonathan Cape, 1995), p. 458.

34 Jan Kott, *Shakespeare Our Contemporary*, trans. by Boleslaw Taborski (London: Methuen, 1965), p. 117.

35 Ibid., p. 118.

36 Ibid., pp 118–19.

37 Ibid., p. 123.

38 Beckett, *Proust and Three Dialogues* (London: Calder and Boyars, 1965), p. 29.

39 This is only in the Quarto text, *The History of King Lear* (Oxford: Oxford University Press, 2001).

40 This passage is deleted from the *Theatrical Notebooks* text but can be found in *Complete Dramatic Works*, p. 106.

41 Beckett, *Molloy* (London: John Calder, 1959), p. 32.

42 Beckett, *Poems 1930–1989* (London: John Calder, 2002), p. 115.

43 Beckett, *Collected Poems*, p. 77.

44 Beckett to Alan Schneider, 29 Dec. 1957, in Beckett, *Disjecta*, p. 109.

CHAPTER 12

Playing Together

William Shakespeare and Frank McGuinness

Helen Heusner Lojek

In 1976, while a postgraduate at University College Dublin, Frank McGuinness played Bolingbroke in Shakespeare's *Richard II*. Joe Long, who directed the performance, later recalled being impressed by the depth of McGuinness's knowledge of Shakespeare, and McGuinness himself has noted that 'everything' he has done since has been influenced by his experience with *Richard II*.[1] In 1979 McGuinness directed a production of *Macbeth* at what was then the New University of Ulster in Coleraine, and for decades he has taught Shakespearean texts to university students.[2] Such external testimony about the importance of Shakespeare for McGuinness is amply supported by internal evidence in multiple McGuinness plays,[3] but it is *Mutabilitie* (1997) that most clearly and most specifically reveals connections between Shakespearean tradition and McGuinness's individual talent. The use of Shakespeare in *Mutabilitie* is a clear example of the extent to which McGuinness's imagination has often been sparked by the works of others.[4] *Mutabilitie*, though, has a more complex and specific intertextuality than other McGuinness plays. If quotes from George Herbert were removed from *Someone Who'll Watch Over Me* (1992), or if John Keats's poems were excised from *There Came a Gypsy Riding* (2007), the plays' narratives – though hardly their themes and resonances – would remain essentially the same. But if Shakespeare were removed from *Mutabilitie*, the play would collapse such is the extent of McGuinness's nuanced national, political and artistic engagement with Shakespeare.[5] McGuinness began working on the play in the mid-1980s, a period of rising critical interest in connections between Shakespeare and Ireland, interest that both fuelled and was fuelled by *Mutabilitie*.[6]

In *Mutabilitie*, McGuinness imagines that Shakespeare has come to Ireland, where he encounters Spenser and an Irish bard (File), and confronts his own role as an artist in times of trouble. The play is often correctly discussed as a text that, while set in the sixteenth century, explores important aspects of the twentieth-century relationship between England and Ireland.[7] For example, when File pleads that the end of her century also be the end to war, she means the end of the sixteenth century and the end of the Munster Wars. Audiences in Ireland and England (where the play premiered), though, would inevitably have thought of their own twentieth-century political realities.[8] File asks whether war must 'continue for another hundred years? [. . .] And another hundred years? [. . .] And another hundred years?'.[9] The double time of the history play is apparent here, with the reiterated questions connecting the conflict of the sixteenth century and the Munster Wars with conflict in the contemporary moment. Tacking four hundred years onto her own era, the File has led listeners to the end of the twentieth century, when Northern Ireland – under the 'rule' of a second Queen Elizabeth – was in the throes of the Troubles that pitted communities against each other and sparked debate about Irish–English relationships. McGuinness's incorporation of such topical political references, and the indirectness with which he addresses twentieth-century tensions, suggest one affinity Shakespearean drama undoubtedly has for him. Both McGuinness and Shakespeare lived in times and cultures marked by intense political debate. Both participate in that debate obliquely and dialectically, creating characters who are powerful spokespersons for various positions. Neither allows politics to preempt entertainment, often highly comic entertainment, as a purpose of drama.[10]

The usefulness of considering Renaissance plays as 'part of a wider discourse' rather than solely in terms of 'authorial engagement' has been noted by Stephen O'Neill.[11] *Mutabilitie* demands the same nuanced approach. Certainly the play participates in late twentieth-century conversation about the Troubles, but there are other, equally important, aspects of the play's engagement in the 'wider discourse' and of the playwright's 'authorial engagement' with Shakespeare. Shakespearean quotations and references are scattered throughout the play, like deliberate teases for scholars hunting evidence of intertextuality, and the structure has parallels with Shakespearean forms and techniques. As Claudia Harris has commented, 'McGuinness's use of historical events intermixed with legendary ones, of comedy underlying tragedy, of a multilayered plot, of wise fools, madmen, and ghosts, of blended styles from poetry to prose, from dialogue to monologue and even soliloquy, and of numerous stories woven into an ornate tapestry of deceit and mishap – all speak Shakespeare.'[12] Such Shakesperiences serve not only to amuse us with a bricolage of erudite references, but also to deepen the play's exploration of the proper role for an artist in times of conflict, and to underline the play's suitability for a fluid, open space reminiscent of Elizabethan stage spaces.

McGuinness has never been a polite playwright: his dramas are outrageous and deliberately unsettling. Often overtly humorous, they exemplify humour that is typically black and always edged; they are aimed at forcing audiences to re-examine their instinctive reactions and reassess their often firmly held beliefs. *Mutabilitie* exemplifies these qualities.[13] When McGuinness provides audiences with a gay, Catholic Will Shakespeare who washes up on the shore of Ireland in quest of land, he is presenting a very human writer and challenging the lifeless stereotype that has become the bard's ubiquitous popular image.

Aspects of the challenge, of course, have clear precedents and some foundation. Textual analyses of the *Sonnets* have long sought to establish Shakespeare's love for another man, and debate over Shakespeare's religion has been equally intense.[14] Suggestions that Shakespeare was not only Catholic but also Irish have been made both seriously and humorously. In Joyce's *Ulysses* John Eglinton asks, 'Has no-one made [Shakespeare] out to be an Irishman?' In O'Neill's *A Long Day's Journey into Night*, James Tyrone asserts that 'the proof' of Shakespeare's Irish Catholicism 'is in the plays'.[15] The humour of other assertions is probably unintentional: a typical entry on the electronic site 'Shakespeare was Irish! I kid you not. . .' suggests it is not an accident that Elsinore is 'Eron Isle' backwards, and thus only a vowel from 'Erin Isle'.[16]

While he claims Shakespeare as a closet Catholic, McGuinness does not quite assert his Irishness. He does, however, allow File to remind us that the common sobriquet 'Bard of Avon' has its roots in the Irish language: 'Bard meaning poet, | River meaning aibhne', File sings repeatedly. In case we do not catch the implications (or in case we are reading and do not realise that in Irish the *bh* has a *v* sound), William spells it out for us: 'Aibhne, aibhne, aibh-aibh. Avon. Aibhne' (24). McGuinness has noted that *bard* and *avon* are two of the very few English words rooted in the Irish language.[17] File's song provides a linguistic link between Shakespeare and Ireland and functions as a border crossing between the apparent binaries of England and Ireland.

McGuinness's Shakespeare is hardly the stuff of heroes. Having washed up on the shores of Ireland in a scene reminiscent of *The Tempest*, the bard demonstrates mundanely human characteristics. It is true that William is instantly recognisable as worthy, despite his ragged appearance, and File sings a prophetic song about a man who 'shall come from a river' and feed the Irish. File's song, though, is full of balanced opposites: the man from the river shall both kill and feed, both lie and heed; and he is both the spear and the fish. Furthermore, William comes 'from the river' because he has leapt into it to avoid the wild Irish who capture the friends he has convinced to come to Ireland and whom he now abandons despite their pleas.

Discussing the origins of his play, McGuinness pointed to the tensions he finds in texts by the historical Shakespeare, whom he described as 'the epitome of English culture and [. . .] the great connector between Protestant England and Catholic England because he has those two wires fused in his theatre. So I thought, what if he comes to Ireland and meets some Gaelic poets like the File while they are all in this tremendous crisis?' It is hard not to hear in this description McGuinness's awareness of the need for a connector between twentieth-century Protestant Ireland and Catholic Ireland, which were involved in another tremendous crisis. McGuinness identified some very human ambiguities in his William and pointed to a surprising model for the character.

> He is everything and nothing. He's not the saviour that the File and the Irish believe – he's much too clever to identify himself with any particular side. The model for him was Edgar in *King Lear* – the way he shifts from the innocent to the madman and can play all these parts. I think he must have been a supreme actor, since the other actors were so jealous of him![18]

William's refusal to identify with a particular side contrasts with both the very English Spenser and the very Irish File, who are 'the troubled embodiments of their own country and politics'. Here too McGuinness's awareness of his own status as an artist is evident. Irish novelists are likely to feel the long reach of James Joyce. Irish poets write shadowed by Yeats and Heaney. A similar 'anxiety of influence' – or perhaps just awareness of similarity – is evident in McGuinness's remarks about Shakespeare. Shakespeare did not identify with any particular side; McGuinness is well known as the Catholic writer from the Republic who (in *Observe the Sons of Ulster*, 1985) displayed respect for the Protestant tradition in Northern Ireland and evinced an effort to understand it – as he has presented respectful portraits of such frequently disrespected groups as women, gays, the innocent, and the insane.

Mutabilitie explores the struggle of artists 'to reconcile their artistic impulses with those of life around them. None of them can escape from their social responsibilities and they know that's what may destroy them'.[19] Yeats struggled with the need to choose between 'Perfection of the life or of the work' ('The Choice', 1932). Heaney identified 'the quarrel between free creative imagination and the constraints of religious, political, and domestic obligation'.[20] McGuinness's plays demonstrate both his desire to engage with the social and political realities shaping his world, and his Shakespeare-like need to engage indirectly; again, through the distance of time or geography.[21]

Philip Edwards has pointed out that much recent writing about Shakespeare has been 'accusatory and contemptuous. Shakespeare has been tried in his absence, and convicted of sharing in the racist denigration which lubricated the ruthless Elizabethan programme of conquest, suppression and occupation'.[22] Michael Billington criticised *Mutabilitie* for a similar unfairness and rejected what he felt was McGuinness's indictment of Shakespeare 'for not having written plays about the suffering that was happening in Ireland in his own day'.[23] Trevor Nunn, who directed the premiere, described the same phenomenon more positively: 'Frank has accused Shakespeare of not telling the story [of Irish suffering under the English], of neglecting that story and therefore by association he's accused the English for generation after generation of never telling the story, of being utterly ignorant of the story.'[24] McGuinness's portrait of Shakespeare in *Mutabilitie*, though, is less accusatory and more nuanced than Nunn's remarks allow. There are undeniable links between the play and painful twentieth-century political realities, but McGuinness's Shakespeare is closer to the Shakespeare identified by Edwards, that is an author 'always outdistancing us in our plodding attempts to fix him. Any serious attempt to deconstruct Shakespeare has to admit that he was there before us, deconstructing himself'.[25] In an essay written the same year *Mutabilitie* premiered, McGuinness identified his own similar sense of Shakespeare's mutability: 'In every scene that he appeared in, he changed character and colour.'[26]

The mutable quality of Shakespeare's texts and characters was illustrated by McGuinness's 1976 performance in *Richard II*. Yeats had described Richard II as a man of 'contemplative virtue . . . lyrical fantasy [and] sweetness of temper' and as a 'vessel of porcelain' who was no match politically for Bolingbroke's 'coarse' and 'remorseless' 'vessel of clay.'[27] The feminine qualities of gentleness and lyricism Yeats found in Richard have long been associated with the Irish; the heartier qualities of Bolingbroke matched the masculine abilities of the conquering English, and so *Richard II* could in a sense be seen as a picture of England prevailing over Ireland.[28] By contrast, McGuinness used his own strong Donegal accent when playing Bolingbroke, creating a marked contrast to the middle-class Dublin accents of the rest of the cast.[29] His Bolingbroke spoke in the accent of Western, presumably most Celtic, Ireland, whereas Richard's vowels were closer to those of the English. The neat Yeatsean formulation of English practicality overcoming Irish musicality was disrupted if not reversed.

McGuinness's plays illustrate another Shakespearean quality that Yeats had noted: 'To pose character against character was an element in Shakespeare's art.'[30] *Mutabilite* poses against each other three artists in times of trouble, and none is a role model. McGuinness's William, for example, is a flawed poet who twice reaches a sticking point in sonnets he is composing (or perhaps reciting: the text is ambiguous). He is able to finish only because the File and later Hugh round out the lines for him. By contrast, the character of Edmund is blocked and cannot complete *The Faerie Queene*, while File has a stunted role in this colonised society and mainly sings the same song over and over. In the play, it is because William connects with the Irish, and because he allows them to influence his texts, that he completes his sonnets and moves on to new compositions. In miniature, this parallels the methods of the historical Shakespeare, who often reworked the plots and characters of his sources.

Mutabilitie deliberately undercuts any undue reverence accorded to theatre. William has arrived in Ireland with two English actors, Richard and Ben, whose names recall the importance of Richard Burbage and Ben Jonson in historical considerations of Shakespeare. The play opens with Ben lamenting a raucous Irish audience that took an axe to the stage during their performance the night before. The early oblique reference to the *Playboy* riots is a reminder that the decorous behaviour often associated with contemporary attendance at Shakespearean plays is not the only way to engage with drama. Similar contrasting notions of artistic appropriateness are evident when Spenser laments the failure of Irish bards to seek to 'better the manners of men'. Instead, Spenser maintains, Irish bards are 'dangerous' and 'desperate', glorifying 'disobedience and rebellious disposition' as they indulge their 'direst fantasies' (46). Later File describes the English theatre she has never seen as the place where the English race now 'speaks to God . . . a holy place of great, good magic' (56–7). She is awed by the ability of theatre to raise the dead, but equally awed that audiences *pay* to attend – in sharp contrast to the less direct financial relationship between bardic storytellers and their listeners, not all of whom were patrons.

McGuinness's play is so loaded with references to Shakespeare that characters' comments about theatre inevitably conjure a background to Shakespearean theatre itself. For instance, there are long quotations from Sonnets 18 and 87; King Sweney's madness is reminiscent of Lear's; William declares they have come to Ireland to 'play [their] parts upon the stage' (22), echoing the 'strut and fret' upon the stage of *Macbeth*; Annas's gathering of herbs evokes Friar Laurence's 'grace and rude will' (25); Hugh and William echo Ben Jonson's remark that Shakespeare had 'small Latin and less Greek' (68); there is a tale 'that's best for winter' (71) and a play within the play whose evocation of Hecuba recalls *Hamlet* (76). Furthermore, towards the end of the play, Hugh declares that the English child left behind will be 'Nurtured like our own, and natured like his own' (100–1), a formulation that is reminiscent of Prospero's contention that Caliban is one 'on whose nature/Nurture can never stick' (IV.I.188–9), and for the English child both nature and nurture apparently *will* contribute to the adult human. Confronting a William newly dragged from the river, Spenser's child says 'Peace be to you, good monster,' modifying the phrasing of Stephano's injunction to Caliban – 'Be you quiet, monster'(IV.I.235) – to add both a reminder of the desireability of peace and an indication that the 'monster' may not be evil.[31] Every observer will discover a favourite Shakespeare echo. My own is Spenser's question 'What is my nation?' (51), a reversal (presumably in impeccable Radio 3 vowels) of the accented 'What ish my nation?' by Macmorris in *Henry V*, a character often cited as the first Stage Irishman. This key echo in a play exploring cultural interrelations undoubtedly resonates most powerfully for audiences familiar with Shakespeare's Macmorris and with the extensive critical dialogue that has whirled about him.[32] On the other hand, the question stands perfectly well without awareness of Macmorris. For 'What is my nation?' is a question that residents of Northern Ireland have repeatedly posed and answered in various ways, and it is a question that often plagues those residents of the Republic or England who have mingled Irish and English backgrounds. But for those who recognise the echo, the shift from Macmorris's non-standard 'ish' to Spenser's standard 'is' provides a reminder that questions of national identity plague people in various segments of society, and that imperialism and immigration have heightened their sharpness. A subtler example of language tensions is the structure of File's discussion of *aibhne* and *river*. She does not say, as an English speaker would be likely to, that *aibhne* means *river*. She says *river* means *aibhne* and thus gives primacy to her native language.[33]

The challenge of dealing with multiple languages on stage is evident in both Shakespeare and McGuinness. In *Mutabilitie* Richard and Ben mock William's attraction to a 'Welsh bit' for whom he wrote 'a part in Welsh because he wouldn't learn English,' and their reference to Owen Glendower (63) reminds us that in *Henry IV, Part One* there is just such a part, for the young boy who played Glendower's daughter, Lady Mortimer. Shakespeare's Hotspur, invited to hear Lady Mortimer sing in Welsh, replies 'I had rather hear Lady, my brach, howl in Irish' (III.1.240). Welsh and Irish are linked as inferior Celtic languages, appropriate targets for jest. And the sounds of Irish are equated with animal howls. Shakespeare's text does not include the Welsh words Glendower and his daughter exchange; stage directions simply indicate that they speak 'in Welsh'. By contrast, *Henry V* – the play in which Macmorris's accent is mocked – includes untranslated dialogue in elementary French, presumably because French is a significant language that the English, including Shakespeare, understand as they could not have understood (or written) Welsh.[34]

In *Mutabilitie*, McGuinness faced a challenge similar to the one Brian Friel faced in *Translations*: characters must be *presumed* to be speaking in Irish, rather than *actually* speaking it, since contemporary Irish audiences, like the Elizabethan English, often cannot understand the Irish language. *Mutabilitie* is set during the time period when English and Irish jostled for linguistic dominance in Ireland.[35] It was written and performed long after English had triumphed and most Irish people, including McGuinness, were native English speakers who learned whatever Irish they knew in school. *Mutabilitie*, then, must present contrasting cultures and realities through the medium of a shared language, and in doing so it demonstrates the triumph of English linguistic imperialism.

McGuinness's dialogue reveals his awareness both of Shakespeare's treatment of Celtic languages and of twentieth-century realities. Echoing Shakespeare's Hotspur, File tells Elizabeth Spenser that 'in certain quarters our voices are referred to as the growling of a dog' (65).[36] And, asked by William to 'Sing – speak to me in your own language', as Shakespeare's Lady Mortimer had done, Hugh replies:

> You are hearing my own language. When the English destroyed us and our tribe, we made a vow. We had lost power to govern our lives and part of that curse was the loss we accepted over the government of our tongue. We do not break our vows. I will not sing nor speak to you in Irish, Englishman. (68)[37]

In a play that seeks in part to measure English and Irish artists and art forms in relation to each other, McGuinness is nonetheless constrained by his own and his audience's lack of fluency in Irish.

A significant difference, of course, is that whereas Shakespeare's Celtic speakers were objects of ridicule, McGuinness's Irish speakers – despite their poverty and political powerlessness – are figures worthy of respect. Significantly, McGuinness was writing after the Downing Street Declaration (1993) and the Framework Documents (1995) had begun laying the basis for settlement of the Troubles in Northern Ireland; both mention the need for 'respect for diverse traditions'.[38] Respect for Irish language culture, powerful in the playwright's native Donegal, is evident in McGuinness's earlier plays, most notably *Mary and Lizzie* (1989). Its appearance in *Mutabilitie* came in the context of expanded political discussion of the need for 'full respect' and 'parity of esteem' for both communities in Northern Ireland. In addition, the Irish speakers in *Mutabilitie* have a source of power not open to the English. Because the Irish are bilingual, they can understand the English in ways the English cannot understand them. In Act Three, the English eat a breakfast served by their Irish servants. The English know the Irish can understand their language, but they speak as though the Irish servants have no ears. It is a classic example of powerful/powerless relationships. The English have all the lines, but the Irish can comment by the manner in which they bear themselves and serve the food. The Irish also take away understandings of the English that far surpass the understandings the English have of them.

McGuinness's handling of the Irish–English colonial relationship also has parallels with the situation of Shakespeare's Caliban, increasingly regarded by recent commentators as a colonised figure. *The Tempest* is full of questions about Caliban's humanity. Caliban observes that the colonisers 'taught me language, and my profit in't | Is, I know how to curse' (*Tempest* 1.2.362–4). In lines that echo Caliban's, McGuinness's Elizabeth declares that the ability of the Irish to speak English explains how they 'learned so early to lie with such excellence'(9). Elizabeth also maintains that the Irish are 'animals', to which Edmund 'roars' back 'They are Irish' (9). The insider joke about the Irish is a typical McGuinness technique, allowing a swift change of tone from presentation of serious issues about the status of the Irish as humans and English language speakers. Parallels with Caliban's situation are clear.

Shakespeare's appearance as a character in *Mutabilitie*, the text's constant references to actual Shakespearean texts, and the fact that McGuinness himself has described this as 'a five-act play in Elizabethan mode', make comparison with Shakespearean plays inevitable.[39] During the period when he was working on the script of *Mutabilitie*, McGuinness was also preparing a version of *Peer Gynt*, and what he said of Ibsen's play applies to some extent to his own work on *Mutabilitie*: 'that formidable energy of Ibsen . . . [rampages] forward, taking the classic five act form and inflating it beyond repair. . ., risking artistic suicide.'[40] Christopher Murray has argued that *Mutabilitie* not only risks but also achieves failure: 'The play is rich in ideas and themes, so rich . . . that it finally collapses under the impossible burden.' Murray also suggests that the play remains important in McGuinness's *oeuvre*, and he convincingly balances Elizabethan regret about the world's changeableness against McGuinness's optimistic view of mutability. His sense that *Mutabilitie* fails, particularly when judged in relation to Shakespeare's history plays, remains his dominant judgement, however. In regretting *Mutabilitie*'s 'Blakean neglect of the logic of plot development',[41] Murray does not overlook the play's many virtues, but he clearly values coherence over nuance and energy.

Few commentators have noted that *Mutabilitie*'s constant references to Shakespeare also suggest how the play might be staged. In a letter to McGuinness written before he staged the opening production of *Mutabilitie*, Trevor Nunn argued that McGuinness's 'extraordinary, ambitious, poetic, magical and profound' play should not be staged in the National Theatre's Lyttleton Theatre, which has a 'large, four-square, uncompromising space' that 'demands narrative and ease of accessibility'. Nunn argued that 'the wrong (proscenium arch) things musn't be demanded' of *Mutabilitie*, and recommended the three-sided configuration of the Cottesloe Theatre, which 'would provide a huge stage space and a tightly packed up close audience'. Nunn noted that McGuinness's 'fine-textured play requires atmosphere, environment, total concentration, firelight, shadows, real unamplified instruments and voices and the kind of proximity that changes an audience'.[42] McGuinness's script begins with a vague stage direction: '*A patch of light in a forest*' and sets the scene with a line of dialogue: 'Ben: This is Ireland' (1). It is a device Shakespeare employed regularly. If his title did not designate a setting, Shakespeare set the scene with dialogue. For example, 'In fair Verona, where we lay our scene' (Prologue) for *Romeo and Juliet* or 'This is Illyria, Lady' (1.2.1–2) in *Twelfth Night*. McGuinness employs a similar technique, suggesting not naturalistic stage sets, but engagement of audiences' imaginations. Draft versions of the text[43] provide additional evidence that McGuinness envisioned a fluid, non-naturalistic set: 'The English live in a castle, the Irish in the forest, but these locations are *suggested* (emphasis added). Ironically, despite Nunn's recognition that *Mutabilitie* needs 'huge stage space' and flexibility, his premiere featured a set that reviewers routinely described as inhibiting the play's magical atmosphere. Georgina Brown described the set as 'a rocky outcrop over which the actors pick their way with some difficulty'. Kate Kellaway lamented its resemblance to 'an adventure playground. The audience surrounds the territory like a moat. The Spenser home is not quite a bouncy castle but you want to step onto [Frawley's] rocky landscape and play with her cardboard-cut-out food'. And David Jays summed up the problem:

> This delicate, dense play gets a production by Trevor Nunn that prefers naturalism and melodrama. Ravens croak and thunder cracks, while Monica Frawley's mossy set harnesses the elements into a picturesque forest. For McGuinness, 'Ireland' is largely a state of mind, but Frawley makes it too substantial . . . [in contrast to] *Mutabilitie*'s greater concern for shades of meaning, of imaginary landscapes and elusive ideas of home.[44]

The Irish premiere, the only other major production of the play, was directed three years later by Michael Caven at the Samuel Beckett Theatre, Trinity College Dublin. Referring to *Mutabilitie*, Caven noted that theatre is 'not about realism. Or real history. It's about imagination and dreams.'[45] Caven's notion of how to use space was markedly different than the notion that informed the London production:

> I knew the first time I read the play that it *must not* be done naturalistically . . . What I wanted to do was to manipulate the total flexibility of space offered by the Beckett Theatre, creating (primarily through height and depth) different places and shifts in time and place that would enable the drama of the piece to continually evolve . . . I wanted to create that Renaissance concept of the above, the middle, and below . . . Light played a fundamental part in creating and defining the imaginative boundaries of those various spaces . . . Scene changes that involve a lot of mechanics slow down the movement and can be fatal. The rational mind kicks back in and resists what the imagination is saying.[46]

Caven's description of how his production took shape is filled with references to Renaissance and Shakespearean theatre, and he utilised clues in the text that reinforce his conception that the play is best presented with theatrical conventions other than those of the proscenium arch or naturalistic theatre.

Preparation of the audience began with the programme. The London programme was filled with discussions of the Munster Wars, explanations of Irish myth and Spenser's *Mutabilitie Cantos*, an essay considering whether Shakespeare had actually gone to Ireland, and pictures of the twentieth-century conflict in Northern Ireland that emphasised the contemporary parallels. The sharply different Dublin programme had a single essay, by Caven, entitled 'A Sacred Theatre of Memory'. As Caven explained elsewhere:

> What an actor needs to know to perform and what an audience needs to watch are not the same thing . . . you can kill an audience dead in their seats if you start producing theatre as academic lecture. So we had to decide, do we need to put great big notes in the program for the audience about the politics of the time; do we need to put stuff in the foyer with pictures and diagrams and all of that? We decided to avoid this as much as possible, because I felt that we had to trust our audience.[47]

Caven trusted not only his audience, but also the script. His decision paid off particularly well in Act III, when a split stage and overlapping dialogue create a complex theatrical effect. McGuinness had used this technique before, most notably in *Observe the Sons of Ulster*. In *Mutabilitie*, twelve actors in four different locales deliver nine pages of overlapping, often one-line, dialogue. Caven's minimalist stage allowed a clear view of all groups, and because the characters had already been fully delineated, the different locales could be imagined without naturalistic scenery. Undistracted by scenery or intrusive naturalistic props, audiences could see the scene's geometry. Clusters of characters delivered parallel expressions of forgiveness. The women were standing, and the men seated, postures that emphasised gender differences and the importance of women. The staging also revealed the extent that forgiveness was extended not only to members of individual groups, but also to other groups and to the audience itself.

The production created a similarly strong focus for its conclusion. Like several previous McGuinness plays, *Mutabilitie* uses eating, a metaphoric breaking of bread, as a sign of hope. The presence of a child is a familiar McGuinness motif indicating hope. The happy resolution of conflict represented by marriage in such Shakespearean plays as *A Midsummer Night's Dream* and *The Winter's Tale* is here represented by the nourishing of a child. The Irish share their sparse provisions with the abandoned English child in their midst, and there is the possibility of reconciliation, a possibility in direct contrast to Spenser's notion in *A View of the State of Ireland* that fostering, particularly if it involved Irish wet nurses, was unnatural and a sure path to degeneration. McGuinness's Irish do not, however, lapse easily or unambiguously into peaceful nurturing of the English child. Hugh protests that there is 'little' milk and refers to the child as a 'hostage'. Furthermore, the minimalist stage permitted Caven to include at the edge of this scene Irishmen with weapons at hand, reminders that violence might well break out again. The presence of the weapons is not demanded by the script, but fits with McGuinness's insistence that the play's 'tiny glitter of hope' does not obscure the fact that 'we're living in dangerous times'.[48] With complex action and a large cast, *Mutabilitie* thus shares Shakespearean drama's appropriateness for flexible stage space in which dialogue and the audience's imagination combine to create a magical albeit fleeting world.

The challenge facing productions of *Mutabilitie* is parallel to the one Henry James identified in an 1896 production of *Cymbeline*, a play he believed took 'little account . . . of the general effort of the theatre of our day to hug closer and closer the scenic illusion. The thing is a florid fairy-tale, of a construction so loose and unpropped that it can scarce be said to stand upright at all, but plays, at its better times, with an indifferent shake of golden locks, in the high, sunny air of delightful poetry.'[49] He might be describing *Mutabilitie*. Yeats, who listed Shakespeare as a favourite author, identified the same tension that James had noted, claiming that efforts he, Synge, and Lady Gregory made to 'create an essentially poetic literature' were defeated by the bitter realism of Catholic writers.[50] A hundred years later, tension between 'scenic illusion' and 'fairy-tale' continue to confront theatre practitioners, and that tension is evident in relation to *Mutabilitie*. Contemporary theatre exists against a 'norm' of realism that does not fit texts such as *Mutabilitie*, and those theatrical practitioners who favour scenic illusion are likely to have difficulty with the play. McGuinness himself, of course, set the framework for such tension. The text's clear references to twentieth-century Northern Ireland almost inevitably lead to adoption of contemporary assumptions about theatrical practice, particularly as it exists in Irish theatre.

In both form and theme, then, *Mutabilitie* raises questions about the uses of the past in history and literature. Has McGuinness adopted the dramatic form of the most revered English playwright because of his affinity for it, or as an act of explosive resistance that allows the empire to speak back? Is his desire to re-tell Shakespeare's story a desire to imagine a version that suits him more, an assumption with Oscar Wilde that 'The one duty we owe to history is to rewrite it'? Or, does his title deliberately focus attention not only on Spenser's *Mutabilitie Cantos*, but also on the mutability of history and literature, reminding us that the unstable past may be brought into fruitful conversation with an equally unstable present? Perhaps McGuinness is seizing revered forms, or recognising in Shakespeare a direct ancestor of his own dramatic intelligence and boldness. Ultimately, it seems best to recognise a case of Shakespeare's tradition and McGuinness's individual talent, an example of T. S. Eliot's understanding that 'not only the best, but the most individual parts of [a writer's] work may be those in which the dead poets, his ancestors, assert their immortality most vigorously'.[51] The play's final communal moment suggests that Spenser's nameless child will be transformed, and his cultural reality will be a new one, a sign of hope that the joined and nurtured powers of multiple pasts, rather than being erased, will inform a new future.

Notes

1   'Writing History', lecture given at the Synge Summer School, Rathdrum, 6 July 1998. Christopher Murray reports that McGuinness also referred to *Richard II* when speaking about *The Tempest* in 1999; see his 'Of Mutabilitie' in *The Theatre of Frank McGuinness: Stages of Mutability*, ed. by Helen Heusner Lojek (Dublin: Carysfort Press, 2002), p. 163. And Hiroko Mikami reports that McGuinness stated *Richard II* was on his mind when he wrote *Mutabilitie*; see her *Frank McGuinness and His Theatre of Paradox* (London: Colin Smythe, 2002), p. 113.

2   First at St Patrick's College Maynooth (which became the National University of Ireland, Maynooth); and since 1997 at University College Dublin.

3   *Carthaginians* (1988) includes a recitation of the names of the dead that warrants comparison with *Henry V* (IV.7.96–110), and a play within the play that has structural and thematic parallels with the 'Rude Mechanicals' in *A Midsummer Night's Dream*. In *Gates of Gold* (2002) Gabriel (like McGuinness and Micheál MacLiammóir, the real life actor on whom Gabriel is based) had acted in *Richard II*, and Conrad's lament for the dying Gabriel reaches for qualities evident in the funeral oration Hilton Edwards, who quoted from the dirge in *Cymbeline* (IV.2.258–81), delivered for MacLiammóir.

4   *Innocence* (1986) owes a large debt to the paintings of sixteenth-century Italian artist Caravaggio, and numerous McGuinness poems refer to works by contemporary Irish artists. The 1998 poem 'Van Gogh in Donegal' (basis of a 1998 Dublin Theatre Festival production by Galway's Macnas Theatre) imagines the painter sailing from Holland to Ireland and getting as far west as Donegal. 'Van Gogh in Donegal' was originally published, under the name T. P. O'Donnell, in *The Ring of Words: Poems from the Daily Telegraph Arvon International Poetry Competition* (London: Sutton Publishing, 1998), reprinted in McGuinness's *The Sea with No Ships* (Loughcrew: Gallery Press, 1999).

5   Similarly, *Innocence* would collapse without the visual and biographical links to Caravaggio.

6   For example, Christopher Highley's *Shakespeare, Spenser, and the Crisis in Ireland* (Cambridge: Cambridge University Press, 1997); Mark Thornton Burnett and Ramona Wray's *Shakespeare and Ireland* (Basingstoke: Palgrave, 1997), a collection of essays for which McGuinness provided a foreword. In 1997, when the play premiered, a conference 'Shakespeare and Ireland' was held at Trinity College Dublin, for which Abbey actors directed by Patrick Mason provided a rehearsed reading of *Mutabilitie*.

7   In 'Writing Twentieth-Century Irish History: *Mutabilitie* (1997)', for example, Anne MacCarthy provides an illuminating review of nationalist and revisionist readings of Irish history, though less than 25 per cent of her essay relates to the play she mentions in the title. *New Hibernia Review*, 6.2 (2002), pp 65–81.

8   The 1997 public reading of *Mutabilitie* in Dublin was not followed by a full Irish production until 2000 in a production directed by Michael Caven at the Samuel Beckett Theatre.

9   Frank McGuinness, *Mutabilitie* (London: Faber & Faber, 1997), pp 58–9. *Mutabilitie* was written over a long period of time and underwent numerous revisions. Performance texts were not identical to each other or to the printed text. I quote only from the printed version.

10   A recent, helpful discussion of such aspects of Shakespearean drama is Andrew Hadfield's *Shakespeare and Republicanism* (Cambridge: Cambridge University Press, 2005).

11 Stephen O'Neill, *Staging Ireland: Representations in Shakespeare and Renaissance Drama* (Dublin: Four Courts Press, 2007), p. 13.

12 Claudia Harris, 'Frank McGuinness's *Mutabilitie*: The Transforming Power of Theatre', *Text & Presentation* 22 (2001), 61.

13 The daringness with which McGuinness presents Shakespeare in *Mutabilitie* comes into sharper focus if we note that www.theactorsshakespeare.com lists over 100 US Shakespeare festivals. Electronic Shakespeare (http://www.wfu.edu) lists 110 in the US and Canada. The Institute of Outdoor Drama (http://www.unc.edu) lists 53 outdoor Shakespeare festivals in the US. Shakespeare is quoted in advertisements and on t-shirts; his works are performed in prisons and elementary schools; the citizens of Lumphanan, Scotland, have laid a stone in memory of Macbeth; there are films and interactive texts and podcasts of his work. No English language education is considered complete until the pupil has encountered at least one Shakespeare text. Such facts are but the tip of the iceberg that preserves Shakespeare's reputation and freezes the western world in admiration of him.

14 See, for example, John Henry DeGroot, *The Shakespeares and 'The Old Faith'* (New York: King's Crown, 1946) and H. Mutschmann and K. Wentersdorf, *Shakespeare and Catholicism* (New York: Sheed and Ward, 1952). See also scholarly works contemporaneous with *Mutabilitie*: David Beauregard, 'New Light on Shakespeare's Catholicism: Prospero's Epilogue in *The Tempest*', *Renascence* 49 (1997), 159–74; Richard Wilson, 'Shakespeare and the Jesuits', *Times Literary Supplement*, 19 December 1997, 11–13; and *Secret Shakespeare: Studies in Theatre, Religion and Resistance* (Manchester: Manchester University Press, 2004).

15 James Joyce, *Ulysses* (New York: Modern Library, 1961), p. 98; Eugene O'Neill, *A Long Day's Journey Into Night* (1940) (New Haven CT: Yale University Press, 1989), p. 127.

16 http://www.indymedia.ie/article/79358–449K [accessed 25 December 2006].

17 Quoted in Jane Edwardes, 'Frank's Spenser', Preview of *Mutabilitie*, *Time Out*, 19–26 November 1997, p. 158.

18 'The Troubles with Shakespeare', Interview with John Whitley, *Daily Telegraph*, 20 November 1997, p. 30.

19 Ibid., p. 30.

20 'Introduction' to *Sweeney Astray: A Version from the Irish* (London: Faber & Faber, 1983), n.p. See also Seamus Heaney's 'Away from It All' in *Station Island*: 'I was stretched between contemplation/of a motionless point/and the command to participate/actively in history.'

21 For a fuller discussion of such issues, see 'Portraits of Artists' in my *Contexts for Frank McGuinness's Drama* (Washington, DC: Catholic University Press, 2004).

22 Philip Edwards, 'Shakespeare, Ireland, Dreamland', *Irish University Review*, 28.2 (1998), 236.

23 Michael Billington, *Guardian*, 24 November 1997.

24 *Clear the Stage*, a Besom production for BBC Northern Ireland, produced by Fionnuala Sweeney, 1998.

25 'Shakespeare, Ireland, Dreamland', pp 236–7.

26 'Foreword', in *Shakespeare and Ireland*.

27 Yeats, 'At Stratford-on-Avon' (1901), *Essays and Introductions* (New York: Macmillan, 1961), p. 106; p. 108.

28 See, for example, Declan Kiberd, *Inventing Ireland: The Literature of the Modern Nation* (New York: Vintage, 1995), pp 268–9. See also Brian Cosgrove's chapter pp 41–3; 46–7. Further discussion of *Richard II* can be found in Christopher Murray, 'Of Mutabilitie' in *The Theatre of Frank McGuinness: Stages of Mutability*, pp 162–74.

29 Joseph Long, personal interview. Dublin, November 2000.

30 *Essays and Introductions*, p. 108.

31 *Booterstown* (1994) has a poem titled 'Prospero's Daughter', and 'Sea-Monsters', in *The Sea with No Ships*, includes the line 'I say, Peace be to you, dear monsters' (25).

32 For a recent illuminating discussion of Macmorris, see O'Neill's *Staging Ireland*.

33 File's wording is an oblique reminder of the ongoing and long-standing conversations about language in Ireland. For example, see Tom Paulin's 1983 Field Day pamphlet 'A New Look at the Language Question'; the 1986 PBS documentary *The Story of English* (the segment on Irish English was titled 'The Loaded Weapon'); and, more recently, Tony Crowley's *War of Words: The Politics of Language in Ireland 1537–2004* (Oxford: Oxford University Press, 2005).

34 In *Speaking Like Magpies* (2005), McGuinness includes brief bits of untranslated Middle Scots dialogue. One character deliberately mistranslates some of the Middle Scots, but only bilingual listeners would have known that for sure. Compare the deliberate mistranslations in Brian Friel's *Translations*, which work differently because the actors are actually speaking English, though we imagine they are speaking Irish.

35 Henry VIII had assumed the title 'King of Ireland' in 1541. Spenser was in Ireland during the 1580s and 1590s.

36 Compare Rosalind in *As You Like It* on the association of *Irish* with *animal*: she connects 'Irish rats' with poetry, referring to supposed ability of Irish bards to enchant rats (III.2.187–9); tired of a conversation, she describes it as the 'howling of Irish wolves' (V.2.110–11).

37 Hugh's 'government of our tongue' echoes Seamus Heaney's use of the same term in a 1987 essay. Seamus Heaney's 'The Government of the Tongue' was a 1986 T. S. Eliot Memorial Lecture at the University of Kent. Faber and Faber (London) published it under that title in 1987. A portion is reprinted in Seamus Heaney, *Finders Keepers: Selected Prose 1971-2001* (NY: Farrar, Straus, Giroux, 2002), pp 196–208.

38 The Downing Street Declaration (15 Dec. 1993) endorses 'full respect for the rights and identities of both traditions in Ireland'. The Framework Documents (22 Feb. 1995) reiterate that language. Subsequently, the Belfast Agreement (10 Apr. 1998) stipulated the importance of 'partnership, equality, mutual respect' for diverse traditions.

39 'Coming Home', An interview with Mic Moroney, *Irish Times*, 29 November 1997, p. 16.

40 'A Long Neck', Introduction to Henrik Ibsen, *Peer Gynt, A Version by Frank McGuinness* (London: Faber & Faber, 1990), p. vi.

41 Christopher Murray, 'Of *Mutabilitie*', in *The Theatre of Frank McGuinness*, pp 162–3.

42 University College Dublin (UCD), Special Collections Library, Letter from Trevor Nunn to Frank McGuinness, 20 Feb. 1997.

43 These are held in the UCD Special Collections Library, to which McGuinness has loaned many of his materials.

44 Review of *Mutabilitie, Plays International,* 4 January 1998, p. 12. Brown's review appeared in the *London Gazette,* November 1997. Kellaway's review was in the *New Statesman,* 28 November 1997, pp 43–4.

45 'Mistaken Identity,' an interview with Joe Jackson, *Hotpress,* 14 September 2000.

46 'A Director's Perspective on *Mutabilitie*', Michael Caven in conversation with Helen Heusner Lojek, in *The Theatre of Frank McGuinness,* pp 181–2.

47 Ibid., p. 180.

48 Quoted in 'Coming Home', Interview with Mic Moroney, *Irish Times,* 29 November 1997, Weekend, p. 16.

49 Henry James, 'Mr Henry Iriving's Production of *Cymbeline*', repr. in Henry James, *The Scenic Art: Notes on Acting and the Drama: 1872–1901,* ed. by Allan Wade (New Brunswick: Rutgers University Press, 1948), p. 282.

50 R. F. Foster, *W. B. Yeats: A Life,* 2 vols (Oxford: Oxford University Press, 2003), II: *The Arch-Poet,* pp 457–8. Foster is citing notes that Horace Reynolds took during a lecture Yeats delivered at Wellesley College in the 1930s.

51 T. S. Eliot, 'Tradition and the Individual Talent', in *The Sacred Wood: Essays on Poetry and Criticism* (New York: Barnes and Noble, 1928).

Index